WOODHOLME

A Black Man's Story of Growing Up Alone

WOODHOLME

A Black Man's Story of Growing Up Alone

D E W A Y N E

W I C K H A M

F A R R A R   S T R A U S   G I R O U X

New York

Copyright © 1995 by DeWayne Wickham
All rights reserved
Printed in the United States of America
Published simultaneously in Canada by HarperCollins*CanadaLtd*
Designed by Fritz Metsch
First edition, 1995

LIBRARY OF CONGRESS CATALOGING-IN-PUBLICATION DATA
Wickham, DeWayne.
Woodholme: a black man's story of growing up alone / DeWayne Wickham. —
1st ed.
p.   cm.
1. Wickham, DeWayne—Childhood and youth.   2. Afro-Americans—
Biography.   3. Unmarried fathers—United States.   4. Afro-American
families.   5. Parental deprivation—Social aspects—United States.
I. Title.
E185.97.W615A3   1995
973'.0496073'0092—dc20   [B]   94-41244 CIP

ACKNOWLEDGMENTS

First and foremost, I want to thank my aunts, Mary Louise Belton, Arline Jackson, and Annette McClain, whose dedication to family brought my siblings and me into their homes—and kept us out of an orphanage—upon the death of my parents. Their love for us flowed from the words they dedicated to their sister—my mother—at her funeral:

> *Sad and sudden was the call,*
> *a bitter grief, a shock severe*
> *it was to part with one so dear.*
> *We often sit and think of you*
> *and speak of how you died.*
> *To think you could not say goodbye*
> *before you closed your eyes.*
> *For all of us you did your best,*
> *oh, God grant you eternal rest.*

This book is a labor of love—and healing—that was at times almost too painful to finish. That I did is due in large part to the prodding of Denise Stinson, my literary agent. Sometimes she was gentle. Other times she was not. But always she made me feel that the story I was struggling to tell was worth my pain.

I am also grateful to my editor, John Glusman, whose faith in me and this project has always been strong—even when I was not. He guided me over the bumpy roads of self-discovery and introspection without tearing the thin skin of my bruised soul. And most important, he allowed me to tell my story my way.

I am also greatly indebted to Bernadette Adams and Raina Harper, whose research uncovered such wonderful information about the people and places I've written about in this book. They were tireless in their efforts. And so, too, was Jeanette Brown, the assistant director of *USA Today*'s library and research center, who helped me restart my engines when the dead ends I ran into caused them to sputter.

A special thanks to John White, who drew me into the craft of journalism, and Allegra Bennett, who for years has challenged me to practice it well—and honestly. They read much of the first draft of my manuscript and offered me some valuable criticisms. This book has benefited greatly from their input.

When *Woodholme* was no more than some raw ideas on a few pieces of paper, Dr. Mary Frances Berry helped me to massage my thoughts and confront the demons that threatened to make the telling of this story too much for me to bear. Since my days as a student at the University of Maryland, where we first met, she has been my teacher, my mentor, and my friend.

Finally, a special thanks to Wanda, who doubles as my wife and best friend. More than anyone else, she has been with me from start to finish of this project. In many ways, this book was as demanding on her as it was on me. For months I was a prisoner of this project, anchored to my computer keyboard like a felon shackled to a ball and chain. Throughout this long period, Wanda never wavered in her support.

In the final analysis, it was her love and understanding that gave me the courage and the strength to write this book.

I love her dearly.

DeWayne Wickham
Owings Mills, Maryland
September 1, 1994

What knowledge is of greatest worth?
it's said someone once asked Socrates.

"Know thyself," he answered.

W O O D H O L M E

A Black Man's Story of Growing Up Alone

CHAPTER 1

The approach was a narrow, tree-lined lane that peeled off
Reisterstown Road with little notice. The only warning
motorists got was a small, one-word sign near the point where
the two roadways merged that simply—no, make that dis-
creetly—announced its destination: Woodholme.

It was the spring of 1961, and I was only fourteen the first
time I made the trip up that winding passage to the Jewish
country club on the hilltop above. My stomach growled loudly
as I took those first uncertain steps toward Woodholme. It
always growled around breakfast time. And most days there
was nothing I could do to quiet it. This one was no different,
since I was only able to scrounge up enough money for the
one-way bus fare to Woodholme.

For much of the way up the road, the private country club's
physical structures and its lush golf course were hidden from
view by a thicket of trees. I'd not been to a golf course before,
nor, for that matter, a country club. And with the exception
of a few visits to Druid Hill Park, the huge public domain
that was then the demarcation line between white and black
Baltimore, in much the same way that New York's Central
Park now separates wealthy whites on its south side from poor
blacks and Hispanics to the north, I had not seen anything
that compared to this warmly bucolic setting.

Interspersed among the lines of oak and maple trees that stood like sentries along the way to Woodholme, the dogwoods and wildflowers were in bloom. The sky was a deeper blue than the one that hung low over the home I'd left behind that morning. And it was sweet with the smell of country air and full of what was for me the unfamiliar sound of birds chirping.

The steady flow of cars up the roadway forced me to walk along its grassy edge. Nobody stopped to offer me a ride. That was my fault because, as I was soon to learn, club members routinely offered a lift to people they found hiking up the road. But not me, at least not on this morning. I didn't want a ride and they probably sensed as much. Most of the way up the road, I hugged the tree line and avoided making eye contact with the drivers who passed me by. I didn't want to get into their cars, having suddenly become self-conscious about the way I looked.

My khaki pants were threadbare and a couple of days over-due for a good washing. My shirt collar was thick with the crust of dried perspiration and its armpits were badly stained. Still, when I left home that morning I thought I looked just fine. But the closer I got to Woodholme—this country retreat for wealthy Jews—the more uncomfortable I became with my appearance, a feeling that only got worse as I made my way up the road.

The ground beneath my feet was wet with the morning dew, which quickly became something of an annoyance as the moisture seeped into my badly worn Converse sneakers. Soon the squishy sound of water-soaked socks pressing against damp rubber soles broke the morning's natural symphony, and slowed my step. It was a little after 7 a.m. when I approached the ridge where the road turns gently to the right, wrapping around the back of a grassy knoll. It was there that I got my first glimpse of Woodholme's golf course.

"Damn" was all I could manage to mutter in amazement at what I saw. From where I stood, the golf course stretched out in three directions. It was a sprawling oasis of trees and well-manicured grass like nothing I had ever seen. A maze of hills and valleys connected by long, narrow strips of turf criss-crossed the great expanse of land that unfolded before me.

In the distance, there was a small stream. Closer by, several poorly formed circles, filled with milk-white sand, cut into the ground. They surrounded a mass of grass packed so tightly, and cut so closely, that it resembled a fine green carpet. Near its center, a little white flag bearing the number 7 flew from a pole that rose up out of a small hole.

Ahead of me, the parking lot was already beginning to fill with the late-model cars of club members arriving for an early round of golf, or game of tennis. They were Cadillacs and Lincolns mostly. But here and there I saw a Jaguar. Next to the wooden booth the parking-lot attendants manned sat a Rolls-Royce.

Off to the left of the parking lot was the clubhouse, a grand, sprawling building with a circular driveway and col-umned entrance that gave the place the look of the southern plantation I'd seen years earlier when my father took me to the movies to see *Gone With the Wind*.

By now the road was wide enough that I could escape the wet grass without fear of being run down by a passing motorist. On the blacktop, the watery sound of my sneakers was even more pronounced. Every step I took left an imprint behind me on the road's surface. As I walked awkwardly past the clubhouse, a steady stream of cars circled under the building's portico. There three black men—each in his early twenties—took turns chauffeuring cars to a parking space.

Even in the cool spring morning air, the men sweated profusely as they hurried to park one car and then raced back to the clubhouse for another. As they ran past me I could hear the sound of coins jangling. Their pockets bulged with the tips already earned in a workday that was just beginning. One of the men, a tall, pocked-faced man with processed hair, slowed as he approached me.

"Hey, man, where do you go to caddie?" I asked him.

"Over there, through the parking lot and down the path," he answered, jabbing his arm over his shoulder in the general direction of the parking lot from which he had just emerged.

Weaving my way through the parked cars, I found a small asphalt walkway on the other side of the now nearly full lot. The path snaked down through a row of trees and shrubbery to the golf pro shop, a small one-story brick building that was tucked neatly behind the first tee, the starting point for each round of golf. A steady flow of white men in brightly colored clothes and spiked shoes went into the building and then quickly reappeared and headed toward the first tee.

The pro shop was a combination golf store and control central for Woodholme's golfers. Its operation was managed by the club's professional golfer. He was a teaching pro, not one of those professional golfers who go about the country competing in tournaments for prize money like Arnold Palmer or Jack Nicklaus. Teaching pros trade the chance for fame and fortune for the security of a steady job and the celebrity that comes with being the country club's resident golf professional. At private clubs like Woodholme, the golf pro is the big fish in the little pond.

As I neared the door to the pro shop I found myself in an even larger sea of white faces. Strangely, they took little notice of me, increasing my discomfort and making my steps less certain. Desperately my eyes searched for a friendly face—a black face. Then I heard the voice.

"Hey, where ya goin'?" it called out to me. The gravelly voice pierced the crowd around me like one of those whistles that dogs hear but humans don't. I was the only one who seemed to notice. Thirty feet away, on the other side of a cinder block wall, an old black man glared at me as though I were about to break some cardinal rule. No doubt about it, if looks could kill, this guy had the face of an assassin.

Henry Thomas was the senior caddie at Woodholme. His small frame, bent low by years of backbreaking labor, disguised the lean, muscular body of a man half his years—an age no one knew for sure, but which rumor put at sixty-something. His skin was black as soot and his hands, calloused, with fingernails that resembled acorns, looked as if they belonged to a blacksmith.

Pop Henry—that's what people called him—knew all of Woodholme's rules of behavior, one of which I was about to violate. The pro shop was off limits to caddies. At Woodholme there were no written rules for caddies, at least none of which I was ever made aware. No, the do's and don'ts that governed our behavior were passed along down a hierarchy from club officials to the golf pro and then to the caddie master, the overseer of Woodholme's caddies.

From that point, Pop Henry just kind of took it upon himself to see to it that the rest of us—by that I mean the black caddies—didn't mess up. He wasn't about to try to tell white folks, even the poor whites who came to Woodholme to caddie, what they could and couldn't do. But on my first day at the Jewish country club, Pop Henry was quick to lecture me.

"I'm here to caddie," I answered the old man.

"Well, boy, if you wanna work here you betta learn to keep yo' mouth shut, steer clear of dat pro shop, and stay outta white folks' way," he said.

Then, with a flick of his head to direct me, he snapped,

"Now git down dere in the caddie shack wit everybody else."

The caddie shack was a single room that clung to the side of the pro shop like a barnacle to the hull of a ship. It had the unmistakable look of something that just didn't belong there. From a distance it appeared to be a dark, brooding place—a dank holding pen for those who daily came to work as porters for the golfers of Woodholme Country Club.

"Where you from, boy?" Pop Henry called out to me, halting my move toward the door that opened into the caddie shack.

"Cherry Hill," I answered.

"Damn, y'all tryin' take over, ain't cha?" he deadpanned. "We got too many of you ole po'-ass niggas out here already."

And more would come.

Cherry Hill was a maze of mostly public housing, with a sprinkling of federally subsidized apartments and low-cost, privately owned homes. As big-city housing projects go, it didn't have the stark and chilling look of Brooklyn's Fort Greene, or Chicago's Robert Taylor Homes, concrete jungles with rows upon rows of high-rise apartments that punctuate the isolation of the people who live in them.

Cherry Hill is different. It consists mostly of two-story town houses spread out over four hundred acres of land. There's a sprinkling of three-story apartment buildings, but nothing as frightening as the two-mile-long line of twenty-eight-story public housing units that line Chicago's Dan Ryan Expressway. For me and the other young black boys who found our way to Woodholme in the early 1960s, the country club was an escape from Cherry Hill—an escape from a life of poverty and despair, and a chance to bring home more money every week than most of the adults we knew could earn legally in seven days. I'd heard about this cash cow called Woodholme from a friend and I wanted to milk it for all I could get. It didn't matter much to me that it took two buses and a long walk up a winding road to get there. That was the easiest part of a tortuous journey that started nearly seven years earlier on the morning of December 17, 1954.

CHAPTER 2

I don't remember much about my third-grade year other than the day I raced from school carrying an envelope full of photographs. Instead of heading home, I took off in the opposite direction. South on Francis Street for about half a block and then a quick right into the alley I often used as a shortcut to the place where my mother worked.

It was Thursday, December 16, 1954. Christmas was a little more than a week away, and my mother, one of two sales clerks—both of them black—was busy with a customer when I burst through the door and into the clothing store of Isidor Cooper.

Isidor Cooper straddled two worlds. A chain-smoker with trembling hands, he was the son of a Jewish immigrant who fled czarist Russia around the turn of the century and settled in Baltimore among the city's growing population of eastern European Jews. In 1948 he opened a small clothing store on the northernmost edge of the city's black business district. It was, to be sure, an upscale shop. Still, Mr. Cooper managed to keep his prices well within the reach of his clientele of mostly working-class black women. He wanted the store to be a place of quality that his black customers could afford, he often said. And it was.

But that wasn't the only reason people came to his shop. Isidor Cooper was generous to a fault—a real soft touch. He often let customers buy on credit, even when their credit record argued against such a decision. "I know the honest ones," he would say. At times, people came to his store looking for a loan, rather than clothing. Even then, he seldom turned anyone away empty-handed. At closing time it was not unusual for Mr. Cooper to offer a female customer a ride home. "You shouldn't walk the streets alone after dark," he'd tell a late shopper, sounding as concerned as any doting father. And then this kindly Jewish merchant would give the woman a ride home.

Once, when I went to his store to ask my mother for five cents to buy some candy, Mr. Cooper overheard her tell me she didn't have any money. Pulling me aside, he asked if I thought I was old enough to assemble some boxes for him. Piled high in one corner of the store were the thin cardboard sheets that folded into the boxes used to package the clothes he sold.

"Sure!" I answered.

"Well, you fold those boxes for me," he said, "and I'll pay you five cents."

Minutes later I walked the half block to the five-and-dime store with the nickel I'd earned and bought a bag of candy. From then on, I had a job. Every day after school I'd go to his store, find an out-of-the-way place on the floor near a rack of clothes, and fold boxes. It was a job one of his employees easily could have done any time business slowed, but Mr. Cooper always let that work await my arrival. And when the job was done, he'd give me a nickel—a payment I quickly converted into a bag of candy corn or jelly beans.

Mr. Cooper's clothing store was located on Pennsylvania Avenue, a two-mile stretch of urban sprawl that was the social and cultural hub of Baltimore's black community. At its upper end, Pennsylvania Avenue becomes Reisterstown Road, a main thoroughfare through Baltimore's Jewish community. People used to jokingly say, "Pennsylvania Avenue is the longest road in the world, because it connects Africa to Israel."

The linkage between blacks and Jews in Baltimore was more than just tongue-in-cheek. At the turn of the century they were tightly tied to each other by discriminatory housing patterns that forced poor Russian Jews to live in close proximity to poor blacks in southern and eastern sections of the city. Many of the merchants who operated businesses in these neighborhoods were Jewish. Over time, the Jews moved out of these ghettoes, but the merchants, like Isidor Cooper, remained for decades.

The point where Africa connected to Israel became a moving target as the outmigration of Jews from Baltimore's inner city and the trailing presence of blacks constantly shifted the intersection of the two communities. By 1954 they joined at the corner of Reisterstown Road and Pennsylvania Avenue.

At the lower end of Pennsylvania Avenue were most of the juke joints and nightclubs that were the favorite haunts of Baltimore's blacks, as well as a nightly lure for others from as far away as Washington and Philadelphia. It was there that places like Ike Dixon's Comedy Club and the Watusi and Millionaire clubs stood within walking distance of the Royal Theater.

The Royal was Baltimore's link in a loosely knit network of playhouses, called the "chitlins circuit," that consisted mostly of stops in northern cities: places like the Uptown, in Philadelphia; the Howard, in Washington; the Regal, in Chicago; the Royal; and, of course, the Apollo, in New York.

Cab Calloway, Count Basie, Nat King Cole, and Dinah Washington all performed at the Royal during the forties and fifties. Sammy Davis, Jr., used to dance on its stage alongside his father and uncle, before he became well known as a singer.

The early sixties brought James Brown, Carla Thomas, Lloyd Price, Martha and the Vandellas, Otis Redding, Maxine Brown, and a long list of other "race music" performers to the Royal. Comedy was also a big part of the shows that played the Royal. Jackie "Moms" Mabley, Dewey "Pigmeat" Markham, and Redd Foxx appeared there often.

Pennsylvania Avenue saw its heyday during the years preceding the social integration that followed passage of the 1964 Civil Rights Act. Back then, the lower end of Pennsylvania Avenue overflowed day and night with black folks. Hustlers. Church people. Pimps and their whores. And panhandlers, too. But mostly there was a broad cross section of working-class blacks—teachers, steelworkers, cabdrivers, and even preachers—prowling the lower end of Pennsylvania Avenue in search of a day's shopping, or a night's entertainment.

The upper end of Pennsylvania Avenue, where Isidor Cooper's clothing store was located, differed from the lower part in much the same way that Broadway differs from SoHo, or Beverly Hills is different from Venice Beach. Where one is full of bright lights, flashy people, and fast-paced action, the other is laid back in both style and substance.

North Avenue is the dividing line for the two ends of Pennsylvania Avenue. Above the intersection of Pennsylvania and North there was a commercial laundry, plus a scattering of appliance, hardware, and secondhand stores. There was also Tickner's—a funeral home for whites only—and, a few doors away, a slaughterhouse where money, not race, was the currency that mattered. Then, at the very top of Pennsylvania Avenue, next door to the Red Fox bar, was the clothing store where my mother worked.

"Here, Ma," I said breathlessly as I stepped between my mother and the customer she was waiting on. My right arm stretched high in an effort to deliver the envelope full of photographs I'd brought from school that day into her gentle hands.

"What is it?" she asked.

"My school pictures," I answered with a big grin and a disarming tilt of the head.

"Are they free?" she snapped, erasing the grin from my face.

"No, ma'am," I answered.

Slowly she pulled the photos from the envelope. Different sizes, they were all the same picture: a single head-and-shoulder shot of an eight-year-old boy with a closely cropped haircut, wearing a plaid shirt that was buttoned at the neck, a broad smile, and the wide-eyed innocence of a deer caught in the bright lights of an approaching car.

The woman she'd been waiting on reacted first. She fussed over my pictures as if they were photos of her own son. It wasn't long before the other women in the store gathered around and started saying how cute the pictures were. That's when my mother's concern about money started to wane.

"Well, maybe we can buy a couple of them," she said with a smile. "Let's see what your father says."

My mother, DeSylvia Chase, arrived in Baltimore in 1938 on the arm of her mother, who had packed up and left Maryland's rural Calvert County to escape an abusive husband. Bessie Chase and her three youngest children—four older ones had already left home—came to Baltimore full of hope for a better life. For a time they all had to sleep in the same bed while awaiting its arrival. Still, life for them in Baltimore was a hell of a lot better than what they left behind in southern Maryland. For black folks, the living was hard in Calvert County. Most of the men were farmers, and the women housewives, who sometimes earned a few extra dollars cleaning the homes and caring for the children of white families.

As far back as anyone remembers, farming was what my mother's family did to make ends meet. My maternal great-grandfather found his way to Calvert County sometime in the last quarter of the nineteenth century. A man of deep mahogany complexion and muscular build, William Howe is believed to have been born in Guam. Nobody knows how that came to be. From his picture, a portrait taken in a Pennsylvania Avenue studio around the turn of the century, he was clearly a man of African ancestry. His marriage to Carrie Gray produced nine children, the second of which was their first daughter, Carrie Elizabeth Howe. From the beginning, everybody called her Bessie.

Bessie Howe was a year older than Leonza Chase when they married in 1913, the same year the Constitution was amended to allow the federal government to tax people's income. The two of them had little reason to be concerned about an income tax. On their marriage license, my grandfather was listed as a farmer, and my grandmother as a "spinster." Ten years later, DeSylvia Virginia Chase, the fifth of seven children, was born to them.

DeSylvia was fifteen when she arrived in Baltimore. She was a pretty girl whose light brown complexion resulted from a long and sexually productive relationship between her father's mother and a white man named O'Leary. For a time, my mother worked as a domestic servant for a Jewish family in The Marlboro, a trendy high-rise on Eutaw Place. She was sixteen when she met and fell in love with John Wickham. That was in 1939, shortly before France and Britain declared war on Germany following its invasion of Poland, an action that launched World War II.

The war industry that sprouted in Baltimore in response to the fighting in Europe created a lot of jobs for blacks; mostly at the shipyards where workers built hundreds of Liberty ships and at the Glen L. Martin plant in Baltimore County where they built bombers and other wartime aircrafts.

Even so, my father had trouble finding and holding on to a job. John Wickham was born in Baltimore in 1922. His father, Trevillian Wickham (everybody called him Dilly), was a porter for the B&O Railroad. He migrated from Richmond to Baltimore in the early years of this century and married Maggie Boyer. Their marriage produced two children, John and Dorothy.

Like my mother, John Wickham was a man of fair complexion, a skin color no doubt influenced by the miscegenation that produced the black branch of the Wickham family tree in antebellum Richmond. Unlike my mother, who was raised in the rural Maryland countryside, my father grew up on the fast streets of a big city. In that way, they were an odd match. Still, it wasn't long after they met that John and Sylvia (that's what her friends called her) became a couple.

He was a smooth-talking, good-looking, street-wise guy who showered her with attention. She was a love-struck country girl full of hope for a future better than her past. Shortly after meeting John, DeSylvia told her sister Arline (pronounced Arleen), "That's the man I'm going to marry."

And so she did. Two years after they met, DeSylvia Chase and John Wickham became husband and wife. But the wedding didn't come until after the arrival of André, my oldest brother. My mother's firstborn, André was fathered by a man she started seeing during a brief breakup of her relationship with John. He couldn't commit to a monogamous relationship and she wouldn't accept anything less. So for a while he went off to satisfy his considerable libido and she started dating another man.

By the time John realized his mistake, DeSylvia was pregnant and had broken off her new relationship—with someone whose identity even to this day remains a mystery to me. Still, John insisted on getting married. The wedding took place in the summer of 1941, just a few weeks after André was born. They were married by the Reverend Matthew W. Saunders, a rather flamboyant man of the cloth who listed his denomination simply as "minister of the gospel." Between Sunday sermons, he operated an employment agency for blacks. For two dollars, Reverend Saunders married my parents in his secular place of business, squeezing in the ceremony between interviews with job seekers and telephone calls to potential employers.

From the start, married life wasn't easy for them. The Japanese attack on Pearl Harbor came less than six months after my parents exchanged their wedding vows. It wasn't long after that that my father got his draft notice. He was ordered to Fort Devens, Massachusetts, for basic training. That was the home of the 366th Infantry, a black army unit that was formed in December 1940.

Several guys from my father's West Baltimore neighborhood ended up in the 366th, including one who was dating Annette Chase, my mother's youngest sister. The Defense Department was reluctant to use black troops in combat, despite the way black units had distinguished themselves in fighting in France during World War I. So my father's unit stayed Stateside longer than most, until it was shipped overseas in March of 1944.

Before he departed, my mother became pregnant again. Her second child—his first—was a boy born to them in January of 1943. They named him John, but from birth everybody's called him by his middle name, Rodney.

Fifteen months later, my father's unit was sent to North Africa. It landed at Casablanca on April 6, 1944, and by the end of the month was in Italy, where it was assigned mostly to guarding airfields. Later that year, with casualties in white combat units spearheading the Allied drive toward Germany running high—and available white replacements low—a call went out to "limited service" units for volunteers. To make up for the heavy losses of white combat troops, General Dwight D. Eisenhower decided that black soldiers could be used as replacements in white combat units.

In less than three months, more than five thousand black soldiers volunteered. My father was one of them. He was reassigned to the 56th Armored Infantry Battalion, of the 12th Armored Division, making him one of the first blacks to serve in an integrated army unit.

Little good came of it. My father was in and out of the stockade during his time with the 56th. The offenses he committed couldn't have been too serious since he was honorably discharged with the rank of corporal soon after the fighting in Europe ended.

Like a lot of black soldiers, he came home to a series of low-paying, dead-end jobs. The tailoring skills he learned at the city's general vocational high school didn't leave him with many real career options. By the time I was born in July of 1946, my father was working as a tailor. A year later, my sister Rise (pronounced Ree-sa) arrived. In 1951, Myron, the last of the children John and DeSylvia shared, was born. Then, five months later, my youngest sister, Sondra, was born—the product of an adulterous relationship my father had had with another woman.

With a wife and five kids at home—and one "in the street," as people like to say of a child born out of wedlock—my father was under increasing pressure to make ends meet. On the December day I showed up at my mother's job full of so much excitement, he was a driver for the Yellow Cab Company—

one of its first black drivers. It was the last job he would ever hold.

After leaving my school pictures with my mother, I went off to play as any eight-year-old boy would do on a late autumn day. André, then thirteen, was in charge of the house when my parents weren't around. He'd fix our dinner, check our homework, and make us come in before it got dark.

Home for us was a first-floor apartment in a two-story brick row house at 2308 Whittier Avenue, a ten-minute walk from my mother's job. My parents slept in the apartment's sole bedroom. The living room doubled as a bedroom for the rest of us. Rise slept on a cot. André, Rodney, and I piled into a single twin bed, and three-year-old Myron slept in a crib.

Usually my mother came home long before we went to bed. With five kids to take care of, home, for her, was hardly a retreat from work. Still, she never shied away from spending time with us. My father's hours were less predictable. He was always around, popping in and out of the house at all hours of the day. But he never seemed to really be there. He was more like a frequent visitor, a guy who showed up at the oddest times, usually with a bag of candy, but who was never really there when you needed him. Still, he managed to come home each night before my bedtime.

But as the hour grew late on the night of December 16, neither of my parents had come home when André anxiously ordered us to bed.

As it turned out, I was the last of the children to see my mother alive. After work, she and my father were spotted outside a grocery store by the man who lived in the apartment above us. That's the last time anyone reported seeing them alive. How they spent their final hours is a mystery. At some point, in the early morning hours of December 17, 1954, my father parked his powder-blue 1950 Plymouth station wagon next to the construction site of a new colored high school, pulled a .32 caliber revolver, and fired two shots—one into the head, the other into the chest—of his wife of thirteen years. Then he placed the gun against the right side of his head and pulled the trigger one last time.

It was about 4:20 a.m. when the police found them. An officer in a radio car on routine patrol noticed my father's head slumped against the window of his car. He was still bleeding from his wound. By the time a doctor arrived, both he and my mother were dead.

Among the personal effects police recovered from the car were a suicide note my father wrote to his mother, a twenty-dollar money order, my parents' wedding rings, and what the police report listed simply as "21 photographs of a colored boy"—my school pictures.

Long before the policemen arrived at our house, André knew something was wrong. He'd stayed up all night looking out the window and waiting for our parents to come home. At some point, he heard a report on the radio about a colored couple found dead in a car, but investigators "were withholding the names of the victims," the announcer said, "until the next of kin could be notified."

That notice came with the crack of dawn. The knock on the door must have startled my brother. As much as he surely wanted our parents to be standing on the porch when he opened the front door, he knew there wasn't much chance that they would be knocking on their own door at that time of the morning.

I can only imagine the raw, mind-numbing fear the two policemen must have seen in André's eyes when they asked him the question they had to ask, but almost certainly knew the answer to.

"Are your parents home?" one of them said.

"No, sir," André answered.

"Anybody else here with you?" the officer wanted to know.

"My sister and brothers," the answer came.

"Any adults?"

"No, sir."

That's when one of the cops asked André if he knew the address of our nearest relative. What happened after that is mostly a blur to me. I remember being in a house full of people, some of them crying. I remember a lot of people hugging and kissing us and then moving away to talk to each other in hushed voices. I remember feeling scared, real scared. And I remember how I started blocking out everything and everybody after Rise leaned over and whispered into my ear the chilling details of what she'd overheard some grownup say happened to our mother and father:

"He shot her two times. Then he shot himself, too. He was mad because he didn't have no money," Rise told me. "They're dead."

I didn't say a thing. Slowly, I began to move away from Rise to find some space of my own in the crowded house. Physically I couldn't get very far, but mentally I was running away from that place and Rise's words as fast as I could.

I don't remember when Isidor Cooper and his wife, Dorothy, came to visit, although I'm told they were among the first to arrive after word of what happened got out. That's understandable. The bond between our two families was strong. Aunt Mary Louise, my mother's oldest sister, worked in the Coopers' home, cleaning house and caring for their two daughters. In the days following my mother's death, Mr. Cooper insisted that my aunt take her place in the store, a job she didn't think she could do. Her father, Leonza Chase, forced his daughters to leave school after the seventh grade. "All they gonna do anyway is git married and have a bunch of babies," he once said. But seven years of schooling was no more than he permitted his sons. The three of them also left school after the seventh grade to go to work.

But Mr. Cooper persisted, and in time Aunt Mary Louise made the jump from domestic worker to sales clerk, a quantum leap back then for a black woman with little formal education.

Some of the Jewish merchants along Pennsylvania Avenue were not well regarded by the area's black residents. People complained that their prices were high and their attitudes toward black folks ranged from condescension to outright hostility. Another sore point was that few of the shop owners employed blacks in anything but the most menial jobs.

Mr. Cooper was different. His sales force was all-black and there was nothing condescending or hostile about the way he dealt with his customers. When business was slow, he would stand out in front of his apparel shop and talk to passersby. It was a simple gesture that made people think of him fondly. When people in the neighborhood complained about "those Jews" they weren't talking about their friend Isidor Cooper.

I suspect there was another, more compelling, reason why Mr. Cooper showed up the day my parents died: he knew firsthand the pain that comes with losing a parent to a violent death.

While traveling near Lynchburg, Virginia, in the summer of 1913, Mr. Cooper's father was savagely beaten and then shot in the back by two white men who attacked him after his horse-drawn wagon blocked the path of their motorcar. David Cooper languished in a local hospital for three weeks before dying of his wound. His son, Isidor, was just three years old at the time.

"It is hard to die so young," David Cooper said in the deathbed statement prosecutors used to convict his two assailants. "I am sorry for my wife and children."

They say Isidor Cooper's hands shook more than usual as

he stood grieving with my family in the hours after my parents died. He moved about the house with an ever-present cigarette hanging from his hand like a sixth finger, consoling some and recalling better times with others. He was like one of the family. In time he left, only to return hours later with new coats for each of the children my parents left behind—gifts intended to protect us from both the coming winter and the chilling realities of the changes our lives were about to undergo. One of them was quick in coming.

The *Afro-American*, Baltimore's biweekly black newspaper, made what happened to my parents its lead, front-page story for two consecutive issues. The first recounted the tragic details of their deaths and the reaction of friends and family members. The second, published just four days before Christmas, reported that the note my father left his mother blamed what he did on his "money worries," including a concern that he couldn't afford "to purchase Christmas gifts" for his children.

In his letter, my father asked his mother to take care of the children he orphaned. The twenty-dollar money order police found on his body was made out to her. It was all he could come up with to help her provide for us. But Maggie Wickham was too sick with cancer to take on the responsibility my father willed to her. She died just about a month after my parents were buried. So it was left to my mother's family to figure out what to do with us.

I don't know how they came to the decision, but it didn't take them long. Rise would move in with Aunt Mary Louise and her husband. Myron would stay with Aunt Arline and her family. André would live with Bessie Chase, our maternal grandmother. And Rodney and I would take up residence with Aunt Annette in the two-bedroom public housing unit she shared with her husband and five children in Cherry Hill.

CHAPTER 3

The first residents moved into Cherry Hill in 1943. At the time, it was the largest public housing project on the East Coast, "a planned community for the colored" from Baltimore's overcrowded inner-city neighborhoods, for those who came to town to work in the war industry, and for black veterans and their widows.

Separated from the rest of the city by the snaking waters of the Patapsco River and a freight train line that runs spine-like along Cherry Hill's western edge, the community was to have had its own schools, fire station, library, and health and social service agencies. It never fully lived up to those expectations. But for a brief while, Cherry Hill was a pleasant enough place. Located on the city's largely undeveloped southern edge, it had a real pastoral quality. Cherry trees (presumably that's how the place got its name) dotted the landscape. Blackberry bushes and crab apple trees grew wild. And the wooded areas that laced through the development were a safe refuge for kids at play.

But by the time I arrived there in 1954, Cherry Hill had already started to fray badly. The community's two elementary schools were overcrowded, forcing many students into portable classrooms. What passed for a library was just a single cramped room with a few shelves of books in the neighborhood's Community Building. And Cherry Hill had no fire station or public health facility.

What it did have was an ample supply of garbage. Tons of foul-smelling, putrid, rat-infested trash, which was trucked into Cherry Hill every day from all over Baltimore to an open-air dump where the constant glow of burning piles of garbage was a local landmark.

From the start, it wasn't easy fitting nine people—two adults and seven children—into a house that was nearly as small as the Whittier Avenue apartment I had been forced to leave. It had just four rooms: a kitchen, living room, and two bedrooms, all with concrete floors. It also had a single bathroom with a tub, no shower. The place was so small that during the day the older kids spent as much time as possible outside. The time of the year, winter or summer, didn't really matter. We hated being shut up in that cramped space. In the summer, without air-conditioning, it sweltered. In the winter, heat poured out of the uncovered radiators like lava from a ruptured volcano.

Most days we usually came inside just in time for dinner —and afterward went back outside until it was time for bed. Putting her newly enlarged family to bed each night was, for Aunt Annette, like trying to fit the proverbial square peg in a round hole.

To start with, she and Uncle Dippy (his real name is Theodore) slept in one of the two bedrooms—a room they shared with their daughter, Robin, and her crib. My cousins Mark and Timmy bedded down on the sleeper couch in the living room. And the four oldest kids—cousins Elmer and Galen plus my brother Rodney and I—shared the other bedroom. Rodney and Elmer slept in one twin bed. Galen, whose nickname was Roach, and I slept in the other.

We lived at 3226 Cherryland Road, the second in a line

of six row houses which anchored a block that dead-ended about a football field away from the edge of the city dump. To be sure, it was public housing. There were no amenities, unless you count the twin sinks in every kitchen. The shallow one was for washing dishes. The deeper one was for doing the family's laundry. Washboards—a necessary accessory on laundry day—were not included.

By government definition, every family on our block was poor; still, most willingly shared what little they did have with a needy neighbor. The funny thing back then about being poor in the midst of a whole community of poor people was that I never fully realized my condition. Sure, I knew that times were tough—dinners of fried salt pork, syrup, and bread to sop it drove that message home. But nobody on our block had it much better, or any worse, than we did.

My mother was the first to be buried. Her funeral came just two days after her death. My father was put to rest three days later. I didn't attend either funeral. That was a mistake. When asked if I wanted to go, I said no.

I was afraid to see them. Scared that I would see the bullet holes. Terrified that they would somehow look strange and haunting. And I was angry that my mother and father had gone away from me forever without even saying goodbye.

They buried my mother in Calvert County, in the cemetery next to the family church. I don't know if Mr. Cooper attended the service, but not long afterward he told Aunt Mary Louise he'd had a tree planted in Israel in memory of my mother. It was for him—as it is for most Jews—a profoundly meaningful act, but the significance of what he had done was lost on my family at the time.

My father was buried in a veterans' cemetery on Baltimore's

western edge. The night before his funeral I saw my father one last time. Call it a dream or a nightmare. Maybe it was just a hallucination. Whatever it was, it seemed very real to me at the time—frightfully real. He appeared in the bedroom, high up near where the corner of the wall in front of me merged into the ceiling. For one terrified, pregnant moment I could not manage a sound. And then I began to scream and cry. My body shook violently. By the time Aunt Annette reached me I was wet with perspiration. Awakened by my cries, my brother and cousins looked on in eerie silence.

"What wrong?" she cried out to me as she entered our bedroom.

"I saw my daddy," I answered her in a voice filled with fear.

"Where?" my aunt asked as she looked nervously about the room.

"Up there, in the ceiling," I said tearfully, pointing to a spot on the wall a few feet away.

Aunt Annette gave the ceiling a quick look, clutched me to her side for a moment, and then walked me slowly into her bedroom and laid me next to her in the bed. "It's okay," she said over and over to me. "It's okay."

But it wasn't okay. And it wouldn't be for a long, long time. Everybody told me that I was my father's favorite child. That's probably true. He used to come home at night with a pocket full of candy—mostly coffee candy—and slip me a piece when others in the family weren't watching. And then there was the time he took the family to Gettysburg to visit the famous Civil War battlefield. I begged my father to buy me a small souvenir from one of the gift shops. He didn't have the money to pay for it, so he just slipped it into his pocket and gave it to me when we got outside.

Once when we were all out in the car together my father

made a quick stop at a tavern. When he came out, he was carrying five hard-boiled eggs—four white and one brown. He gave one white egg each to my sister and brothers. "You get white eggs because you were born in white hospitals," he told them. Then he handed me the brown egg and with a big smile explained, "This is for you, because you were born in a black hospital." My father always found ways like that to single me out, to make me feel special.

I thought he was singling me out the night I saw him in my bedroom. I was afraid he had come to take me with him, to do to me what he had done to my mother. He killed her, I thought, and now he'd come back for me.

Even after Rise told me what my father had done, I still loved him. But I also hated him for the unspeakable thing he did that tore apart our family. I wanted my mother back. I wanted to be back in the bed I shared with my brothers in the house on Whittier Avenue, not the one I was sleeping in with a cousin I barely knew. I missed my friends and the special closeness I'd had with my sister. She always wanted to tag along with me during my journeys through our West Baltimore neighborhood, and while most of the time I protested her presence, she usually came anyway. I missed her.

I missed André's protective voice calling out from the back porch for me to come home for the sandwiches he always fixed to get us by until our mother came home to make dinner.

And maybe most of all, I missed Rodney, the brother I had known before the deaths of our parents. He talked to me then, as much as any eleven-year-old boy speaks to his eight-year-old brother. But not afterward. Whenever I tried to bring up with him the life we left behind on Whittier Avenue, all I got in return was an icy stare.

Aunt Annette got me through that night all right, calming my fears with some soothing words and the cuddling warmth of her body. But she wasn't able to quiet the voice deep inside me that cried out for the answers to questions I was afraid to ask.

Why did this man who used to cradle me in his arms and slip coffee candy into my fingers shoot my mother? What could she have done to make him so mad? And why did they both have to die?

No one ever answered the questions the voice inside me asked, and so I quickly learned to block them out. The less I thought about my parents, the more I suppressed my memory of them, the harder it became for that angry voice inside of me to be heard.

After moving in with Aunt Annette's family, I never ate another piece of coffee candy—and in all the time since then I've never had a drop of coffee. For many years, just the smell of the stuff made me nauseous.

After my father's funeral my new life began to take hold. A new school. New friends. A new home and neighbors. They all helped insulate me from the people and things that were too painful a reminder of all that I wanted to forget.

The report in the *Afro-American* about my father being despondent because he couldn't afford to buy Christmas gifts for his children really got to a lot of people. Gifts poured into my old elementary school after teachers there appealed for toys to make sure there was something under the tree for us on Christmas Day. In just a matter of days, the donations filled several large boxes. The school held a ceremony to hand over the gifts to us, but I was too ashamed of what had happened to my parents to go. Somehow, Aunt Annette arranged to have two of the boxes delivered to her house. One was big enough to hold a refrigerator. The other was about the size that a large television would come in. My aunt let Rodney and me have our pick of the toys, and split the rest among her children. That was fine with me, since many of the toys were things I didn't want or duplicates of those I did.

After Christmas, my aunt enrolled me in P.S. 159, one of Cherry Hill's two elementary schools. Mrs. Foster, my homeroom teacher, knew about the awful thing that had happened to my parents. I think my aunt told her the day she walked me to class and had a whispered conversation with my teacher after I sat down. Whatever she said must have jerked Mrs. Foster's heartstrings. She treated me special, as if I were one of her own children—squeezing and cuddling me more than any of the other children in the class.

Every day Mrs. Foster sent two boys to pick up the free milk and graham crackers that the children in the school were given during the morning break. To be trusted with the responsibility of getting the right order and bringing it back to the classroom intact was a big deal to a bunch of third graders. I was one of the boys Mrs. Foster chose to make the daily pickup. Each morning the two of us would go to the pickup area and get a half-pint carton of milk and graham crackers for every student in our class. Then we'd return to class and hand out the milk and crackers, a duty that gave us some real power, since we decided who got the chocolate milk.

Just about everyone in the class wanted chocolate milk. But the milk we got was always evenly divided between chocolate and white. Why? I'm not sure, but the fact that it was made me a big shot in the class. Nobody messed with me if they ever wanted to get a carton of chocolate milk. Aside from giving my favorites among the girls in the class extra graham crackers, I didn't put the power I had to much use. But because I could, nobody wanted to get on my bad side.

I think Mrs. Foster knew what she was doing when she

gave me that job. It was a shield against the kinds of hurtful things children often say to each other. She knew she couldn't be next to me every moment of the school day to stop the prying questions or deflect the ugly words. So instead she gave me a power over my classmates that in a way protected me from all of that.

There was a strong sense of community among the people who resided along the section of Cherryland Road where I lived. The women talked to each other over the backyard clotheslines or across the metal rails that divided the front porches. The men, none of whom owned a car, would often walk together to and from the bus stop or occasionally sit side by side in the shade of the trees that dotted the small hill behind the row houses.

There wasn't a single-parent family on our block the year I moved in with my aunt. Every mother had a husband and every husband had a job. But still the families all struggled just to survive. The jobs the men had were all menial. Without the surplus food some of the families got from the city's welfare agency, the money the men earned would not have been enough to make ends meet—especially when you consider all the mouths most of the families on our block had to feed. The Garretts had eight children. The Blackwells had six. The Craddocks, three. On one side of my aunt lived the Yateses and their three kids. On the other side were the Georges, with eight children.

Every day the small strip of land in back of the line of row houses became a crowded playground. Mostly the boys shot marbles and played catch with a tattered old ball—and the girls jumped rope and played jacks. But occasionally we would all take to the streets together to go skating. Street skating was the craze in Cherry Hill. Just about every kid in the neighborhood had a set of the cheap metal skates. Sometimes the street in front of our homes would fill up with kids on skates. And when that happened, it wasn't long before the call went out for a line.

The first time I saw that happen, I had no idea what a line was—or, more important, how it worked. But I quickly found out. Usually the person who called for a line would take off, skating down the middle of the street as fast as he could with a hand extended out behind him. Quickly another skater would grab hold and offer a hand to someone else. In a matter of seconds a long line of skaters would be rolling down the street, each one holding on to another. The last person in the line was either a daredevil or someone who had no idea what was about to happen.

I was in the latter category the first time I joined a group of skaters in the street and found myself at the end of one of those lines. There were at least a dozen of us strung together like paper cutouts, racing down the middle of Cherryland Road. Suddenly the lead skater screeched to a stop. As he did, his trailing arm whipped the person behind him forward, creating a domino effect. One after another, each skater did the same thing, until the guy in front of me got his turn. As he put on the brakes and his arm sprung forward he let go of my hand, and I was propelled forward like a stone fired from a slingshot.

Out of control, I flapped my arms in a desperate attempt to keep my balance. But that only made the other skaters laugh harder as my feet raced out ahead of me and I crashed to the ground. I landed on my backside, my butt skidding along the concrete street until I rolled to a stop against the curb in front of my aunt's house. The seat of my pants was ripped and my behind was bruised, but after a moment's hesitation I bounced to my feet and skated away as if it were no big deal. I spent the next couple of days in the house healing my wounded bottom, but on the streets outside I had earned a reputation for toughness that kept a lot of guys off my back.

Aunt Mary Louise, who also lived in Cherry Hill, was a devoutly religious woman. She was a member of the local Presbyterian church, which was pastored by the Reverend Edgar Ward. He was a quiet man, not given to great demonstrations of religious fervor. And as a result his sermons were pretty boring.

The Presbyterian church was located near the intersection of Cherry Hill and Cherryland Roads, across the street from St. Veronica's Catholic church. An AME and Baptist church shared the lot next to it. Since she had custody of Rise, Aunt Mary Louise made sure that my sister attended services every Sunday at her church. She also somehow managed to convince Aunt Annette that of all her charges, Roach and I, too (we were just six months apart in age), should join the church. To do that, we had to attend its dreaded Thursday afternoon confirmation class.

The class was taught by Valeria Murphy, a matronly woman who ran it like a military boot camp. Any infraction of her rules usually resulted in a swift slap of your knuckles from the eighteen-inch ruler she wielded. And if that weren't bad enough, Miss Murphy was also our Sunday School teacher. Thursdays and Sundays were my worst days. I seldom studied my religious lessons and she always punished me when she caught me unprepared. Still, I somehow managed to complete my training, but not without some unexpected help from Miss Murphy.

I'd already been attending church for a few months when the first Mother's Day without my mother came around. As I dressed for church that Sunday morning, Aunt Annette came into the room with two small flowers. The red one she pinned on the lapel of Roach's suit coat, and the white one she attached to mine.

The red flower means that your mother is alive, she said to us. The white one means that she is dead. I wore my flower like a scarlet letter. I was afraid of the attention it would bring me—the notice it would call to my mother's death, a loss I had been able to deal with only by acting as though it never happened. And now I was being made to walk straight up Cherryland Road and into church wearing a white flower like a big neon sign bearing the words: "My mom is dead."

The closer we got to the church, the more crowded the streets became. Here and there I saw a man or woman wearing a white flower, but the children all wore red ones. All, that is, except me.

I had nearly made it into the church when the incident happened.

"You got on the wrong flower," a little girl said to me. I ignored her, but she persisted.

"Don't he, Ma?" she asked the large woman to whose arm she was tethered.

"Is your mother dead, boy?" the woman asked in a voice that seemed to come out of a loudspeaker.

"Yes, ma'am," I answered in a whisper.

"Well, then he's got on the right flower," she seemed to shout to the little girl.

I couldn't stop the water in my eyes from streaming down the sides of my face. As much as I tried to blink back my tears, they kept coming. The door to the church was just a few steps away. I wanted to get inside and lose myself in the larger than normal crowd of worshippers the Mother's Day service attracted. But before I could do that, Miss Murphy draped her arm around my fallen shoulders.

"Come with me," she said, in a voice much softer than any she had ever spoken to me with before.

"Now go ahead and cry if you want to," she said as we entered the small room at the rear of the church where my confirmation classes were held. "It's Mother's Day, and if you miss your mother, it's okay to cry," she said while cradling me in her arms. And cry I did. Tears that should have been shed the day my parents died. Tears that had been stored up inside for months and now flowed with the force of a river.

Afterward, not a word of what happened was ever spoken, but our relationship was forever changed. In confirmation class, Miss Murphy was still a stern taskmaster, but I was a far more willing student. The following year I was baptized and took my first Holy Communion.

Feeding and clothing seven children was tough enough for Annette and Theodore McClain, but when my aunt gave birth to her sixth child the pressure of providing for them, plus Rodney and me, was more than their marriage could stand. One day Uncle Dippy just left home and never returned. Before that, the family was barely able to make ends meet. After his departure, we couldn't—at least, not in the way we had before. The salary my uncle brought home from his maintenance job at the Calvert Liquor distillery was enough to pay the rent and feed us two meals a day. Breakfast usually consisted of a bowl of cold cereal covered with a watered-down cup of Pet milk. Dinner, while having a lot more variety, was predictable. On Fridays we had fried fish. Dinner on Saturdays usually consisted of baked beans and hot dogs, the house brand that the A & P sold in packs of twenty. On Sundays, Aunt Annette fed us fried chicken. Some days, when the food money was running short, we'd have pancakes or a pot of navy beans for supper.

But when Uncle Dippy left, my aunt had to really scramble to feed us. Sometimes dinner consisted of a tin of King syrup and a loaf of bread for sopping. Fried pork fat, which we called fatback, also became a staple in our house. So did Spam and potted ham. Aunt Annette found one creative way after another to put dinner on the table each day. Sometimes that meant sending one of the children to the store bus for one or two items to round out a meal. The store bus was an old school bus that had been converted into a grocery store on wheels. It could usually be found nearby on Bethune Road, or farther away near the end of Seagull Avenue.

The advantage of going to the store bus was that just about everything could be bought in individual units. You could buy one egg, or a couple of cigarettes. If you only wanted— or could only afford—four slices of cheese, you could buy that, too, on the store bus. Regular customers could also get food on credit from the store bus.

The disadvantage of doing business with the old black man who operated the mobile grocery store was that his prices were sky-high. But for people who couldn't afford to buy a dozen eggs, it mattered little that the price they paid for one at the store bus was double the unit cost of a single egg at the A & P. The only thing that mattered was that this store on wheels would sell them a single egg and the A & P wouldn't.

Not long after Uncle Dippy left, my aunt started working full-time as a barmaid to help make ends meet. A proud woman, she wouldn't go on welfare like some of the others on our block. And she never joined the women who walked the short distance to the city dump to pick through mounds of garbage for something to eat. Shopping at the dump, as the kids on my street called it, was something more than a few families did.

One neighborhood woman regularly walked among the heaps of burning garbage, scavenging with a stick in one hand to fend off rats, and a leather shopping bag in the other to carry away whatever edible food she found. Because of its closeness to Baltimore's harbor, Cherry Hill's trash dump got most of the fruits and vegetables that failed to clear customs at the port. And every time trucks loaded with these foods rolled down our block on their way to the dump, people would come out of their homes and "go shopping."

A lot of people from all over Cherry Hill prowled the dump for food to eat. I used to go there with friends in search of bananas, mounds of which were sometimes trucked to the dump. The yellow ones we ate before we got home. The green ones we'd hide in a closet until they ripened.

The dump had one small incinerator. Most of the garbage was stacked high on acres of open field. When the piles of garbage were ignited, the putrid smell of burning trash mixed with tiny particles of ash to foul the air. For most of the people of Cherry Hill there were pitifully few chances to escape this awful pollution of the body and mind.

There were times when I went to the dump in search of prey, not food. Ty and I often went there to hunt rats. Ty's real name is Ellwood William Gary Johnson. How that mouthful got reduced to two letters I don't know. What I do know is that neither of us had much fear of the oversized rodents that made the dump their home.

We started out chasing rats between the burning trash piles, beating them with sticks as they raced from one for the cover of another. Then one year Ty's father bought him a BB gun. Ads for BB guns used to appear on the backs of the worn comic books that got passed between kids in my neighborhood. But until Mr. Johnson came home that day with the long box under his arm, I didn't think anyone I knew could afford to own one.

Armed with the BB gun, Ty and I went to the dump one day determined to bag us some rats. Using a long stick, I pounded the trash piles, causing the rats to scatter. Ty stood just a few feet away firing rapidly at the fleeing rodents as I jumped up and down to avoid the rats all about me. All the while, I was shouting at the top of my voice.

"Get 'em. Get 'em."

The force of the BB's was hardly enough to kill a rat, especially ones that had grown as large as those we found at the dump. But it stunned them long enough for me to strike the fatal blow with the stick I was wielding. After a few hours of this sport, we paraded home like triumphant African warriors returning from a successful hunt. Tied to the sticks that hung from our shoulders were the bodies of the rats we killed. The sight of us walking up the street from the dump with dead rats dangling from a rope drew a knot of curious, squealing children—and the wrath of Ty's mother.

From the safety of her front porch, Mrs. Johnson ordered us to throw the dead rats into a storm drain, where their bodies were left to slowly rot. For days after that, our block reeked of an awful odor that seeped out of the sewer along with the swarms of flies that fed on the rotting carcasses.

Staying out of trouble was a real problem for the children on my block. With the exception of a small, fenced-in cemented area that housed a monkey bar, seesaw, and sliding board, there wasn't a playground within a mile of us. So when it came to play, we improvised. At times that meant stealing from Farmer Brown.

It's a good bet the aging white man with the snow-white

head of hair and beard who lived in the clapboard house across from the city dump was named neither Farmer nor Brown, although his home certainly had the look of a farm. There were chickens and dogs in a yard beaten bare of grass. And cords of firewood were stacked high near the rear door of the house, which sat just a few yards off the road that stretched from the dump entrance all the way to Hanover Street, a major thoroughfare bordering Cherry Hill's eastern edge.

Out back of Farmer Brown's house was a thicket of woods. The trees wrapped around his property on three sides, forming a horseshoe-like perimeter that separated him from everybody else in Cherry Hill. His isolation—and the surly look he gave those kids who got a glimpse of him when they ventured down the dump road—gave rise to some terrifying rumors about this old white man.

Farmer Brown, it was said, hated black children—especially the black boys he caught in his fruit trees. He had apple trees. Pear trees and peach trees, too. And bushes and bushes of blackberries, which grew plump and juicy in the summer. It was all too tempting for me and my friends to pass up—despite what we were sure would be our fate if we fell into the hands of Farmer Brown.

It was said that years earlier a kid from Bethune Road had been captured by a shotgun-toting Farmer Brown as the youngster sat perched high atop one of the man's apple trees. The youngster's shirt bulged with the unmistakable evidence of his thievery. The boy was last seen being marched into the old man's backyard, where he was forced to open a trapdoor and descend into the basement, a hellish abyss from which he never emerged. And that, the story goes, is what happened to the children who pleaded for mercy. Those who didn't were shot on the spot and their bodies chopped up and fed to his dogs.

It didn't matter that no one remembered the names of the

old man's victims, or could explain how so much was known of his cruelties but still he avoided arrest. All that was important to know was that you took your life in your hands to steal from Farmer Brown.

Only a fool would climb into one of Farmer Brown's trees without a lookout. Someone had to remain on the ground to signal his approach should Farmer Brown try to sneak up on the thieves he spotted in his fruit trees. That job usually went to the faint of heart—someone who was unwilling to brave either the climb or the increased chance of capture that came with being in the tree, instead of on the ground, when danger approached. Most of the time when Ty and I climbed up into one of the fruit trees, Roach stayed on the ground as our lookout. Once we'd stuffed enough fruit down the necks of our shirts we would drop out of the tree and beat a quick retreat. When we got home the three of us would split up the fruit. Roach always got the worst of the batch—those with worms or bruises—because he took the fewest risks.

As it turned out, he was overpaid.

One summer day while high up in one of the pear trees I heard a violent rustling of bushes and then the muffled sound of Roach's voice.

"Here comes Farmer Brown," he cried out. His words came from the clump of bushes that he disappeared into before sounding the alarm. Ty was out of his tree in a flash, but my descent was more difficult. He got away. I didn't.

When I hit the ground my knees buckled and my right ankle gave way. Some of the overripe pears beneath my shirt squashed against my chest. In a second I was on my feet, but it was too late. I was a prisoner.

"Why are you stealing from me, boy?" the old man asked.

The throbbing pain in my ankle was nothing compared to the fear that gave my heart a frenzied beat. For a moment everything around me was blurred by the tears that welled in my eyes. I wanted to beg for mercy, but instead I tried to lie my way to freedom.

"I wasn't stealing from you, Mr. Farmer Brown," I said.

"Open up your shirt," he commanded me.

I did. The pears fell to my feet and just as quickly I changed my story.

"I didn't mean to steal from you, Mr. Farmer Brown," I said, sure now that my end was near. "I'm sorry, please don't shoot me," I pleaded.

"Shoot you, with what?" he asked.

In his hand, Farmer Brown clutched a broken tree limb, not the shotgun he was said to always carry. And the bloodhounds that he supposedly used to track down the boys who came daily to steal his fruit were actually two scroungy-looking mutts, more interested in the pears I'd dropped than me.

"You don't have to steal my fruit," he said. "I've got plenty here. If you want some, just knock on my door and ask for it. That's all you got to do, okay?"

"Yes, sir."

"Now pick yourself up a couple of them pears and git," he said with a stern look and a gentle nod of his head.

By the time I got home, Roach had told his mother that Farmer Brown caught me stealing his fruit. Aunt Annette was hot. She made me throw away the pears I had, refusing to believe my story that the old white man had given them to me.

Later, I told Ty, Roach, and the rest of the neighborhood kids that Farmer Brown had tried to carry me off to his basement, but I wrestled away from him and escaped.

To keep us out of Farmer Brown's fruit trees—and out of

trouble—Aunt Annette decided to send Roach and me to the movies just about every Saturday. In the winter when the weather was cold and there was little to do on the streets of Cherry Hill, spending Saturdays in the Hill Theater was something we looked forward to. But not in the summertime.

"Here, take this money and go to the movies," Aunt Annette would say early on Saturday mornings as she handed us each twenty-five cents. "And don't come home until it's dark."

In the summertime that meant going off to the movies around nine in the morning and staying there until the sun went down. Even with two feature films, a serial, cartoons, and previews to watch, we had to see everything three times before it was time to head home.

It cost fourteen cents for children under the age of thirteen to get into Cherry Hill's lone movie theater. That left us eleven cents each for food. I usually invested a nickel of my money in a box of Jujyfruit. Buying the candy was something of a crapshoot. The advantage is that Jujyfruit—which comes in assorted colors: red, yellow, orange, green, and black—can last for hours. The disadvantage is there's no telling how many black and green pieces are in a box. I hate the black and green Jujyfruit. The only thing they are good for is chucking. I used to sling them about the Hill Theater once the lights went out, often beaning unsuspecting moviegoers in the back of the head.

"Hey, who threw that?" a voice would cry out in the darkness when I hit my mark. The question was answered only with silence—and in time another barrage of black and green Jujyfruit. Eventually this series of attacks would set off a wave of shouting that caused the theater's manager, Morris Q. Norris, to turn off the projector and turn on the lights to warn us about our behavior.

Mr. Norris was a tall, thin black man who always wore a suit and tie. He patrolled the aisles of the movie house like a schoolteacher bent upon catching the class clown at play. If forced to, he'd toss an unrepentant troublemaker out of the theater.

Once, after paying the fourteen cents admission, Gus Green, a classmate of mine, rushed straight down the aisle to the emergency door off to the right of the screen and kicked it open. Shards of sunlight leaped through the open door, followed quickly by a half dozen or so of Gus's friends. They were little more than blinding silhouettes who scattered in every direction, disappearing into the theater's seats.

Gus was not so lucky.

From the rear of the theater, Mr. Norris saw him open the emergency door and, like a heat-seeking missile, locked in on Gus's chubby body as he scrambled for a seat. Before an usher could shut the sprung door, Mr. Norris had Gus firmly in his grip. He marched him straight up the aisle, into the lobby, and out the front door, loosening his hold on Gus only after depositing him on the sidewalk beyond the theater's marquee.

That was the exception. Usually Mr. Norris just took the offending moviegoer to his office for a quick lecture on behavior and then returned him to his seat. That's exactly what happened to me the day he caught me raining black and green Jujyfruit on some people a few rows away.

"Remember," Mr. Norris said, "I've got my eyes on you." That was the problem. One look into Mr. Norris's eyes and you knew they were way too gentle to intimidate anyone.

CHAPTER 4

The city's housing department had all but finished building public housing in Cherry Hill the year I moved there. But as the public housing units filled up, and the waiting list for vacancies grew, private developers stepped in and started building a mix of low-income apartment complexes. The rapid growth in the community's population of school-age children was more than Cherry Hill's two elementary schools could accommodate by the fall of 1955.

Both P.S. 159 and P.S. 160 were badly overcrowded that year. To deal with the overflow, some teachers had to instruct two grade levels at once. School officials also had several portable classrooms set up on the playground in back of P.S. 159's two-story building. Still that wasn't enough. So hundreds of children were bused from Cherry Hill to elementary schools in Westport and Mount Winans.

Back then, Westport was a working-class white neighborhood of wood-framed row houses that had the area's only full-fledged public library and fire station. The year before, the Supreme Court had opened the way for black kids from Cherry Hill to go to P.S. 225 in Westport when it voted to end racial discrimination in public schools.

Westport was an easy target for school integration in Baltimore. It was a small community of white folks with little political influence, wedged between the two larger black neighborhoods of Mount Winans and Cherry Hill. Westport sat on Baltimore's southern edge, next to the parkway that connects the city to Washington, D.C. To the west of Westport is Mount Winans, an aging black community of single-unit clapboard houses and a scattering of public housing.

Instead of going to the fourth grade in Cherry Hill, I was bused to P.S. 156, a one-story brick schoolhouse on a quiet side street in Mount Winans. The route took me right past P.S. 225, which had a series of ugly racial clashes that year as whites outside the school protested the arrival of black students.

Mount Winans's elementary school was so small that the same room served as the school's gym, cafeteria, and auditorium. Everything—except classroom space—was in short supply there. We had to write or draw on both sides of the paper teachers gave us, except, of course, when one side of the paper had already been used by another class. There was just one textbook for every two students in my class, a handicap we overcame by sitting two abreast so that we could all read our lessons.

After completing both the fourth and fifth grades in Mount Winans, I attended the sixth grade at P.S. 163, a brand-new elementary school in Cherry Hill that was built on the field just behind P.S. 159. Because mine was the school's first sixth-grade class, the graduation ceremony turned out to be quite a big deal. A lot of white people came. I guess they were officials from the department of education and maybe a few politicians. We spent weeks rehearsing the ceremony, which included songs, dramatic readings, and a closing dance exercise around the maypole in the school yard.

Instead of coming to my graduation, Aunt Annette went to work that day. The family's only breadwinner, she told me she couldn't afford to take the day off. Nobody from my family came. I remember looking at all my classmates, surrounded by their parents and other relatives, and wishing that my mother and father could be there. It was just a fleeting thought, there one moment and gone the next. I couldn't indulge myself in the idea because to miss my parents was to acknowledge their loss, and I still wasn't ready to do that.

After the ceremony, I wandered off with a couple of friends to play in a thicket of woods just beyond the school playground. We climbed trees, searched for wild berries, and sat talking on the large branches of a fallen tree until we realized it was getting late.

It wasn't until I got home and was scolded by my aunt for messing up my clothes that I realized I'd left the little certificate they gave me at graduation in the woods. But as it turned out, that was okay. No one else noticed that I had come home empty-handed.

My two years at Cherry Hill Junior High School were bittersweet. For the first time since I'd moved to Cherry Hill I was in the same class with both Chester and Danny, my two closest friends. We had a lot of good times together. With them I could let down my shields. I could crawl outside of the cocoon inside of which I spent so much time hiding from the truth of what happened to my parents. They didn't ask me questions about the mother and father I never mentioned, or crack on me about my worn clothes. They didn't, but others did. To fend them off, I became pretty good at dissing people. I was always cracking on someone. Slamming them about the way they looked, about the clothes they wore, or just calling into question their intelligence. Anything to keep them laughing at someone other than me.

It wasn't long before Bernice Brown, my homeroom teacher in both the seventh and eighth grades, branded me one of the class clowns. The other cutup was a guy named Tyrone Langston. Every day Tyrone and I would get something going before homeroom ended. We didn't work as a team so much as we were constantly trying to outperform each other.

One day Tyrone used rubber bands to attach a small mirror to the top of one of his shoes. Then he tried to position his foot so he could look up Rose Hall's skirt. In the seventh grade, Rose could have been a body double for Sophia Loren. She had a Coke-bottle figure: a bulging bust line, a tiny waist, and a butt so round and shapely that it could—and often did—stop traffic.

Like most of the guys in our class, Tyrone wanted to see more of her. But his plan fizzled when Rose caught him trying to position his foot between her legs as the two of them sat side by side in our homeroom class one morning.

"Boy, what's wrong with you?" Rose screamed, slapping playfully at Tyrone's head.

"Nothing. Nothing. I ain't doing anything," he answered with nervous laughter as he fended off her attack.

Mrs. Brown, a small woman with a piercing glare and heavy hand, stepped between the two of them as Tyrone dropped to the floor to retrieve his mirror.

"He tried to look up my dress," Rose shouted.

Seeing the mirror on Tyrone's shoe, Mrs. Brown didn't wait for an explanation. Grabbing him by the shirt, she pulled Tyrone toward her and slapped his head with her free hand as he protested his innocence. When Tyrone let out a delayed moan, the classroom erupted in laughter.

Tyrone and I had a lot in common.

His family, too, was dirt-poor. Watching him eat his lunch every day was a real adventure. Whatever he had for dinner the night before usually made it into his lunch. One day it was fried fishheads. Another time it was meat loaf. My lunches weren't much better. Sandwiches made of potted ham and grape jelly were one of my staples. And so were egg salad sandwiches, which could really stink up a locker on a hot day.

Between us, Tyrone and I didn't have enough changes of clothes to keep from having to wear the same thing twice in a single week.

One of my running gags was to predict what Tyrone would wear to school the next day, right down to his socks. The funny thing is that he probably had more clothes than I did. But if I kept people laughing at him, they didn't seem to notice how bad off I was.

Mrs. Brown tried mightily to keep me and Tyrone under control. Eventually, she just decided to isolate us from the rest of our homeroom classmates by seating Tyrone in one rear corner of the classroom and me in the other. There wasn't another student within ten feet of us. But that hardly stopped our nonstop Heckle and Jeckle routine. Most days we came up with original jokes and side-splitting ad-libs. On occasion, though, we got an unintended assist from one of the targets of our humor.

When it came to textbooks, Cherry Hill Junior High was only slightly better off than the elementary school I attended in Mount Winans. At best, the school had just enough history books for students to have individual copies to read from while in class, but far short of what was needed for every seventh grader to have a book to take home each day for study. So instead of reading the book as a homework assignment, we read it aloud in class. The teacher would call on students at random to read a few paragraphs from the book. This would go on until the section to be covered that day had been read.

One day our lesson covered the French Revolution, and the teacher called on a guy named Joseph Bunn to read a passage. Bunn was a big guy whose name became the focus of a lot of bad jokes—most of them behind his back—because of his strong body odor. On a couple of occasions Tyrone cracked on him to his face and just barely escaped getting his butt whipped. Well, Bunn began to read this passage about how somebody he called "Nappy Leon" gained control of France.

"Nappy who?" I cried out from my seat.

"Nappy Leon," Tyrone answered me on cue as everyone in the class, including the teacher, started laughing at Bunn's butchering of Napoleon's name.

Bunn didn't think what we did was very funny. In the hallway after class, he singled me out by making a big scene of challenging me to a fight behind the gym after school. I wasn't going to let him make a chump out of me in front of all the students who were gathered around us, so I made an equally big scene of accepting his challenge.

When the last bell of the school day rang, I slipped out a side door and took the long way home. Bunn, who lived in Mount Winans, waited for me until the crowd that had assembled to watch us get it on had pretty much dispersed and the school bus that took him home was about to leave. At that point he broke off his vigil and raced across the parking lot and hopped aboard.

After that, he stalked me around the school for a few days, but I fended him off by always joking about the showdown he wanted—and by staying close to my boys until his anger faded.

Sometimes all the clowning in the world couldn't hide how poor my family was. In the seventh grade, I wore Converse sneakers to school every day. Even during a snowstorm. When

I wore a hole in the bottom of the sneakers, I stuffed them with cardboard in a failed effort to keep my feet dry. Joseph Bunn was the first to notice my makeshift soles. It was his chance to get even—and he did. He rode my back all day. Even Danny and Chester were laughing at me. There was nothing I could do to get him off my back until my aunt found the money to buy me another pair of sneakers.

When I went to the eighth grade, Aunt Annette decided to buy me a pair of brogans—the kind with steel plates in the toes and metal taps on the bottom—to wear to school. As hard as I was on sneakers, she figured I needed something on my feet that wouldn't wear out so fast. The first day I walked into school, with those taps clacking against the concrete floors with every step I took, Joseph Bunn started cracking on me right away.

"Man, where'd you get them combat boots from?" Bunn said in the hallway outside of our homeroom. The knot of boys around us snickered in anticipation of yet another clash between us.

"From your mother," I shot back.

That was a mistake. Bunn lunged for me. I slipped his grasp and took off running down the hall with him in hot pursuit. Fortunately for me, there was a teacher nearby who ordered us to stop. As I broke my stride I skidded right past the teacher. The taps on the bottom of my shoes caused me to slide across the polished concrete floor like someone skating on ice. By the time I careened to a stop, all the guys around me were clamoring to get a closer look at the brogans I was wearing.

Within a few weeks, half the guys in my class were wearing brogans with steel taps—including Joseph Bunn. What started out for me as an embarrassing sign of my family's poverty had turned into a fashion statement at Cherry Hill Junior High.

In the summer between the eighth and ninth grades, Aunt Annette moved the family out of Cherry Hill. Five and a half years after Rodney and I joined her family, she packed us all up and moved into a three-bedroom row house on a quiet street in west Baltimore, an integrated neighborhood that was rapidly shifting from white to black. It was for me a short-lived exodus from Cherry Hill.

One-forty-one South Hilton Street was a far nicer place than the concrete-floored housing unit we left behind on Cherryland Road. In addition to the bedrooms and bath on the second floor, there was a living room, dining room, and kitchen on the first floor, plus a basement.

We had a lot of space but very little furniture. Just an old couch and chair in the living room and a worn table and chairs in the kitchen. Our dining room was empty, and there were no beds in the bedroom I shared with Rodney, Roach, and Elmer. We slept two each on old mattresses laid flat on the floor.

Roach and I got up early the morning after we moved in and went out front to sit on the steps of the large wooden porch that overlooked the flow of cars and people up and down Hilton Street. He was excited about our move, glad to have escaped Cherry Hill's housing project. But for me the move was pretty traumatic. Already I missed the friends I'd left behind. They were the buffer between the life I'd had on Whittier Avenue and the new one that started the morning after the deaths of my parents. Now I would have to start all over.

As I sat on the steps that morning, my old fears returned.

I worried that the new friends I was about to make would want to know why I lived with my aunt, and not my mother and father. I was scared they'd ask what had happened to my parents. And I was terrified that Roach, or one of my other cousins, would tell them the truth. So I ducked back into the house when I sighted two black boys headed our way, while Roach stayed put and quickly made friends with them.

Allen and Buck Hall lived on the next block. Their father, a widower, was a bartender at Steve's Pink Pony, a popular west Baltimore bar. Mr. Hall raised his six children in the two-story house at 201 South Hilton Street with a lot of help from Patricia, his teenage daughter. She was the surrogate mother to her sister and four brothers.

The Halls' house was the center of activity for many of the neighborhood's black kids. The summer days all seemed to begin there. Allen, a short kid with a raspy voice, usually organized the day's events: a trip across the Edmondson Avenue bridge, a hike along the train tracks to Bloomingdale Park, or a game of softball on the vacant lot on Lohrs Lane, just behind the unit block of South Hilton Street. He was always the one who got things going.

One day when the neighborhood guys were a player short for a softball game, Roach dragged me out of the house to fill the last spot in the lineup. Allen had arranged a game against a group of guys from a nearby community who routinely trounced the Hilton Street team. He stuck me in right field, where sandlot teams often hide their weakest defensive players. Knowing that there was a newcomer in right field, the players on the opposing team tried to hit everything in my direction. But after I made a couple of good catches they started to hit the ball elsewhere.

Allen was thrilled. He quickly found out that not only could I catch, I could hit, too. I got two hits in the game.

My first hit was a single that tore the glove off the third baseman's hand. The other was a home run hit deep to left field with two guys on base. The ball landed in the parking lot of a soft-drink warehouse, missing a truck stacked high with bottles of Hires root beer by just a few feet.

The three runs my homer produced gave the Hilton Street boys their first victory that summer over the visiting team, and made me an instant hero. After that, I didn't worry much about being asked embarrassing questions.

Aunt Annette's work hours got longer and her temper shorter after we moved into the house on Hilton Street. She went to work in the morning and often stayed on the job until late at night, when barmaids earned the best tips. The children—all eight of us—were pretty much left to fend for ourselves for long stretches of the day. It's not that she was neglectful, just that she couldn't be in two places at once, and God knows she needed to work.

When school started that fall, I entered the ninth grade at P.S. 91, Gwynns Falls Junior High, an interracial school three blocks away. It was a real culture shock. I'd never gone to school with whites—or, for that matter, seen so many in one place, at the same time. With the exception of Farmer Brown, I rarely saw any white people in Cherry Hill. Most of them were the merchants who operated businesses in the strip mall that was Cherry Hill's shopping center. Few whites ventured out into the streets of Cherry Hill. Those who did were mostly policemen and bill collectors.

My English teacher at Gwynns Falls Junior High was an attractive black woman named Delores Augustus. She had a well-deserved reputation for toughness and a low tolerance for those who treated her classroom like a playground. From the beginning she singled me out, calling on me in class even when I didn't raise my hand and taking me to task when she found me hanging around with the wrong crowd. I tried to steer clear of her, but our paths always seemed to cross.

The first semester of my ninth-grade year was largely uneventful. I was an average student and pretty popular among blacks at the school. There wasn't much socializing between the races. The only real integration that took place in the school was in the classroom, where black and white students sat next to each other. The rest of the school day there was a sort of mutually agreed upon segregation in place that dictated seating arrangements in the cafeteria and where students gathered outside during recess.

If anything, Aunt Annette seemed to struggle more to keep the family afloat after she moved us out of Cherry Hill. Elmer, her oldest son, enlisted in the Navy; and Rodney, then a high school senior, spent most of his day shuttling between school and Cherry Hill, where most of his friends lived. But even with two fewer mouths to feed, times got tougher in our house.

At the beginning of the school year, Aunt Annette gave me twenty dollars to buy some clothes and supplies for class. Even then it was a challenge to make the money stretch that far. I bought two pairs of khaki pants and a couple of shirts from a surplus store; I got a good deal on a pair of shoes at a pawnshop, and still had enough left over to buy a loose-leaf notebook. But as the school year went on, I increasingly had to make some tough decisions about how to spend the little money my aunt gave me.

By the spring semester, those decisions became even tougher.

At one point I went so long without a haircut that I was

too embarrassed to go to school. I stayed away for an entire week. On the fifth day of my absence, I answered a knock at my door in the middle of the school day to find Delores Augustus, my English teacher, staring me in the eyes.

"Come on, you're going with me," she said sternly. And with that, Mrs. Augustus marched me up Hilton Street two blocks and then right on Baltimore Street to the barbershop a half block from the corner. She ordered me into a chair, handed the barber a dollar, and told him to cut my hair. "I will see you in school on Monday," she said in a commanding voice as she headed for the door.

I never found out how she discovered the reason for my absence from school that week, although I suspected it was Allen who told her. When I returned to school, Mrs. Augustus made no mention of her visit to my home. She did, however, give me extra homework to make up for the time I missed from her class.

The special attention I got from my ninth-grade English teacher kept me in school, but it didn't keep me out of trouble. As graduation approached, I came perilously close to going to jail instead of high school. My partner in crime was a classmate named Floyd Maxie. Like me, Floyd came from a poor family. Unlike me, he was not even an average student. But for a short period during the spring semester of my ninth-grade year, the two of us were inseparable. We were also a shakedown team.

Before class, as students milled around outside the school building, and on the playground during the lunch break, Floyd and I teamed up to extort money from white male students. It wasn't a racial thing. We targeted them because they had money. Most of the black students didn't. Floyd and I were one of several two-man teams of black students who preyed upon the weakest of the white boys at P.S. 91. Our approach was simple. I would walk up to our mark and say, "Hey, man, lend me a quarter." Floyd would stand nearby with a surly look on his face, pounding his right fist into his open left hand. If the kid barked at my request, Floyd would step forward and back up my words—with a chilling emphasis.

"He said, lend him a quarter, chump," Floyd would say in a voice meant to leave no doubt of the fate that awaited anyone who turned me down. Nobody did. During our two-week reign of terror, we netted about five dollars in coins—and a trip to the police station.

It was during a graduation rehearsal that the cops came for us. One morning several officers walked into the auditorium where the ninth-grade classes had been assembled to practice our parts in the ceremony that was little more than a week off. One of the cops took to the stage and conferred briefly with the school's vice principal, who then stepped to a microphone and read off the names of six students the police had come to get. Floyd's was the first name on the list. Mine was the last.

The officers paraded the six of us out a side door and into a waiting patrol wagon, where two other students who had been pulled out of their classes were already seated. During the short ride to the police station none of us said a word. Then, as we were being led out of the wagon, Floyd elbowed me in the side to get my attention.

"Don't tell on me" was all he managed to say through clenched teeth as the cops led us off into separate interrogation rooms. For several hours, two police officers, one white and the other black, questioned me. They said they knew I was one of the black kids who had been taking money from white students. They told me they had witnesses. They said that

instead of graduating I was going to be put in a home for
juvenile delinquents—unless I gave them the name of the guy
I had teamed up with. If I turned him in, they said, they
would let me go back to school.

I was more afraid of Floyd than I was of them. I stuck to
my story. "I don't know what you're talkin' 'bout," I said,
over and over again.

Finally they let me go. I don't know if they were convinced
by my denials, or simply frustrated in their attempt to break
me. Whatever the case, they released me. The white officer
drove me back to school. As he pulled his marked patrol car
into the circular driveway, I opened the door to get out before
he could stop it.

"Hey," he said as I jumped from the car, "the next time
you won't be so lucky."

There wouldn't be a next time.

The four hours I spent in the police station passed slowly.
I was scared, real scared. I'd heard stories about what happened
to young boys in jail. I'd never been more frightened or felt
more alone than when I was sitting in that interrogation room.
I wanted to call someone for help, but I didn't know how to
reach Aunt Annette on her job. Besides, I didn't want her to
know the trouble I'd gotten into. In the middle of my interrogation, I thought about the stories I'd heard about the time
my father spent in military stockades, and wondered if I was
destined for a similar fate.

I knew the only chance I had to get out of there was to
keep denying any knowledge of the crimes the cops were asking
me about. And that's just what I did. Even then I wasn't sure
the cops would let me go free, but I knew if they did, I'd
never get myself in a mess like that again.

Walking home from school that day, I wondered what
happened to Floyd. The next day when I went back to class he

wasn't there. He didn't return to school and I never saw or heard from him again.

Aunt Annette did not attend my ninth-grade graduation. Instead, she went to work that morning. Aunt Arline was the only member of my family to show up, and she left as soon as it was over. After the ceremony, most of my classmates stood around on the campus taking pictures with family members and teachers. I wanted to get as far away as possible. As I headed for a side door, I saw Mrs. Augustus in the middle of a crowd of people. She looked at me and smiled. I wanted to say something, to thank her for all she had done for me, but I didn't know how. So I just waved to her and then slipped quickly out the door.

I'll never know how much of a sacrifice it was for Aunt Annette to take my brother and me into her home after the deaths of our parents. And at age fourteen I wasn't very appreciative of what she had done. In the weeks after my graduation we clashed often—mostly about money. She was getting a small government survivor's benefit check for me, and I couldn't understand why some of that money wasn't finding its way to my pockets. 141 South Hilton Street became an increasingly hostile environment. One of us had to get out, and since my name wasn't on the lease, I left. I spent the first night out of the house in the back of a truck behind the soft-drink warehouse. The next day Willie Lloyd, a neighborhood friend, took me into his house, and his father insisted I spend the night on their couch.

I caught a bus to Cherry Hill the following morning and moved into the apartment that André, then a student at Morgan State College, shared with Rodney, who had graduated from high school and was working as a stock clerk at Montgomery Ward. My brothers managed to pay the rent and put some food on the table, but if I wanted more than that, I needed to find a summer job.

Ray, a guy I knew from the Hilton Street neighborhood, told me about Woodholme Country Club. "If you're willing to do some hard work," he said, "you can make enough money during the summer to get through the entire school year."

"Doing what?" I asked.

"Caddying," he answered. "Man, guys are making twelve to twenty dollars a day out there," Ray whispered, his eyes surveying our surroundings for eavesdroppers. "You want in?"

"Damn right. What do I have to do?"

"Meet me there tomorrow morning, 'bout seven o'clock," Ray said. "I'll hook you up with the Man." After getting directions to Woodholme from Ray, I asked one last question. "Where do I meet you?"

"In the caddie shack, man," he said sharply, as though the answer was obvious to all but the biggest of idiots.

CHAPTER 5

The benches that protruded from the walls of the caddie shack were packed with dozens of lounging bodies, nearly all of them belonging to young blacks who, like me, had come to Woodholme in search of work. There were just three white guys, all in their early teens, sitting uncomfortably amid a group of black caddies when I walked in looking for Ray. It was such an eerie scene, the three of them squeezed into the single space controlled by black folks in this enclave of white wealth and power.

In one corner of the room a crap game was already under way. A group of guys hovered over a pair of dice and a small pile of crumpled dollar bills. In another area of the caddie shack three guys playing tonk, a favorite card game of black kids, tried to convince a fourth one to join them and ante up the twenty-five cents' price of the game so that the pot could expand to a dollar, the cost of admission into the crap game. One would-be caddie sat quietly reading a book while the guy next to him sold doughnuts out of a brown paper bag.

"How much for a honey-dipped?" someone asked.

"Ten cents," came the answer.

"Shit, man, I can buy two for a fuckin' dime."

"Where?"

"On the avenue."

"What avenue you talkin' 'bout, man?" the seller said with a hoarse chuckle.

"Pennsylvania Avenue," his customer shot back.

"Yeah, but that's a thirty-five-cent bus ride from here, ain't it?" the doughnut seller said with a smirk, drawing some supportive banter from the people around him.

"So what you gonna do, spend thirty-five cents to save a nickel, or give me a dime for this here doughnut?"

"Here, man, gimme the goddamn doughnut," the customer said, tossing two nickels into the lap of the doughnut salesman, causing the banter to give way to a wail of laughter.

The caddie shack was a dungeon-like space illuminated by a single bulb and the streams of sunlight that leaked in through a small window and two doorways. One of them, the front door Pop Henry had pointed me to, was at the bottom of a gentle slope of asphalt that flowed from the pro shop to a shed on the other side of the caddie shack where the electric golf carts were kept. The back door opened onto a large patio at the rear of the pro shop's basement. From a window above, the caddie master would call caddies when he had work for them.

Inside the caddie shack, the floor had an uneven roughness that made the daily crap games a contest of nerves as well as one of chance. The dice often failed to land flat when thrown to the ground, an outcome that regularly brought the cry of "cocked dice" from someone on the losing end of the roll. "Cocked dice" is to craps what a foul ball is to baseball, or an out-of-bounds pass is to football. It's not supposed to count. But in Woodholme's caddie shack, a cry of "cocked dice" usually had to be backed up by a lot of tough talk to make it stick.

The bathroom, which was cut into a wall the caddie shack shared with the basement of the pro shop, had a single toilet and small sink. With no ventilation system, its foul air leaked back into the caddie shack, giving the room the smell of an outhouse. But there were few complaints. For most of us who caddied at Woodholme, the country club was a dream come true. And no one wanted to complain too loudly about conditions in the caddie shack and risk turning that dream into a nightmare.

I found Ray wedged into a corner of the caddie shack, looking a lot less confident than he had the day before. All his bluster was gone, replaced by the uncertainties of a caddie's daily existence.

"So where's the Man?" I asked him, getting straight to the point of my being there.

"What man?" he answered in a barely audible voice.

"The Man I need to see about caddying," I shot back. "That Man."

"Oh, he's upstairs," Ray said. "Don't worry, I'll hook you up with him."

He didn't. He couldn't. Ray barely knew the Man.

Charlie Mannion (the Man's real name) had been at Woodholme for sixteen years when I first showed up there. He was a scrawny fourteen-year-old white kid when he started working as a caddie in 1945, nearly a decade before the club got its first black caddie. Two years later, Mannion dropped out of school and went to work in the pro shop, stocking shelves, selling golf supplies, and eventually teaching the game of golf to some of the club's young members.

Mannion seldom smiled, at least not around the caddies he commanded. There was little reason to. The stern face and arched brow he constantly displayed were the makings of the mask he wore to keep caddies from nagging him endlessly about "getting a bag"—one of the terms we used to describe the job of caddying.

In addition to controlling when and how often caddies got

to work, Mannion also ran Woodholme's equivalent of the company store: a snack bar he operated with the help of Pop Henry from a basement window at the rear of the pro shop that overlooked the patio. Hot dogs, cupcakes, crackers, soft drinks, candy, and a small array of sandwiches could all be purchased at the snack bar. And as with any monopoly—his was the only sanctioned food service operation at Woodholme where a caddie could get something to eat—the prices he charged were inflated. But after lugging a couple of heavy bags of golf clubs over nearly four miles of rippling terrain in the dead of summer, most caddies gladly paid what Mannion asked for a soda to quench their thirst or a hot dog to satisfy their hunger.

I did, though not my first day at Woodholme. I didn't have a cent in my pocket when I settled into a small space on the bench inside the caddie shack that day. I languished there for hours, waiting for Mannion to notice me during one of his occasional forays into the caddie shack and to give me some work.

As Pop Henry had made it all too clear, I wasn't the only one from Cherry Hill who found his way to Woodholme. Nearly a dozen other guys from "the Hill" were already there when I arrived in the spring of 1961. To my surprise, I didn't know any of them. They all came from what we called the front of Cherry Hill, near Slater and Berea Roads. That was about as far away from where I lived as you could get and still be in Cherry Hill. But not knowing them didn't matter because there was a special bond between Cherry Hill residents, a kind of tribalism, that allied us. At Woodholme that bond drew me immediately into the protective circle the guys from Cherry Hill created for themselves. We were like members of a clan who were separated by great distances, but united by an inviolable loyalty to one another.

Iney Gray was the first member of the Cherry Hill clan I

encountered at Woodholme. A thin, wiry guy with deep, piercing eyes and a slight stutter, Iney overheard me say something to Ray about Cherry Hill my first day at the country club, and his eyes lit up.

"Yu-yu-you from the Hill?" he asked with a big smile, his words echoing with a stutterer's rhythm. "Wa-wa-what part?"

"Cherryland Road, near Seagull Avenue," I answered, identifying myself with the section of Cherry Hill where I'd lived for six years before Aunt Annette moved me to west Baltimore, rather than with the area several blocks away I'd just moved into with my brothers.

"What about you?" I asked.

"Fi-Fi-Fisk Road. Be-be-behind the Community Building," he answered, referring to the large public building that housed Cherry Hill's library and a mix of social services.

Homer Gray, Iney's brother, also caddied at Woodholme. So did Barry and Ernie Ward, Reggie Shellington, and "big John" Henry. They, and most of the rest of the Cherry Hill contingent, came from a cluster of old public housing units at the northern tip of the community. Barry was responsible for getting many of them to Woodholme. He drove a '55 Chevy that he used to ferry guys to the golf course for the same price it cost to take a bus there. The difference, of course, was that Barry took you all the way to Woodholme, the bus didn't. Which probably explains why he called his car the "caddie wagon."

Reggie, a short, dark-skinned man in his early twenties, was the croupier of the caddie shack. He always had a deck of cards and a pair of dice in his pockets and never passed up an opportunity to launch a game of chance. Reggie walked with a hustler's swagger, as if, to paraphrase Maya Angelou, he had diamonds at the meeting of his thighs. He didn't, but rumor had it John Henry did.

John Henry—everyone called him by two names—was an ex-Marine whose body rippled with muscles. The short sleeves of his shirts looked as if they had been painted on his arms. His shoulders were broad and his waist narrow. His legs appeared muscular, but not muscle-bound. People said he was a "knockout artist"—someone who could turn out your lights with one mighty swing of his fist. They also said John Henry was hung like a horse, a really big horse. Some of the guys jokingly called him "el ropo." But never to his face. Whatever the size of his penis, John Henry didn't like being the subject of such talk. Once when he overheard someone joking about his penis size, John Henry freaked out. He smashed his fist into the guy's chest. It was a left jab, thrown with the quickness of Sugar Ray Robinson and the power of Sonny Liston—and it landed with a loud thump. There were just a few of us in the caddie shack when this happened, so the incident was replayed verbally throughout the day as other caddies came in from a round of golf.

"Man, it was a two-punch fight," one spectator gleefully recounted to a group of returning caddies. "John Henry hit him, and he hit the floor." After that, there wasn't much more talk about the size of John Henry's sexual organ.

By midafternoon of my first day at Woodholme, most of the caddies had gotten bags and were on the golf course working. Some, having already completed one round of golf, were back on the course a second time, caddying for someone else. But a few of us, all newcomers, hadn't gotten any work when Mannion took his first notice of me.

"You new?" he asked.

"Yes, sir," I answered anxiously.

"Ever caddie before?"

"No, sir."

"Hmmm," he grunted before turning to Ray. "And how about you?" he asked my friend, who, like me, had yet to get any work that day.

"Yeah, I've been here all week," Ray snapped, abandoning all pretense of the closeness he had claimed the day before to Woodholme's caddie master.

"And I'm ready to walk today, man. I'll take a single or a double," he told Mannion. "Anything to make some money."

Most golfers play the game in groups of twos and fours. And most caddies at Woodholme—the experienced ones—carried two bags of clubs, one on each shoulder, during a round of golf. Caddies were paid four dollars per bag for a full (eighteen holes) round of golf, which took about four hours to play.

The club's worst golfers usually played alone, or with other duffers. We called them "snakes," because instead of lofting the golf ball into the air with every swing, they more often than not struck it so poorly that it just slithered across the ground. New and inexperienced caddies usually got the call whenever one of these players came out for a round of golf. Since both these golfers and their caddies knew next to nothing about the game, they were generally thought to be deserving of each other.

Maybe so. But caddies unfortunate enough to get the bag of one of these snakes worked a lot harder and earned less money than those who got to carry the bags of more talented golfers. That's because the poor play of the snakes caused novice caddies to wander all about the golf course in pursuit of errant shots, usually stretching an eighteen-hole round to more than five hours of playing time. And since those who caddied for these poor players usually carried just one bag, they would be paid only half of what the experienced caddies earned.

It wasn't long after Ray pleaded with Mannion for work that the caddie master leaned out of the window overlooking the patio and called his name. Ray leaped quickly to his feet and, with a cocky I-told-you-so tilt of his head, dashed off toward the Dutch door from behind which Mannion doled out the golf bags of club members about to tee off.

Ray got a single—the bag of old man Shapiro, Woodholme's biggest snake. The good news was that he only played nine holes. The bad news was that he tried to play at all. Caddying for him was a job that turned Woodholme's golf course into an obstacle course. Whenever word reached the caddie shack that old man Shapiro was headed toward the pro shop, caddies would disappear into the nearby woods. But Ray as much as asked for his bag. And as far as I was concerned, he lucked out. Three hours after leaving, Ray returned to the caddie shack with the two dollars he'd earned and an anguished look on his face. By then, I'd been at Woodholme for nearly twelve hours and hadn't earned a cent.

"Boy, you been here all day and ain't walked?" Pop Henry asked when he found me sitting alone in a corner of the caddie shack late that day. "Well, git on in dere and ask the Man for some bus fare home," he said, his leathery skin and rotting teeth unable to mask his honest concern. "If you here all day and don't walk, you s'pose to git caddie welfare."

Nobody remembers when the country club started handing out caddie welfare, but the best guess is that the practice followed the arrival of black caddies. Just like the federal government's program, the money to fund Woodholme's welfare payments came from a tax. Every time club members played a round of golf, they were assessed a small fee. That money, in turn, was paid out in two-dollar allotments to caddies who spent the day at Woodholme without getting any work. I never did figure out why they called it "welfare."

Welfare is what you give to people who don't have a job. We were ready, willing, and able to work. The two dollars we collected on days we sat around for nearly twelve hours looking for work without success wasn't welfare. It was an unemployment benefit.

In truth, caddie welfare was the thanks you got for waiting all day for work that never came. It was a handout that made it possible for those caddies who didn't earn money one day to return the next and try again. More often than not, it went to the newest caddies, guys whose lack of experience left them languishing in the caddie shack while others made money hauling oversized bags full of golf clubs around Woodholme's hilly course—an act we referred to simply as "walking."

I went to the door of the pro shop and peered in. An older, heavyset man noticed me first. He was Carroll McMasters, the club's aging golf professional, who had been head pro at Woodholme since 1935. He didn't speak a word, but instead cleared his throat to get Mannion's attention and then nodded in my direction as if to say, "See what he wants." Mannion sprang across the room toward me.

"What do you want?" he asked, his voice low so as not to disturb the few club members inside the pro shop.

"Can I get some caddie welfare?" I answered, struggling, as I did not want my eyes to make contact with his. Up until that very moment, welfare was a handout my family had done without—something we were too proud to accept. But unless I wanted to walk the many miles that separated Woodholme from Cherry Hill, I had to swallow my pride. It didn't go down easy.

Mannion went behind a counter, dug out a couple of dollar bills, and returned to the door and handed them to me.

"You coming back tomorrow morning?" he asked.

"Yes, sir," I answered.

"Well, get here by six-thirty for caddie class, so you can learn something about this job," he said, his eyes reading my body language for a sign of deceit.

"Okay," I answered softly, still avoiding the eye contact he was after as I turned away to begin my long journey back to Cherry Hill. Ray never returned to Woodholme, but I did, bright and early the next day.

Caddie class was two hours of instruction—given over two days—about the basic rules of golf and the game's etiquette. Golf is very much a game of etiquette. There's a protocol to every action. The player farthest away from the hole hits first. When striking the ball, players often cause a small plot of grass, called a divot, to go flying into the air. Divots must be carefully replaced, a job that usually falls to the caddie. It's considered a fairly grave offense for a person to talk while another player hits his ball and an act of golf sacrilege for someone to lie about their score.

After the second day of instruction I was declared a "B" caddie, a rather dubious distinction that came with a badge to be worn whenever I was sent out onto the golf course to work. The letter "B" was the designation given to those caddies who were allowed to carry just one bag per round of golf. It meant they didn't have the skills or experience to take on the harder—but financially more rewarding—job of lugging two bags of clubs around the golf course.

The golf bag is the player's equivalent of a mobile home. Just about everything he or she might ever need on the golf course is stuffed into one of its many pockets: golf clubs; balls and tees; rain clothes and umbrella; shoes, sweaters, and hats—all combine to push the weight of the average golf bag well over fifty pounds.

Hauling one of these bags across four miles of golf course was tough enough. Making the trek with one hanging off each shoulder was a backbreaking experience that every caddie craved for reasons of simple mathematics.

After the caddie classes, Mannion started giving me work. Soon I was earning forty dollars or more in a six-day work week as a single caddie. It wasn't long after my arrival at Woodholme that Mannion made me an "A" caddie. There was no test required for this promotion; no more caddie classes to attend. When I had caddied several times without a complaint about my work reaching the pro shop, Mannion decided to give me the chance to carry two bags—and make some real money.

My first time out as an "A" caddie, I got the bags of two women in their thirties who took to the golf course one Monday afternoon. Monday was ladies' day at Woodholme. On other days of the week there were restrictions of one sort or another on when women could play a round of golf. On Mondays the golf course belonged to them.

When Mannion gave me their bags I was relieved. Women golfers usually don't hit golf balls as far, or as wildly, as do most men. Caddying for them was a big break, I thought— a relatively painless way to break in as an "A" caddie. And there was one other advantage: women's golf bags, for some odd reason, were not nearly as heavy as those of men.

And so with two golf bags dangling clumsily from my shoulders I made my way to the first tee with the badge of an "A" caddie pinned to my shirt. It was late June, and the heat and humidity of Maryland's summer had arrived early. The afternoon air was heavy and hard to breathe. Woodholme's first tee was sandwiched between two rows of tall trees. Their arching branches turned the ground beneath them into an oasis from the sun's bright rays, staving off the moment when I would have to suffer the full heat of the blazing sun.

The first to tee off was a slightly plump woman dressed in plaid Bermuda shorts and a white, sleeveless blouse.

"What's your name, caddie?" she asked while pulling a club from one of the golf bags still hanging precariously from my shoulders.

"DeWayne," I answered, surprised that she wanted to know.

The women of Woodholme were, for caddies, forbidden fruit. It's not that we lusted after them so much as it was that white men, I believe, have always feared that, given the chance to do so, black men would lust after white women. At Woodholme, some caddies certainly did, but not me. That's because white women were still very much of a mystery to me. Up until the moment I stepped onto the first tee with those two white women, most of my contacts with white people had been with men. The beat cop in Cherry Hill. The milkman. The mailman. And the bill collector who came to our block every Saturday morning, calling out the name Charles Fish as he went door to door to get the payments his customers weren't trusted to make any other way.

Only years later did I come to understand that Charles Fish was the name of the store from which so many people in Cherry Hill bought on credit—everything from irons to bedroom sets—and not the money collector's name.

There was another reason. At the time, the memory of what had happened to Emmett Till, the fourteen-year-old black boy who was kidnapped and murdered after being accused of whistling at a white Mississippi woman, was still fresh in my mind. Not long after Rodney and I had moved in with Aunt Annette's family, I saw a picture of Emmett Till in *Jet* magazine. He was laid out in a casket, his mutilated and partially decomposed body serving as a grotesque reminder of what white men were capable of doing when they think a black man—or boy—shows some sexual interest in a white woman.

Of course, Maryland was not Mississippi. White men in

my home state never acted out their rage so freely against black men. But at fourteen, I had no way of drawing such distinctions between the behavior of white men of Money, Mississippi, and those of Baltimore. I just knew I didn't want to end up like Emmett Till.

Even in my ninth-grade class at P.S. 91, I had virtually no contact with white girls. Our separation was enforced as much by school rules as by my own fears. The gyms for the school's boys and girls were at opposite ends of the building. And hallway lockers were assigned on the basis of gender. Seating in the school's cafeteria was also divided by sex. During recess, girls and boys were not allowed to commingle in the school yard.

And in much the same way Woodholme's black caddies were kept at a safe distance from the club's women. I guess that was another of the country club's unwritten rules. With rare exception, it was the club's men who would offer us rides to and from the bus stop. And Mannion was very selective about which caddies he would send out onto the golf course with the women of Woodholme, especially the younger women.

Still, it didn't dawn on me until the very moment I stepped onto the tee that I had passed a test even more important than the rules of play taught to me at the early-morning caddie classes. I was seen as someone who could be trusted alone on the golf course with the young women of Woodholme.

The first woman on the tee stood over her golf ball for what seemed like a lifetime before finally jerking her club into motion. The ball sprang into the air in an odd trajectory, sort of like a tennis ball being lobbed over a net. It landed in the middle of the fairway, about 150 yards away. Her playing partner, an attractive, shapely woman with milk-white skin that smelled of roses, made more efficient use of her time on the tee, clubbing her ball quickly.

The golf ball leaped into the air, heading straight out into the fairway before slicing sharply to the right and landing in the high grass, called "rough," that straddles the fairways of every golf hole.

With that shaky beginning the three of us set out on what, for me at least, was an unforgettable round of golf. By the time the two women finished playing the first hole, my shirt was soaked with perspiration. I don't know how many times I'd heard the saying "the shortest distance between two points is a straight line" before that day, but the lesson became painfully clear to me by the time the three of us headed toward the second tee. They had zigzagged their way through the first hole, slicing, hooking, and dribbling their golf balls in every direction. With seventeen more holes to go, I was already exhausted. My shoulders ached, my legs were tired, and I sweated profusely as the women stopped to wash their golf balls before playing the second hole. It was then that one of the women—the cute, shapely one—started talking about an extramarital affair she was having with a man who was also a member of the country club.

I was shocked, although I acted as though I either didn't hear or couldn't decipher her thinly veiled admission of the tryst she was having. She spoke in titillating detail about the time the two of them slipped away from a late-night party and rolled about in the grass near the ninth hole one hot summer night. All this within earshot of me—her caddie. I couldn't believe what was happening. It was as if I were peeking into someone's bedroom, leering in on a most intimate moment.

I'd barely recovered from the shock when the two women

started to play the second hole. Again, the plump woman drove her ball straight into the fairway; the other woman sliced her ball into the rough. Finding a golf ball in the fairway is easy. The little white sphere can be seen from hundreds of yards away when it comes to rest atop the finely cut grass. But when a golf ball ends up in the rough's tall grass, locating it is often difficult—and sometimes impossible. So I immediately set out with the woman whose ball was in the rough to find it before my memory of its general location started to fade.

As we walked away from her playing partner, the woman looked over her shoulder several times as though to measure the separation. Then, when the spacing was just right, she farted. The sound was unmistakable, a staccato eruption of body gas. She didn't look at me, and she didn't offer me a word of apology. And why should she? By now it was all too clear to me that I didn't matter to her. My being around hadn't mattered when she shared her adulterous secret. And it surely didn't matter when she had to fart. I was the "Invisible Man" Ralph Ellison had written about in 1952—one of those black men white people so often don't see, not because we're hidden from their view, but because they choose not to acknowledge our presence.

Much to my surprise, when they finished the last hole, the women each gave me the four-dollar fee plus a fifty-cent tip, for the eighteen-hole round of golf. Later that day Mannion gave me the bags of two middle-aged men who played only nine holes. They paid me two dollars apiece. I left Woodholme that day having earned thirteen dollars, just a buck short of what my brothers paid every week to rent the apartment in which we lived.

With thirteen dollars I could buy a complete outfit of clothes—shoes, pants, and a shirt—with enough left over for the cost of admission to Cherry Hill's movie theater and the price of popcorn and soda. Monday was the slowest day of the week for Woodholme's caddies. Most didn't bother showing up.

I did. I liked the slow, less competitive play of the club's women golfers. They put less pressure on themselves and their caddies. Golf to them was just a game, not the contest it almost always became among the men.

It was during one of my Monday outings to the country club that I first met Richard Kress. Richard literally grew up on Woodholme's golf course. Before he was old enough to play the course, he crisscrossed it with Carroll Hitchcock, the club's head greenskeeper. He learned a lot about caring for a golf course: stuff about grass, fertilizers, irrigation that would bore most youngsters to tears. But not Richard, whose grandfather was one of the club's founders.

Woodholme Country Club opened in the summer of 1927 as a retreat for the wealthiest of the Eastern European Jews who came to the United States around the turn of the century. A good number of them found their way to Baltimore, a city some of the newly arrived Jews called America's Jerusalem. Their migration to the United States sounded an alarm among more than a few people, including many Jews of German ancestry in Baltimore, who had come to this country years earlier. They feared the arrival of poorer, Eastern European Jews would increase anti-Jewish sentiments in the city and cause problems for Baltimore's growing Jewish business community.

Even after some of the Eastern European Jews started to obtain both wealth and position in Baltimore, they continued to be shunned by many in the city's more established community of German Jews. They were not allowed to become members of the Suburban Club, the city's only Jewish country club at the turn of the century. So instead the Eastern European Jews set up their own social club on Eutaw Place, just a few blocks from the apartment building where my mother and grandmother would later work as domestic servants. It was called the Amity Club.

In 1926 the Amity Club's members purchased a large piece of land just beyond Baltimore's city limits for use as a country club. A year later, Woodholme Country Club opened with ninety-two members and a nine-hole golf course. One of the founding members was Richard's grandfather, a man named Louis Kahn.

Richard's family came to the United States from Latvia and Russia in the 1890s. Like Kahn, his grandmother's brothers, A. B. Hirschman and Leon Hirschman were also members of the Amity Club and later founding members of Woodholme, which was more than twice Richard's age when the two of us met in 1961. He was sixteen and already an avid golfer.

Woodholme was one of the centers of Jewish life in Baltimore. In those days the club had a party just about every Saturday night that was open to all members. There were no private parties. No VIP affairs. Woodholme wasn't that kind of place. It was a family club. Some nights the club would hold bingo games. Other times a member who owned some theaters would set up a screen and projector on the patio near the swimming pool and show one of the latest films, sometimes before it was even released.

Most Saturdays a band would begin setting up under the outdoor pavilion at the rear of the clubhouse right around dusk, just about the time the last caddies were preparing to go home. It was then that Woodholme's night life came alive. The sounds of music rippled through the evening air as cars coming up the hill to Woodholme passed caddies hoping to get a ride in the opposite direction, and pulled slowly under the clubhouse portico, carrying couples out for an evening of dinner and dancing.

William Kress was Richard's father. Willie, as his friends called him, was an orthodontist on the teaching staff at the University of Maryland's Dental School. He was a quiet man who often gave caddies free dental work. Pop Henry got a mouthful of false teeth—the caddies called it a "new grille" —from him, free of charge.

But as generous as he was to caddies in need of dental work, the elder Kress was demanding of his son. When Richard started going to Woodholme almost every day to play golf, his father told him to get a job to help pay the cost of his outings.

And he did. Richard got a job caddying at the Suburban Club. The rules of Woodholme prohibited the children of members from caddying at the club, so he traveled the few miles down Reisterstown Road to Suburban to work. With the money he made there, Richard would return to Woodholme and take to the practice tee to hit some balls. Like many good golfers, Richard had his own bag of practice balls he brought to Woodholme. The club's practice range was down past the golf cart shed. There golfers would stand on the practice tee and hit one ball after another out into a pasture-like field that sloped down off the tee for about fifty yards before rising sharply back toward a thick line of trees.

The flight of the balls was measured by a series of markers ranging in distance from 100 to 250 yards from the practice tee. It was often the case that several golfers would hit balls off the practice tee at the same time. Most used specially marked balls belonging to the club. Others, like Richard, hit their personal stock of balls, which had to be recovered immediately by a caddie—a job known as "shagging."

On the list of things caddies really hated, shagging balls

was second only to caddying for old man Shapiro. Because in addition to being a ball retriever, you were also the target at which golfers aimed their shots. Golf is a game of precision. It's not enough for serious golfers to strike a golf ball cleanly; they try to hit each shot as close as possible to a desired location. On Woodholme's practice tee, that usually meant hitting balls right at the caddie who had been sent into the field to retrieve your balls.

The caddie would go to a designated spot and the golfer would then hit a series of balls right at him—the closer the better, since accuracy was the goal. After a while the golfer would wave the caddie to a new location and hit another batch of balls his way. This would go on until he had hit all of his balls into the field. Throughout this process, the caddie would dash about picking up his golfer's balls and depositing them into a shag bag, a small leather pouch that looks a lot like a bowling ball bag. After about an hour of this torture the golfer would pay the caddie a dollar and send him back to the caddie shack. There was at least one advantage to being stuck with such duty: if you shagged for a golfer who was about to play, Mannion would let you caddie for him as well.

That's how I first got to caddie for Richard. He just appeared one day outside the pro shop with his big red golf bag and matching shag bag, anxious to hit some practice balls. It must have been around 5 p.m., the time of day most golfers have already taken to the course and when the caddies who weren't working could start thinking about going home. I had made about twelve dollars that day and was ready to start my ninety-minute journey home when the call came from Mannion.

"DeWayne, round front," he yelled out to me from his window.

"You wanna shag for Richard Kress?" Mannion asked me

when I made my way to the front of the pro shop. "He's a good golfer," he added in a consoling tone. The question caught me off guard. Mannion told caddies what to do, he never asked. It was totally out of character for him to put the question to me—and equally out of character for me to accept. I hated having to shag balls. But I never turned down a chance to make money at Woodholme.

From the beginning, Richard and I got along. He was just a year older, but far more mature and self-confident than I was then. Before sending me into the field, he asked my name and wanted to know where I lived and went to school. He seemed a bit surprised to hear that I would be attending Baltimore City College that fall. City College was actually a high school for boys, one of Baltimore's most prestigious public schools. It was a large structure on a sprawling hill in the northeast section of the city that had a large number of Jews in its student body. The building looked like an old English castle. Instead of red bricks, its walls were made of big blocks of gray stone, stacked from the ground all the way up to the top of a tower that rose high into the sky. Everybody called the school the "castle on the hill."

Getting into City College was no easy task. You had to be one of the better students to gain admission. It wasn't my grades that got me in; it was the scores I made on the standardized exams I took in junior high that got me admitted. My counselor said they indicated I had a lot of potential.

That I had been accepted into City College apparently impressed Richard as much as his young golf game impressed me. He was good. He had a picture-perfect swing. The ball flew through the air like a missile and landed every time within a few steps of where I was standing. Shagging for him was the easiest buck I'd made at Woodholme.

"I'm playing tomorrow," Richard said when I returned his

balls to the practice tee. "Do you want to caddie for me?"
"Sure," I said.

"Okay, I'll tell Mannion," Richard said before walking off.

At the front of the clubhouse, along the road that winds away from Woodholme toward Reisterstown Road, caddies huddled under a large maple tree when they were finished working and waited for a departing golfer to offer them a ride to the bus stop. There was no need to stick out a thumb; the fact that you were there was all that was needed to signal your desire.

By the time I made my way to that big tree there were four other caddies sitting under its branches. It was late and most of the golfers had already gone home. Other club members were beginning to arrive for dinner. The chance of us all getting a ride down the road didn't seem very good, until a pink '59 Cadillac pulled alongside us.

"What y'all gonna do, sit there all night?" Sugar Ray, a fellow caddie, said in his soft, almost girlish voice. "I'll take you to Pennsylvania and Fulton for thirty-five cents," he offered.

The corner of Pennsylvania and Fulton was the transfer point for those of us trying to get to Cherry Hill. It had a sort of carnival atmosphere to it. It was a way station that black folks reached before venturing north along Reisterstown Road into the largely Jewish neighborhoods that lay ahead.

The intersection bustled with action. There was always a crowd of people there. On the sidewalk outside of the Red Fox bar, Bootsy the Midget operated a shoeshine stand. And nearby in the street, Ernest Stewart, a heavyset man from Cherry Hill, darted in and out of traffic washing car windows for the spare change some of the drivers would give him.

And just one door east of the intersection on Fulton was Luigi's, a soul food restaurant run by an Italian man who had the good sense to stay out of the kitchen. He never stirred far from his cash register, leaving it to the black women who worked for him to cook, take orders, and serve up plates piled high with southern cooking. Luigi's was the place where many of Woodholme's black caddies rendezvoused at the end of the workday.

Getting there most of the time was just a matter of hitching a ride to the bus stop, climbing aboard a bus, and paying the thirty-five cents required for the bus ride and a transfer that would get you the rest of the way home. Giving Sugar Ray that much money just to get as far as Luigi's was an offensive idea, but one that had an understandable appeal given the lateness of the hour and the fact that Woodholme's parking lot was now nearly empty of cars that would be leaving any time soon.

It was no accident that Sugar Ray showed up when he did. He always hung around trying to catch a group of his fellow caddies without a ride so he could make a little extra money. That day he had us right where he wanted us. After a couple of moments of futile bargaining and angry words, the five of us piled into Sugar Ray's pink Cadillac and waited for him to pull off.

The car didn't move—and Sugar Ray didn't say a word. Finally someone spoke up.

"Why we sittin' here?"

" 'Cause" was Sugar Ray's one-word answer.

" 'Cause what?" someone else asked.

" 'Cause I ain't moving till y'all give me some ducats."

"Man, ain't nobody tryin' to rip you off," another caddie said. "You gonna git yo' money."

"Hey, just like the bus driver," Sugar Ray answered, "I'm gonna git it before I move."

And he did.

Sugar Ray started caddying at Woodholme in 1956. He was one of the club's first black caddies. A cherubic man, whose processed hair and mouth full of gold teeth gave him the look of a dandy, he was at twenty-six an old caddie when I first came to Woodholme. By the time most caddies got beyond their teens they were long gone from Woodholme. But not Sugar Ray—Woodholme was his base of operation, his steady income in a life fast with action and full of chance.

A country hustler, when he was twelve he used to sneak onto a golf course in Chapel Hill, North Carolina, in search of lost balls. Once he collected a bag full, he'd post himself on the second hole, out of sight of the club's staff, and sell them to the players who came by. Sugar Ray left the south in the early fifties and headed for the high life of New York City.

Eventually he ended up in Baltimore, a slow town where a country slick of his talents could make a better living. Cards and pool were his tools. He used both to keep himself in fine clothes and the company of easy women.

Most guys at Woodholme thought he was just an ass kisser because of the way he always pandered to Mannion. But that was just another of his hustles. Most nights, Sugar Ray played in a band at some of the dives on Pennsylvania Avenue, a gig that kept him up until the early hours of the morning.

So instead of arriving at Woodholme around 7 a.m. like many of the other "A" caddies, Sugar Ray often would not show up until 10 or 11 a.m. Caddies were usually assigned work on the basis of when they arrived at the golf course.

Sugar Ray managed to get around this practice by sucking up to the caddie master.

"Morning, boss," he'd call out with a big smile as he'd come walking down the path hours after other caddies had arrived. "Want me to clean some golf clubs?" he'd ask, offering to help ready the bags for club members. No job was too small or too menial for Sugar Ray. And no amount of pandering was too much for him to ensure that he got work ahead of many of those who arrived before him at Woodholme.

Of course, Mannion knew what Sugar Ray was up to. His lips would draw tight as if he'd been forced to suck a lemon every time Sugar Ray started his foot-shuffling act. But Sugar Ray would always win him over and by day's end earn more money than most of the other caddies.

I liked Sugar Ray. There was something about him that appealed to me. Outwardly at least, nothing bothered him. He was always cool. He had a ready smile and a quick answer for every situation. And when it came to conning people, he was just as much at ease with hustling white folks like Mannion as he was with trying to trick one of Woodholme's black caddies.

There was, however, one thing about Sugar Ray that bothered me. He was a painfully slow driver. The world seemed to pass us by as he crept along Reisterstown Road toward the intersection of Pennsylvania and Fulton. I could have taken a bus and been seated at a table inside Luigi's with a plate of fried chicken, collard greens, and potato salad in front of me by the time he pulled his car to the curb a half block from the restaurant.

"See you boys in the mornin'," he said with a flashy smile of his gold teeth as he deposited us onto a sidewalk, just across the street from where Isidor Cooper operated his clothing store.

"Fuck you, Sugar Ray," one of the guys called back to him. The words brought an even bigger smile to Sugar Ray's face as he honked his horn and drove away.

Inside the restaurant, Iney and Homer sat at one table finishing off the heaping plates of food that cost them each less than two dollars. William Cross, another member of the Cherry Hill clan from Iney's neighborhood, was seated at the counter. He was just finishing his meal, wiping the plate nearly clean with one last swipe of a piece of the homemade roll that came with his food.

"What's it gonna be, honey?" the waitress asked before my bottom had a chance to settle onto the stool.

"Can I see a menu?" I asked politely.

"A menu? Lord, child, y'all come in here every day and the menu never changes and still you want to see a menu," she said, while turning to fetch one. Just as she put it in front of me, Iney leaped to his feet and cried out, "He-he-here comes the 37." With that he dropped a couple of dollars on his table and bolted for the front door, followed by his brother and everyone else in Luigi's whose final destination was Cherry Hill. 37 was the designation the Baltimore Transit Company gave to its bus that went to Cherry Hill. The number was a beacon to poor black folks trying to get home to Cherry Hill and a warning to white bus riders who traveled the No. 28 bus line that the final destination of this bus was the black housing project. Cherry Hill was the end of the line for the 37. When it turned around and headed out of Cherry Hill, through downtown and out into the northwestern reaches of the city, the bus changed its number back to 28, the same as the other buses that traveled its route outside of the Hill.

But when the bus got to the other end of the line, near Gwynn Oak Park, the amusement complex just across the city line in Baltimore County, the 28 bus became a 37 again. No other bus belonging to the private-run, public transportation company changed its number that way. But then the 37 was the only bus that went to Cherry Hill. Other southbound buses running along the identical route branched off into white neighborhoods as they neared Cherry Hill. They were all marked with the number 28. This, no doubt, was done to ensure that white riders didn't end up in the black ghetto by mistake. Whatever the reason, the coming of the 37 was a welcome sight to us. Whenever it neared the crossroads where Pennsylvania Avenue merges into Reisterstown Road, leaning heavily to the left as it turned onto Fulton Avenue, and lumbered to a stop right in front of Luigi's, most of the caddies inside would race for the door, anxious to get home to Cherry Hill.

CHAPTER 6

It didn't matter where we lived in Cherry Hill, most of us stayed on the bus until it came to a stop in front of Pressman Brothers, a supermarket and drugstore complex owned by a Jewish family. Across the street from Pressman Brothers was the Cherry Hill shopping center, a small L-shaped strip mall with an A & P food store at one end and a fast-food carryout at the other. In between the two was a mix of commercial establishments, including a barber and beauty shop, a hardware store, liquor store, pool hall, women's clothing store, a Laundromat and cleaners, the Hill Theater, and Singer's, a men's clothing store.

The shopping center was Cherry Hill's village square, a gathering place for the young and old. The sidewalks outside the stores were usually crowded with shoppers—and people who just went there to hang out. It was as much the social hub of the community as its economic center, a place to see and be seen.

In the early evenings of late spring and summer, teenage girls in Bermuda shorts and pedal-pusher pants descended upon the shopping center for an ice cream cone or cherry Coke— but mostly just to see and be seen. Young men would strut about the parking lot like cocks in a barnyard. Hanging out in the shopping center was a mating ritual that returning caddies could ill afford to miss by bothering to go straight home from work to bathe and change into clean clothes. With our pockets bulging with money, we didn't think it mattered much to others that we reeked of a day's hard labor. Besides, the shopping center was where I'd almost always find Danny and Chester.

The three of us were as tight as a sailor's knot. Where one went, the others usually followed. Most evenings our outings began at the shopping center. When I started working at Woodholme, I tried to get Danny and Chester to come along. But no matter how tight money was for them—and it was— they weren't ready to abandon a summer of fun for the back-breaking work of caddying.

So every day when I returned to Cherry Hill I headed straight for the shopping center in search of my two friends. And most days I found them there—somewhere on the narrow stretch of sidewalk between the liquor store and the pool hall. Too young to get inside either business, they'd usually just hang around outside acting as though they could. Once in a while they'd convince someone of age to go into the liquor store to buy them a bottle of wine, preferably Thunderbird, Purple Cow, or Richards Wild Irish Rose. Cheap wine, the sweet-tasting kind that went down easy and didn't have much aftereffect—except for the foul breath and throbbing headache it produced the next morning—was their favorite.

"C'mon, man, take a swig," Danny said, shoving the paper bag containing the wine bottle against my chest one night after he and Chester "copped a jug of wine."

"Naa, I pass, man," I answered, pushing the bottle away with a sweeping motion of my right hand.

Danny laughed. He always laughed at my refusal to get high. I think he saw it as a weakness—the one thing he was certain he could outdo me in. The two of us were athletes.

Basketball, football, baseball, we played them all on neighborhood teams that competed in leagues set up by the Recreation Department. I was naturally athletic. Danny, on the other hand, played the games with a lot more heart than skill. Even in pickup games he was among the last guys selected for the team. But that didn't stop him from playing with reckless abandon. He would dive for balls on the asphalt softball playing field behind the Community Building. In pickup touch football games he'd volunteer to block the biggest players on the opposing team, and on the basketball court he would play a wild, blistering defense that more often than not left him sprawled on the ground while the guy he guarded glided in for an easy lay-up. But whenever a league championship—or just bragging rights—was on the line, Danny usually got replaced in the game by a more skilled player.

It was only when it came to drinking liquor or smoking pot that Danny became a starting player and I was left standing on the sidelines. I didn't do either. It wasn't that I was such a do-gooder. I just didn't see the sense in getting bombed out of my mind and stumbling about in the night ducking the cops and most adults while pretending to be a grownup. Besides, the run-in I had had with cops while at P.S. 91 was enough trouble to last me a lifetime. Danny saw my refusal to get high as a weakness he always delighted in making fun of.

"Yeah, big boy, you always pass, don't ya?" he said, his normally high voice dropping down into the range of Broderick Crawford, the barrel-chested actor who starred in *Highway Patrol*, a popular 1950s television series.

"Hey, Danny, stop messing with him," Chester said, only halfheartedly playing the peacemaker. "You know he gets high on Pepsi."

"That's a boy's drink," Danny shot back; "this is a man's drink. It puts lead in your pencil."

Like a lot of other guys our age, Danny believed the cheap wine he drank was an aphrodisiac. A few gulps and boom, he'd get an erection bigger and harder than the ones we all got the first time he snuck his father's *Playboy* magazine out of the house and we rushed into the woods to gawk at its revealing pictures.

"From what I hear, nigga, you need a lot more than some lead in your pencil," I said.

"What you tryin' to say, man?" Danny asked, his voice now higher than normal.

"What I'm sayin' is that the word on the street is that your pencil is a stub."

"I got your stub, nigga. I got your stub," Danny cried out in singsong fashion. "I got your stub right here," he said, clenching his crotch tightly with his right hand.

"I know you do, Danny," I said, looking at what he clutched in his hand. "I know you do."

Cherry Hill's pool hall was the other magnet to which the three of us were usually drawn. It was wedged in between the hardware store and the Laundromat, sixty feet or so from the liquor store. When the shopping center first opened, the A & P occupied this space. But years later, when the regional food store chain built a much larger building on the far end of the shopping center, a pool hall opened in its old location.

You had to be at least eighteen to get in to shoot a ten-cent game of pool, though anyone could enter the place to buy the cold sodas and snacks that were sold from behind a counter just inside the door. Once, when I was about fourteen, I went in to buy a soda and then lingered near the door watching the older guys shoot pool until the manager, a gruff old man with a deep voice, caught a glimpse of me there.

"Git outta here, boy," he snapped.

"Yeah, boy, git yo' young ass outta here," a tall, hulking teenager said as he rose from a nearby bench and approached me.

"And gimme that soda," he snapped, snatching the bottle from my grip with one hand and shoving me back against the door with his other.

"Give the boy his soda, Keno," the manager said.

"Oh, I was just playing with him," the older teenager answered, extending his arm as though to give me back my soda.

"Well, I ain't playing with you," the manager answered. "Give the boy his soda so he can git outta here."

"Here, chump, take your soda," Keno said.

As I reached for the bottle, he loosened his grip on it and let the soda crash onto the pool hall's wooden floor.

"Now you gonna clean that up," the manager yelled, all but forgetting about me as he pivoted on his heels to face Keno.

"Don't mess with me, old man," Keno answered as I backed out of the dimly lit room and onto the sun-drenched sidewalk.

Keno was the pool hall bully. He wasn't the baddest dude in the place, but he was the one people feared the most. That's because Keno was unpredictable; some said crazy. Whatever the case, he kept the pool hall—and much of the rest of the shopping center—in turmoil. Keno walked with a sort of primal bounce in his step. And even when he stood still, his body never did. He always seemed ready to pounce upon his next victim.

Once he entered the pool hall only to find that all of the tables were taken. But as wild and unpredictable as Keno was, he was no fool. He picked his targets carefully. This day it was a guy named Flag.

"Gimme your stick," Keno said to Flag, who was playing a game of nine-ball with a friend.

"Go on, Keno, leave me alone," Flag said. His tone was tough, but his words were pleading.

"Nigga, I said give me the goddamn stick," Keno responded in a booming voice as he moved menacingly toward Flag. Flag had no intention of backing down, but nobody thought he had much chance of winning a fight with Keno, either. Before Keno could get his hands on Flag the manager came out of a back room and stepped in between the two of them.

"Keno, either sit down and wait for a table to clear, or get out," he shouted. "I don't want no stuff out of you today."

Keno stood there, his eyes seeming to stare through the manager at Flag, who was trying not to look too relieved. Keno's entire body shook with rage—and then all of a sudden, he started to laugh. His laughter was as intense as the rage he had shown moments earlier.

"Ah, man, I was just joking," he said, his head and shoulders bobbing as if he were having some sort of spasm.

"Well, then sit down and wait your turn," the manager said, pushing Keno back toward the bench that hung from a nearby wall. And there Keno sat quietly for more than an hour while Flag and his friend shot one game of pool after another until without warning he leaped from his seat, grabbed a pool stick from a wall rack, and smashed it into the back of Flag's head, knocking him out cold.

Needless to say, I tried mightily—though not always successfully—to keep my distance from Keno.

Friday nights were the busiest at the Cherry Hill shopping center. In the early evening, the sweet smell of pressing oil, the pungent odor of burning hair, and the cackling sounds of laughter oozed out of the beauty shop. A large picture window let people outside see, but not hear, what was going on inside where, it was jokingly said, the women of Cherry Hill went to get their hair "fried, dyed, and laid to the side."

The A & P was packed with folks who did their grocery shopping on Fridays to avoid the crowd that showed up on Saturdays. The liquor store was busy with people out to buy enough drink to last them through a long night of partying. Those who didn't usually ended up going to an after-hours joint where liquor was sold illegally in the wee hours of the morning and where they paid through the nose for cheap booze.

Half a shopping center away, customers dashed into the dry cleaners to pick up clothes, sometimes asking the clerk if they could "split the ticket." That meant paying for some clothes and leaving the rest for pickup another time. The request angered the manager. It also left her with the choice of getting part of the money a customer owed or none at all. In a community where people often took weeks to pick up their clothes from the cleaners, the manager's decision— though grudging—was usually to accept the partial payment.

Friday nights were also a busy time for Heavy, the barber. Men and boys in need of a clipping sat waiting for a chance to get into his chair until well past the 9 p.m. closing time. The late closings were due as much to the time Heavy spent bobbing in and out of the small shop chasing people away from his late-model Cadillac he always parked just out front as they were to the many heads he had to cut. Most boys got a Quo Vadis, a style that became popular after the 1951 MGM movie by the same name found its way into black theaters. Their hair was closely cut with clippers, and a razor was used to produce a rounded look similar to the hairstyles in the movie.

Outside the barbershop you could hear the sound of music wafting through the hardware store's open door and mixing with the ambient noises of a community readying for a night of play. The hardware store was the place people went to buy the latest records, the music of performers like Lloyd Price, Sam Cooke, and Jeanette "Baby" Washington. They sold a few albums, but mostly 45s, the staple of house parties. The small discs, which carried a single song on each side, cost sixty-nine cents, and every time someone bought a record, the clerk dropped it onto a turntable and let it play. A speaker outside the hardware store's front door pushed the sound into the shopping center's parking lot. The practice was meant to test the record for defects, and to promote sales.

Sometime shortly before 8 p.m. on Friday nights a crowd would begin gathering for the last show at the Hill Theater. Standing ramrod-straight under the marquee, Mr. Norris would greet passersby and court customers. For sixty cents, the admission charged everyone over the age of thirteen, a moviegoer could see two feature-length films, a cartoon, a serial, and the coming attractions—an evening's entertainment that would last until nearly midnight. The Friday night late show at the Hill Theater was for couples: a few husbands and wives, but mostly younger guys and their dates. It was no place for three teenage boys on the cusp between childhood and the sexual awareness of puberty. So Chester, Danny, and I usually steered clear of the movies on Friday nights.

Instead, we just whiled away our time finding creative ways to do nothing of any real significance. To begin with, that meant queuing up at the counter inside the Simple Simon carryout to order submarine sandwiches. "Half a cheese steak with fried onions and lots of hot peppers" was the big seller. Then, with our sandwich in one hand and the large watered-down fountain soda in the other, the three of us would take a slow ritualistic stroll across the parking lot toward Singer's Men's Shop, which was strategically located about halfway between the liquor store and the pool hall.

The two windows of the clothing store had always been a great attraction to me. The one to the left of the door was the larger, maybe six feet in length and about as tall, and it always displayed the sharpest—and latest—of fashions. Suits. Topcoats. Sharkskin slacks, Ban-Lon shirts, and the double-knit sweaters that were the hot styles back then. The smaller window to the right of the entrance held a cramped offering of shoes ranging from the long, pointed "tiptoe blades" to penny loafers. Every time I passed Singer's, I'd stop to see the new fashions, as if I could actually afford to buy something from the store.

"Man, what you lookin' at?" Ruben asked one day as he caught me peering into Singer's windows. Ruben had lived just a couple of doors from me on Cherryland Road, and while we were never the closest of friends, he always seemed to be nearby whenever Chester, Danny, and I got together.

Like a lot of other guys who hung out in the shopping center, Ruben had mixed feelings about Mr. Singer's store. He liked the flashy clothing that filled the shop's windows, but complained that the prices were too high.

"Man, you never pay him the asking price for his stuff. You can Jew that rascal down," I heard Ruben say once long before I had enough money to go inside the clothing store to purchase anything. The common wisdom among those in Cherry Hill who claimed any special knowledge of Jews was that the merchants among them inflated their prices when doing business with black folks. So in order to get a fair price, blacks had to haggle with them until they lowered the cost —a process we came to call "Jewing down."

"It don't matter what's there," Ruben said, "you can't afford it."

"I don't see you in there buyin' nothin'," I shot back.

"No, and you don't see me hangin' round this window all

the time, like you, wishin' I could, either," he said, interspersing his words with laughter.

"Man, ain't neither one of you niggas got a pot to piss in," Chester interrupted, in his strangely protective way. "So why don't you just get off of it." We did—get off the subject, that is—but I never got over the sting of Ruben's words. He was right; all I could afford to do was gawk at the clothes in Mr. Singer's windows as though I were peeking into a fantasy world. In the real world in which I lived, my entire wardrobe fit into a single dresser drawer.

But that changed after I went to work at Woodholme. I stashed away a lot of what I earned my first few weeks at the country club. And then one day I walked inside Singer's Men's Shop with nearly $200 in my pocket.

Actually, I was no stranger to Mr. Singer, or his store. André often went there to shop. Once he took me in the store to buy me a pair of Converse sneakers and khaki pants, the staple of my wardrobe. But this time I was going in on my own to shop for clothes—clothes that I would wear to school when the fall semester started at City College. Chester and Danny waited outside. Watching me shop for clothes was not their idea of a fun-filled Friday night. Eventually they wandered off in the direction of the pool hall, where they said they'd wait for me.

"What can I do for you, young man?" Mr. Singer asked the moment I entered his store.

Julius Singer was a small man, about five foot three or five foot four, and like most of the other merchants in Cherry Hill's shopping center, he, too, was Jewish. The inside of his store was fresh with the smell of piles of new clothes and bulged with all manner of low-cost but fashionable clothing. Just to the right of the entrance, a waist-high counter stretched the length of the wall. Inside the glass case were the best clothes

Mr. Singer had to offer, mostly alpaca and double-knit sweaters. Behind the counter were boxes of shoes stacked from floor to ceiling. The main floor of the store, a highly polished rectangular stretch of hardwood, was a maze of large wooden tables stacked high with pants and other clothing items, a scene that left me a little breathless as I looked at them for the first time with money to spend.

"I got a job, Mr. Singer, and I want to get some school clothes," I said softly in answer to his question.

"You got the money to get what you want?"

"Not all of it. Not now, anyway."

"So where are you working?"

"Woodholme Country Club."

"Doing what?"

"I'm a caddie."

"Come back here with me," he said, snaking a trail for me to follow past the staggered display tables and into a rear storage room that doubled as an office. The space was as sloppy as his showroom was neat. For the next fifteen minutes, Mr. Singer gave me a soft-spoken lecture on the benefits of good credit—and the perils that befall those who don't pay their bills.

"I know you're an orphan," he said. It was the first time I'd heard anyone call me that, and the word stung. "But I think you're a good boy like your brother, so I'm going to give you a chance.

"You pick out what you want—but only what you can afford to buy—and give me a deposit. I'll put the clothes aside. You can give me some money every week until the bill is paid," he said.

"Can I trust you to do that?" he asked.

"Yes, sir," I answered, the excitement in my voice betraying my feelings.

It took me until nearly closing time to forage through stacks of pants, racks of coats, and the piles of shirts Mr. Singer pulled from his display case to choose the clothes I wanted. When done, I'd bought enough clothes to fill two suitcases: an overcoat and car coat, several pairs of pants (none of them khaki), some shirts, sweaters, and socks, two pairs of shoes, plus a dozen pair of white boxer shorts and matching undershirts. The total cost was about $250. I didn't haggle over the price. Maybe I should have, but I was too excited to question the cost of the clothes I was buying. I gave Mr. Singer a $125 down payment. He set aside the clothes I'd chosen in the storage room—and I promised to pay the balance of my bill in equal installments over the next five weeks.

It hardly registered with me at the time that after making me listen to his lecture on credit, what Mr. Singer offered me was something else altogether. I really didn't know the difference between buying on credit and putting something on a layaway. What I did know was that my life would never be the same after that night. How could it be? From that moment on, I was no longer a kid waiting for an older brother to buy him something to wear. I could now take care of myself, and manhood, I thought, was just around the corner.

But Chester and Danny were not. They had grown tired of waiting for me and wandered off, so I went home for the night. No one else was there when I arrived at the small town house at 611 Bridgeview Road. André, who worked evenings at a department store after his college classes, sometimes spent the night with a friend who lived close to Morgan's northeast Baltimore campus. This was one of those nights. And Rodney, who worked the 11 p.m. to 7 a.m. shift in the stock room of Montgomery Ward's warehouse, was out in the streets and would not be home before going to work. So I sat there, alone in that little sliver of a living room, looking at the payment book Mr. Singer had given me. That night I slept with a hand wrapped tightly around the book, clinging to it as if it were my passport to the good life I so desperately craved.

CHAPTER 7

As it turned out, my new life began pretty much the same
way the old one ended. When I arrived at Woodholme
that morning, Mannion had two golf bags waiting for me.
One belonged to Richard Kress; the other, to his father. William Kress was a man with a thin smile who looked strangely
out of place at Woodholme. Although he was a better-than-
average golfer, the elder Kress never seemed very comfortable
in the country club environment. He loved the game of golf,
but I think he would have been just as happy playing on a
public course as at Woodholme.

Richard, on the other hand, could not separate the two—
at least not at the impressionable age of sixteen. For him,
Woodholme and golf were synonymous. The fun was not just
in playing the game but in competing against the country
club's best golfers. Richard was a gladiator and Woodholme's
golf course was his arena. He spent endless hours on the practice
tee honing his golf skills, and by the time we met he was
already one of Woodholme's best golfers, though he had yet
to prove it in competition. But his chance would soon come.

It wasn't long after I put all those clothes on layaway that
Chester decided to give caddying a try—a very brief try. A
plump kid with a dark complexion and wavy black hair, Chester announced that he would caddie just long enough to earn

$32.50, the price of the tassel shoes he wanted. He didn't have much choice.

Getting his mother to give him that much money for a single pair of shoes was out of the question. $32.50 was a pretty big chunk of the money she brought home every week. Chester knew that if he really wanted those tassel shoes on his feet he'd have to come up with the money to buy them on his own.

Chester's parents migrated north from rural Alabama in the early 1940s. Dorothy Shaw moved first to Washington, and into the home of an aunt who worked in the kitchen of Franklin and Eleanor Roosevelt's White House. She wanted to be near her hometown sweetheart, who came north after landing a job with the railroad. Like the son he fathered in 1947, his name, too, was Chester Milner.

After their marriage, Chester and Dorothy Milner set up house in Fairfield, a small community of public housing and clapboard homes near the large oil storage tanks that cluttered the outer bank of Baltimore's harbor. There she gave birth to a second son. By the time Dorothy moved her two boys to Cherry Hill in 1952, she was separated from her husband. Not long after that, she went to work as a domestic for a white family in north Baltimore.

"I'm just gonna work long enough to get you some Easter clothes," she told her sons the first time she left them with a baby-sitter to go to work. But with two growing boys to raise—and Easter coming every year—she had little choice but to hold on to her job.

I don't know what attracted me to Chester, or him to me. In many ways we were surely opposites. I was athletic, he was not. In elementary and junior high school, I was a fairly good student, and although Chester was bright, he never put forth much effort in class. He was always neatly dressed. Most days

I looked a bit tattered. I didn't mind hard work. Chester almost always did. And for a while it was this last distinction that kept Chester away from Woodholme.

"Man, I ain't goin' out there and lug them damn golf bags around," he would say whenever I pressed him to go with me to the country club. But it wasn't long after I started working at Woodholme that Chester decided to give caddying a try— at least long enough to come up with the money he needed to buy those tassel shoes.

As it turned out, his first day at Woodholme was a lot like mine. He sat around the caddie shack for hours without getting any work. At the end of the day, Chester had to ask Mannion for caddie welfare to get home. But over the next couple of days he earned enough money to put the shoes he wanted on layaway. Five weeks later he was wearing them. And by then he, too, was hooked on Woodholme—though he never was quite as faithful as I was when it came to showing up for work. Chester's mother had to roust him from bed most days to get him to make the early morning trip to Woodholme.

"C'mon, Pete," she'd call out to him by his nickname, "it's time for you to go to work."

"Ah, Ma, it's gonna be hot today," he'd usually answer in a pleading voice. "I don't want to go out there and have a sunstroke."

It was a game they played. She would wake him each morning and he'd act as though he was putting his life at risk to make the money he so badly needed.

Chester had barely started caddying at Woodholme when planning for the Calcutta got under way. The Calcutta was one of two major golf tournaments held each year at Woodholme. The other was the club championship. Of the two contests, the Calcutta was by far the most popular—and most coveted—of Woodholme's tournaments. The club championship, which was held over the Labor Day weekend, was a contest of individual skill. It was played like most professional golf tournaments, in which the player who records the lowest score after several rounds is declared the winner. From the outset, the field of contenders was small. Only the very best players at Woodholme had a chance of winning.

The Calcutta, on the other hand, was a best-ball competition in which sixteen teams of four players each competed for bragging rights and a share of the betting pool, which totaled thousands of dollars. The members of each team played as though they were one, recording just a single score per hole—the lowest score made among the team's players. Thus the name "best ball."

In golf, amateur players are given handicaps based on their average score over a number of rounds of play. For example, a player whose average score is 80 on a golf course that should be played in 71 strokes is given a handicap of 9—meaning that 9 strokes are subtracted from the player's score during an eighteen-hole match. Giving amateur golfers a handicap is like staggering the start in the 100-meter dash to ensure that runners of varying speed have the same chance of finishing first. In a tournament like the Calcutta, handicaps are used to even out the competition between amateur golfers, thus making it possible for any competitor who matches or exceeds his average score to have a real chance of leading his team to victory.

Forty-eight of the sixty-four club members who comprised the sixteen teams were chosen at random, their names being drawn from a hat. The sixteen team captains were usually selected by the club's golf committee. But every year the selection process was haunted by rumors that someone, somehow, had managed to get around the luck of the draw to build a winning team.

Whatever the process, once the teams were chosen, interest among club members—and caddies—in the Calcutta soared. The posting of the team rosters set off a frenzy of activity among club members anxious to bet on the tournament's outcome. Some would go so far as to pull caddies aside and question them about how well members of the different teams had been playing in the days leading up to the tournament.

All of this intelligence had to be gathered in short order because two weeks after the teams were selected, they were auctioned off to the highest bidders. The auction usually took place behind the clubhouse, on the dance floor adjacent to the swimming pool. It was a major social event, attracting scores of club members.

Bushels of Maryland's blue crabs, steamed until their shells turned a bright red, were eaten and washed down with gallons of cold beer before the bidding got under way. Once the bidding started, club members paid hundreds of dollars to gain a stake in a team—an ownership they shared with team members. The money raised at the auction was split between the members of the tournament's top three finishing teams and their non-playing owners.

Caddies, too, had a financial interest in the outcome of the Calcutta. Just as club members competed for a chance to share in the winnings of the tournament's top teams, caddies jockeyed for bags to carry. That's because golfers on teams that finished in the money were usually very generous to their caddies, paying them four or five times the normal fee.

With that kind of money at stake, caddies lobbied Mannion heavily for "a good bag" in the Calcutta—one belonging to a player whose team was thought to have a decent chance of finishing in the money. That usually meant caddying for someone like Jack Land, Morty Silverman, Bernie Savage, Arnold Plant, Albert Aaron, or J. W. Shapiro.

Of those players, the most-sought-after bags belonged to Albert Aaron and J. W. Shapiro. Both excellent golfers, they had well-earned reputations as players who put a high value on winning.

Aaron, a tall, dapper lawyer, was the owner of the Rolls-Royce that always sat alongside the parking lot attendant's booth. He was a ruggedly handsome man who possessed the soft-spoken charm of Cary Grant and—on the golf course— the swashbuckling reputation of Errol Flynn. A fiercely competitive player, Aaron loved winning as much as he liked the attention his golf game and good looks brought him.

J. W. Shapiro also liked to win.

And at times winning was more important to him than how he played the game, according to a well-worn story that Woodholme members love to tell. Shapiro, whose dark complexion and jet-black hair made him look anything but Jewish to me, spent his summers in Baltimore and his winters in Palm Beach, where he was also a member of a Jewish country club in that east Florida playground of the rich and famous.

At Woodholme, Shapiro had a 6 handicap. But when asked his handicap at the Palm Beach club, Shapiro said it was 12. The extra strokes Shapiro falsely claimed were supposed to give him the edge in his matches with members of the club. At least, that's what he thought. But much to his frustration, Shapiro was routinely beaten by a couple of Palm Beach golfers whom he suspected of also lying about their handicaps.

It didn't take Shapiro long to come up with a scheme to get even.

One day he showed up at the Palm Beach club with a

guest, a man he introduced as Dick Schwartz, a Woodholme Country Club member who had come to town to pay him a visit. But the guy was neither Jewish nor a Woodholme member. He was actually Dick Whetzle, the young professional golfer from Texas who replaced Carroll McMasters as Woodholme's resident pro during my first year at the club.

Shapiro bragged that he and his friend from Woodholme could beat the two Palm Beach club members in a head-to-head match. The men took the bait, agreeing to a "best-ball" eighteen-hole match. The two of them against Shapiro and Schwartz.

The match lasted just two holes.

On the first hole, a par-four, Whetzle hit a big slice off the tee and into the rough, a location from which most amateur golfers would find it difficult to recover. The two Palm Beach golfers could barely conceal their delight. But then Whetzle hit his next shot over some trees and onto the putting green. The ball stopped a few feet from the hole. While his playing partner and two opponents each finished the hole in four strokes, Whetzle sunk his putt for a three—and a win for himself and Shapiro.

The second hole was a long par-three. To get from the tee to the putting green, the players had to hit their balls nearly twice the length of a football field into the face of a stiff wind and avoid landing in the pond, near the front of the green.

Whetzle hit his ball first. Taking a 1-iron from his bag, he tossed a few blades of grass into the air to measure the direction and force of the wind and then took a mighty swing. His ball leaped off the tee like a bullet fired from a rifle and sailed low—"quail-high," as the Texan was fond of saying— under the wind straight toward the putting green.

Seconds later, it rolled to a stop just feet from the hole.

Without saying a word, the two Palm Beach golfers started walking off the course.

"Wait a minute, where are you going?" Shapiro called out to them.

"This match is over," one of the men yelled back to him, his voice quivering with rage.

"Why?" Shapiro pleaded, barely able to contain his laughter.

"Because there's not a Jew alive who can hit a shot like that," came the answer.

When the pairings for the 1961 Calcutta tournament were finally announced, Richard Kress was one of three golfers teamed with Albert Aaron. Richard couldn't have been happier. Twice before, his father had been on winning teams in the Calcutta tournament, each time bringing home a share of the betting pool and a coveted silver putter—the trophy given to each member of the winning team. Being on Aaron's team meant that in his first Calcutta, Richard had a pretty good chance of bringing home a silver putter of his own. It also meant that as Richard's caddie I had a pretty good chance of making a lot of money during the three-day tournament.

Aaron's team was a heavy betting favorite to be among the top three finishers in the tournament. But after the first two days of play, his team trailed the tournament leaders by several strokes. Richard had played well enough, but neither he nor Aaron had been able to rally their team.

Then, with just ten holes remaining in the tournament, Richard got hot—red-hot. He played the ninth hole, a par-four, in just three strokes. Next Richard birdied the tenth hole, pulling his team closer to the tournament leader. The eleventh hole was a par-five. It was also a hole on which Richard received one of his handicap strokes. This gave him a real advantage. Whatever he scored on the hole would be reduced by one stroke. The better he played on the eleventh hole, the better his team's chances of overtaking the tournament leaders.

As the members of Aaron's team stood on the eleventh tee, all the pressure was hanging on Richard's slender young shoulders. Well, maybe not all the pressure. Strangely, my heartbeat quickened and my palms were wet with sweat as I pulled a club from his golf bag and handed it to Richard so he could tee off.

Nobody had to tell Richard what was expected of him. He knew. He'd been through this situation dozens of times on the practice tee, simulating hundreds of pressure-packed situations where the outcome of a golf match depended on his one shot, or the way he played a single hole. And now that it was happening for real, Richard seemed not to feel the pressure. After all, this was the tournament he had been training for—one of those chances in life we all get but few of us handle well—for a moment of stardom.

My first shot at stardom came in the fourth grade, when Curtis Carter and I played a duet during a school band concert. His instrument was the violin, mine the trombone. Of all the students in my elementary school's band, the two of us were chosen to play "Twinkle, Twinkle, Little Star" during the concert.

I choked. The sounds that came out of my trombone that day sounded like the wailing cries of a dying elephant, far worse than anything I produced during my many hours of practice. And poor Curtis—his chance at stardom was wiped out by the awful noise I created.

It wasn't that I hadn't prepared for that moment. For months the roving music teacher who came to my school once a week had taught me how to play that very song on the old trombone the school loaned me. After school each day I practiced at home, often incurring the taunts of friends and the complaints of family members for my fledgling trombone play.

One day, after an hour's practice in my bedroom, I took the trombone apart and washed the mouthpiece in the bathroom sink. The cleaning left a dark, oily residue in the sink that my aunt discovered moments later. When she found out it had come from my trombone she was mad as hell.

"Why didn't you clean up this mess?" she angrily said.

"I don't know," I answered meekly.

"You don't know? What do you mean you don't know? Didn't you see the mess you made?"

"No, ma'am."

Aunt Annette glared at me for a moment, frowned her face in disbelief, and said, "Boy, you're so dumb, you don't know your ass from a hole in the ground."

In the hallway outside the bathroom I could hear some of my cousins laughing at their mother's words—and at me. I wanted to run away and hide, but I had nowhere to go. I was upset at my aunt for what she said and embarrassed by the laughter coming from the hallway. But most of all, I was mad with my father for putting me in that situation. If he hadn't pulled that trigger, if he could have found a way to work out whatever it was that sent him into such a deadly rage, I would not have suffered that humiliation—because I wouldn't have been there to begin with.

My music teacher had great hopes for me. She said I had talent. I was one of her prize students. If I stuck with my lessons and practiced hard, she told me, I might end up at Baltimore's famed Peabody Institute.

But any chance of that happening was beaten down by my aunt's disparaging words and the grating sounds that came out of my trombone during the duet I played with Curtis. Of course, there would be other opportunities, other chances to claim at least a few moments of fame, but that was my first one and I blew it.

Or did I? I mean, how can you blow the chance to gain something you really don't want? With stardom comes recognition. People take notice of you. They fuss over you—and then invariably say something like: "Your parents must really be proud of you."

On the day of our concert, a lot of proud parents and relatives showed up. It seemed as if every band member, except me, had someone there to cheer them on as our music teacher introduced each of us after our opening performance. Aunt Annette wasn't there. She never made it to any of my school events. Or PTA meetings. After the day she enrolled me in a third-grade class I was on my own.

She wasn't there in the audience the day Curtis and I stood for our duet. She wasn't on the playground at P.S. 163 for my sixth-grade graduation ceremony. And she wasn't there the day I graduated from junior high school.

I didn't set out to fail. But as Curtis and I stood before the microphone, looking out into the crowded auditorium— and the proud face of his mother—I didn't want to succeed, either. I was afraid of the attention, and prying questions, success would surely bring.

Failure, for me, was a lot easier to deal with.

Like the basketball player who cries out for the chance to take the final shot with just three seconds left in the game and his team losing by a single point, Richard craved his chance at stardom. Standing there on the eleventh tee, with all that attention focused on him, was the moment he had spent all those afternoons on the practice tee preparing for. This was

Richard's chance to show others at Woodholme, especially Aaron, just how good a golfer he really was.

His shot off the eleventh tee was perfect. It rolled to a stop in the fairway more than 250 yards away. Two shots later, his ball was on the putting green, some thirty feet from the hole. If Richard could finish the hole in just two more strokes, for a total of five, his handicap would reduce his score to four— and pull his team another stroke closer to the tournament leaders. If he managed to do it with just a single putt, he'd score a three on the par-five hole and almost certainly put his team in a position to win the tournament.

Richard's ball sat on the right-hand side of the putting green. The hole was to the left. From where he stood, the ground sloped gently, almost unnoticeably, to the right toward the pro shop, which was just a few yards away from the putting green. Just the slightest mistake in aim and the ball could slide right past the hole and leave Richard with another difficult putt to make.

Aaron, whose ball was farthest from the hole, was the first to putt. His ball was on the front edge of the putting surface, about forty feet from the hole and to the left of Richard's position. Instead of hitting it toward the hole, Aaron putted his golf ball in the opposite direction—toward Richard. It stopped a few inches beyond the spot where Richard's came to rest.

Aaron had managed to put his ball in nearly the same alignment with the hole as that of Richard's. And since his ball was still the farthest away, he had to putt again. This time Aaron studied the flow of the terrain carefully, eyeing the rippling earth over which his ball would travel. Then he putted. His ball started out to the left of the hole and then curved slightly to the right and toward the pin. It missed dropping in the hole by just fractions of an inch, but Aaron had accomplished what he set out to do. He sacrificed his own score on the eleventh hole to show Richard how his ball would break when his turn came to putt. It was a lesson the young golfer learned well.

Richard studied the path his ball had to travel to the hole one last time and then placed his putter into position. Slowly he drew the club back and then pushed it forward in a pendulum motion, causing his ball to roll across the green. Like Aaron's ball, his also started out left of the hole and then moved slightly to the right. But then it rolled right across the center of the hole and disappeared into the cup below.

Thump!

Ordinarily, the sound of a ball dropping into the hole of a putting green is barely audible. But when Richard's ball hit the bottom of the cup it loosed a sound that was heard above the din of celebration that began the moment it disappeared from view.

It was a scene stolen from the Masters, professional golf's most prestigious tournament. The crowd of club members standing near the eleventh hole erupted in cheers. Aaron and the other team members celebrated wildly. Unwilling to lose his composure at this long-awaited moment, Richard simply smiled as he turned to hand me his putter. We didn't speak. We didn't need to. We knew better than the others what had just happened. Richard had catapulted himself to the top of the list of Woodholme's best golfers. And then, having single-handedly moved his team into contention for the tournament title, Richard walked off the putting green to accept the ad-ulation of the club members into whose midst he disappeared. There were still seven holes to go in the tournament, but for all intents and purposes the event was over. The momentum had swung sharply in favor of the team led by Albert Aaron and his star member—young Richard Kress.

After the final hole was played and Aaron's team had secured its victory, Richard's father walked over to me and gave me thirty dollars for carrying his son's bag that day. Thirty bucks for hauling a single golf bag eighteen holes. That was almost eight times the going rate.

In the caddie shack, I was treated like a returning hero. After all, it was my guy who had rallied his team to win the Calcutta with the putt he made on the eleventh hole. And so while Richard stood in front of the pro shop basking in the afterglow of his victory, I was around back in the middle of a group of caddies explaining how "we" had just won "our" first Calcutta.

I spent the rest of the summer with my head in the clouds. In the short span of a few weeks, I'd been transformed from a kid who couldn't afford the price of a haircut into someone for whom money—at least when it came to my basic needs —was no object. My life, I thought, had taken an irreversible turn for the good.

During the summer of 1961, I earned and spent hundreds of dollars; hardly a king's ransom, but certainly a princely sum to me. Two weeks before school opened I made the final payment and got my clothes out of layaway. The day I went to pick them up was something of a holiday for me. It was a Saturday, but I didn't go to Woodholme. Instead, I was standing in front of Singer's Men's Shop at 9 a.m. when the store opened. After settling my account with Mr. Singer, I headed home with my new clothes.

I didn't live very far from the shopping center, but it took me twice as long as usual to walk the distance. That's because I took a circuitous route through the shopping center, down past the pool hall and carryout, before pointing myself in the direction of home. It was a victory lap—a few moments of uncontrolled pride during which I not-so-subtly flaunted the bags of new clothes I carried.

Throughout my first nine years of school, I had borne the brunt of so many cruel jokes about the way I dressed, from the sneakers full of holes I'd worn to school in a snowstorm, to the battered Thom McAn shoes with the flapping soles that a classmate caught me trying to staple closed, and the gray and brown khaki pants that were a standard part of my wardrobe. They all produced a lot of laughter at my expense. But as I was about to enter the tenth grade, all of that was going to change—and I wanted everyone to know it.

CHAPTER 8

The last days of the summer of 1961 were the best days of my life. It was a fun time, free of the worries and fears that had become so much a part of my existence since the deaths of my parents. With the clothes I put on layaway paid for, I began to spend my money freely, as though there were no tomorrow. I should have put some aside for school. But having a pocket full of money was a new experience for me and I was determined to take full advantage of it.

For my fifteenth birthday, I went with some friends to the Royal Theater to see a stage show. Afterward we walked across the street to "Moms," a gritty soul food restaurant that James Brown used to frequent every time he came to Baltimore to perform. For dinner I had hog maws and chitterlings, and some hot peach cobbler for dessert. It may not have been the same as an evening at the "21" Club, but it was a big thrill for me.

The next day I woke up early and broke open the packs of underwear I'd bought from Mr. Singer. I now had four or five times as many white boxer shorts and T-shirts as I'd owned at any one time in my life.

I tossed them into a sink of hot water, bleach, and soap powder and let them soak for a few minutes. It wasn't that they needed the cleaning. After all, they were brand-new. But that didn't stop me from plunging a washing board into the sink and rubbing the underwear against its rippled metal until my knuckles were raw with pain. Why? On the one hand, I wanted to show off my new clothes. But on the other, I didn't want to draw attention to just how threadbare I had been before landing a job at Woodholme. So I washed my new underwear to make them look used. Just as I didn't want my friends teasing me about wearing raggedy drawers, I didn't want them getting on me about wearing new ones, either.

The town house my brothers and I lived in on Bridgeview Road was one of a line of eight that stretched the length of our block. The back of our building faced the rear of yet another row of red brick town homes. The two buildings were connected by wire fences that stretched between both ends, closing off general access to the backyard to all but the people who lived in the two buildings.

In the middle of the backyard was a clothesline nearly as long as the buildings it served, on which I hung my freshly washed, brand-new underwear. While it dried in the hot summer air, I walked across the vacant lot that separated my block from the shopping center to pick up a few items from the drugstore. I couldn't have been gone more than thirty minutes. But as it turned out, that was too long.

Someone stole my underwear.

All that was left of my wash was the clothespins that were scattered about the ground. I couldn't believe it. Who in hell would steal somebody's drawers? What kind of person would want to get up every morning and put on someone else's underwear? The more I thought about it, the angrier I got. My eyes were wet with tears, but I fought them back. I hadn't really cried in years, not since that Mother's Day in 1955 when Aunt Annette pinned the white flower on my lapel and sent me off to church. God knows, there were lots of times I wanted to, but crying was a weakness I felt I couldn't afford to show.

Besides, the bulk of the clothes I'd worked all summer to buy were safe in my bedroom closet. And while I didn't have any money saved, I had time to earn enough at Woodholme to replace my stolen underwear before school started.

It could have been worse. The thief could have gotten inside the house and taken the rest of my new clothes. He didn't, but my cousin Barry did. Barry was Aunt Arline's oldest son, three years my senior. He was born before my aunt married Thomas "Buddy" Jackson, a mailman well known for his fondness for booze and fast-pitch softball, a game he played for years in an adult league in Druid Hill Park.

Uncle Buddy and his stepson were often at odds, arguing over one thing or another. A few days after my underwear disappeared, Barry showed up at our door with a sad tale about how he had been put out of the house by his stepfather. His breath reeked of liquor and his story was full of holes, but still André agreed to let him stay with us until things cooled off between him and Uncle Buddy. That turned out to be a big mistake.

The Purple Cow was Rodney's pride and joy. A 1953 Oldsmobile, the car was my brother's first. And like the cheap wine it got its name from, its color, too, was a deep purple.

One night not long after he moved in, Barry talked Rodney into letting him use the Purple Cow to drive to the state Motor Vehicle Administration headquarters in nearby Glen Burnie to pick up his girlfriend, who worked there. I was sitting outside on the steps when Barry brushed by me, hopped into Rodney's car, leaned out the window, and asked if I wanted to go for a ride. I couldn't believe it. Rodney never let me near his car. He got mad once when he caught me and Chester just leaning against it, and yelled at us. Now he was letting Barry take it for a drive.

I jumped in the front seat, rolled down the window, and

hung awkwardly out of the opening for everyone to see me as Barry drove my brother's car out of Cherry Hill. The ride to Glen Burnie was uneventful, except for the smell of alcohol that seeped out of Barry's mouth every time he spoke. It wasn't until we arrived at the Motor Vehicle Administration, which also housed a state police barracks, that I started to worry. I mean, here I was pulling up in a purple car with a driver who was obviously drunk. There were cops and motor vehicle officials all around, but somehow Barry managed to pick up his girlfriend without drawing attention to himself. She sat in the front, next to Barry. I stretched out on the backseat for the ride home.

When Barry pulled the Purple Cow out onto Ritchie Highway and pointed it in the direction of Cherry Hill I was relieved. We'd be home in a few minutes and I'd be out of harm's way. I was wrong. Barry couldn't resist the urge to show off. He pressed down hard on the gas pedal, causing the Oldsmobile to surge forward up a steep stretch of highway. As the car rushed over the rise in the road and started down the other side, the Purple Cow's speed increased, hurtling it toward a car that was stopped at a red light about fifty yards away.

Barry reacted too slowly. He slammed on the brakes, but not in time to keep the Purple Cow from rear-ending the car. Fortunately, neither the lone white woman in the car he struck nor anyone in the Purple Cow was injured. Most of the damage was done to the other car. A state trooper from the nearby barracks was at the accident scene in minutes and asked to see Barry's driver's license. After fumbling through his wallet for a few moments, Barry said he'd left it home.

"What's your name, boy?" the white officer asked.

"John Rodney Wickham," Barry answered, giving my brother's name instead of his own.

"Spell it," the trooper ordered him.

"J-o-h-n," Barry spelled out the letters of my brother's first name.

"Spell Rodney for me," the trooper pressed him.

"Rodney?"

"Yeah, spell it."

For what seemed like a lifetime, Barry didn't say a word. Then he turned to me and asked, "How do you spell Rodney?"

"R-o-d-n-e-y," I answered softly.

"R-o-d-n-e-y," Barry repeated the spelling to the trooper. Right then I knew he was headed for the county jail and I was in for a long night. It had to be obvious to the officer that Barry was not John Rodney Wickham and probably didn't have a driver's license of his own. But instead of arresting Barry, the trooper asked him for the car's registration and insurance information.

While I sat there waiting for Barry to be arrested, the trooper moved back and forth between his car and that of the woman Barry had plowed into. Finally he returned to our car and gave Barry a ticket—made out, of course, to John Rodney Wickham. As it turned out, the trooper knew the woman whose car Barry hit and thought the insurance that covered Rodney's car wouldn't pay for her repairs if, as he suspected, it was being driven by an unlicensed driver. So instead of arresting Barry, he let him go.

Not long after that, Barry moved out. He didn't announce his departure. I went to Woodholme that morning and returned to find him gone. Also gone were my topcoat and several of the shirts and sweaters I'd bought for school—clothes I never got the chance to wear and had no money to replace. It took me a few days to track Barry down. When I did, he claimed he had borrowed the clothes to wear to his new job and would return them to me as soon as he got a paycheck and was able to buy some things of his own.

It didn't take me long to find out that there was no new job, no paycheck on the way, and little chance that I would get back the clothes, which I later learned my cousin had pawned. The opening of school was just a few days away and much of what I'd spent the summer working for was gone. The money. The clothes. And the self-esteem that came with them.

I didn't have anyone to turn to. No one to really talk to about what I was feeling. I sank deeper into my cocoon. As badly as I needed the money, I started missing days at Woodholme. Some days I got on a bus in the morning, rode to the end of the line, and then returned home. I needed some time alone to think things through.

One weekend late in August, I caught a bus out to Memorial Stadium, where the Orioles played. The stadium sits on a broad stretch of Thirty-third Street, just a block away from City College, in northeast Baltimore. Actually, the six-lane roadway in front of the stadium is called Babe Ruth Plaza in honor of the native Baltimorean who played most of his baseball for the New York Yankees. Like a lot of black boys who grew up when I did, I started paying attention to major league baseball around the time teams began hiring black players.

When the St. Louis Browns moved to Baltimore for the 1954 season there wasn't a single black player on the team that changed its name to the Orioles. But in 1956 two black players—first baseman Bob Boyd and pitcher Connie Johnson—were on the team's opening day roster, and I quickly became a rabid fan. I listened to just about every game on radio. Once or twice I got to attend a game, along with a busload of other poor kids who were given free tickets by the Recreation Department. But it wasn't until I started working at Woodholme that I could afford to go to a game on my own.

Most baseball fans remember 1961 as the year the Yankees' Roger Maris hit sixty-one home runs, breaking the single-season record held by Babe Ruth. But in Baltimore that was the year of "Diamond" Jim Gentile, a hard-hitting first baseman who put up some impressive numbers of his own. He finished the season with a .302 batting average, 46 home runs, and 141 runs batted in. In just about any other baseball season those kinds of numbers would make a player a national hero, but outside of Baltimore, Gentile's 1961 performance was overshadowed by that of Maris.

Images of what it must have been like in Memorial Stadium that year flashed through my head as I sank into a seat near the top of the left-field bleachers that day. From there I could see the rows of neatly manicured lawns in front of the homes that wrapped around three sides of the stadium. To the left, off in the distance, the red-brick structure of Baltimore's Veterans Hospital etched the skyline. Ahead of me, beyond the playing field and the right-field bleachers, the tower at the top of City College seemed to touch the clouds.

You can see much of Baltimore from the top of the school's tower: as far east as the cemetery on North Avenue where John Wilkes Booth is buried, south to the harbor, all the way west to the Forest Park section of the city, and north to Morgan State College and beyond. But that view was reserved for graduating seniors. It would be three years before I would enjoy that rite of passage.

I was about to become the second person in my family to attend City. André had graduated from the school in 1959. He was a brilliant student—a language major who took classes in Latin, French, and Spanish. He graduated near the top of his class, a feat that brought him much attention but few offers of academic scholarships. While white students with lower grades went off to Ivy League schools, André enrolled at Morgan, a historically black college just a couple of miles away. By the time I arrived at City two years later, teachers still remembered my brother—and as a result expected much of me.

Unfortunately, I didn't live up to their expectations.

City College was more than a school for bright students; it also attracted many of Baltimore's top athletes. The school routinely produced the city's best football and basketball teams and many of its track stars. More than anything else, I wanted to add my name to its list of standout performers.

Tryouts for City's football team got under way several weeks before school opened. I was among the dozens of students who showed up to compete for a place on the team. On the playing fields of Cherry Hill and west Baltimore I had been a pretty good football player. I could run and catch the football with the best in my neighborhood; a small universe, to be sure, but one that I thought was pretty competitive when it came to sports. So when a coach asked all the players to line up according to the positions we were trying out for, I didn't move.

"You here for the team, son?" he called out to me.

"Yes, sir," I answered.

"Well, then get in a line."

"I don't know which line to get in."

"What position do you play?"

"Running back . . ."

"Okay."

". . . and receiver."

"Well, now that's a problem, isn't it," he said in a voice

that was unsympathetic to my problem. "Listen, son, there's a line for running backs and one for tight ends. Get in one of them and stop wasting my time."

Forced to decide, I got in the line with the most white boys. It was a snap decision, but one that I thought made a lot of sense at the time. The only white athletes I knew, I'd met during my ninth-grade year at P.S. 91. They were all awkward and slow afoot, hardly any competition for someone with my skills. And so I stepped into the line for tight ends because almost everyone in it was white, while most of the guys in the line for running backs were black.

That was a big mistake.

The white guys in line were a different breed from those whom I encountered at P.S. 91. While they may not have been the fastest guys on the field, they could catch a football. More important, they were big, hulking guys. Their height and weight were advantages I could not overcome.

City College played a brand of power football in which the tight end's primary job was blocking for running backs, not catching passes thrown by the quarterback. And as I quickly found out, the white boys I lined up with could block with a vengeance.

I was cut from the varsity squad after just two days of practice and dispatched to a distant part of the practice field where the junior varsity team trained. Determined not to repeat my earlier mistake, I told the junior varsity coach I was a running back. It hardly seemed to matter. The self-confidence I brandished the first day of varsity practice was shattered. On the junior varsity squad I could do nothing right. I fumbled the ball, botched my running assignments, got into arguments, and committed the cardinal sin of blaming other players for my poor performance.

Three days after joining the junior varsity squad I was

dropped from the team—cut for the second time in a week. Despite all the warning signs, the decision came as a real shock to me. It was hard enough to accept being reassigned to the junior varsity football team, but it was devastating to be told that I wasn't good enough to make a squad of "wannabes."

The week I spent trying out for City's football teams put a big dent in my pride. It also cost me the money I could have earned caddying at Woodholme. The latter I could easily make up. The former would be hard to repair.

On the first day of school, I rode the No. 28 bus out of Cherry Hill and transferred downtown to the No. 3. By the time the pale green bus reached Thirty-third Street, it was packed full of students. Just across the street from Memorial Stadium, the bus stopped to discharge dozens of giggling girls who were on their way to Eastern High School. An all-girls school, Eastern was a huge red-brick building, easily a block square, that sat alone on a piece of land nearly as large as that which held the stadium.

Eastern High was the sister school to City College. The girls of Eastern would crowd into the stands at City's sporting events, to cheer the all-boys school on to victory. It was mostly the boys of City who escorted Eastern girls to their proms, or took them out for a date on Saturday nights. On the street outside the two schools, the student bodies of both looked like one as they mingled together on the grassy knolls that linked their two campuses.

The next stop for the No. 3 bus was at the corner of Thirty-third Street and The Alameda. When the doors opened, the boys emptied out and began the climb up the long line of steps to the "castle on the hill."

Behind my bus, several others discharged wave after wave

of teenage boys onto the school's campus. Not sure exactly where to go, I just followed the flow of students. It swept me inside the cavernous old school building, and moments later I found myself in my homeroom.

There were just a handful of black students in my class, no more than five or six out of about thirty-five students. But they all seemed more like the white guys in my class than like me. They had that preppie look—button-down shirts, tapered pants, and shoes that ranged from desert boots to penny loafers. It wasn't the kind of dress that I saw a lot of in Cherry Hill, especially not in the windows of Singer's Men's Shop.

But if my classmates looked strange to me, I must have seemed like something of a fashion leper to them, from the bright yellow double-knit shirt I wore to the imitation Italian shoes on my feet. Clothes, though, weren't the only reason I didn't fit in at City College. There was something else— something far more compelling—that would chase me away.

Fear.

Fear of the unknown. Fear of competition. Fear of life outside the protective cocoon I'd spent much of the last seven years hiding inside. The kind of fear that can chill your bones and make your palms sweat all at once. Seven years after the deaths of my parents, I still hovered, psychologically, in the shadow of that great tragedy. I still shuddered at the thought that someone might find out that my family had been torn apart by my father's murderous rage. And somewhere deep inside, I worried that someone's prying questions about my parents would force me to confront my own feelings about what happened to them. All those years I'd avoided doing that. I didn't want to think about my parents because I didn't know what to think of them.

Could I hate the man who took my mother's life, and still love the father I had known? Would I love my mother any less if I allowed myself to wonder if she might have done something to spark what my father did? I was too afraid of the answers to these questions to let them linger long in my consciousness.

From the moment I walked into that classroom at City College I was afraid my secret wouldn't be safe there, scared that I would be forced to relive in public the horrible event that continued to plague me privately. From the first day of school when the English teacher asked each student in my class to "tell us something about yourself and your family," my mind was racing away from City College. And it wouldn't be long before my body followed.

CHAPTER 9

"So how's school?" Richard Kress asked me one Saturday morning in late September.

A fall chill had emptied the unheated caddie shack and forced everyone out onto the patio, where rays of sunlight pierced through the large tree branches hanging overhead. While the start of school had taken me away from Woodholme most weekdays, I still went to the country club on weekends to make what money I could.

"It's all right," I answered as nonchalantly as I could.

"You sure?"

"Yeah, I'm sure. Why you askin'?"

"Because I hear you're not doing so good," Richard said in a hushed voice.

"Who told you that?" I wanted to know, my mind racing ahead of the question in a desperate attempt to figure out which of my classmates might have spoken to Richard.

His answer caught me off guard.

"Your French teacher," he said. "That's who told me."

Frieda Glass was my French teacher. She was hard to look at. Her face had been badly disfigured by skin cancer. Except her eyes, which were gentle and inviting, and every time I looked at them they seemed to plead for a chance to help me. In her own way, she tried in vain to get me through her class.

She was cautious in her approach to me, not knowing how I would respond to an outright offer of help. Once she had me come back to her class after school, supposedly for being a couple of minutes late, and then spent an hour going over a homework assignment with me. Another time she asked me to help her move some books from a storage area. She turned the work into a private French lesson.

"En français. En français," Miss Glass said when I asked in English which books to pull from the storage room shelves. It was her way of gently nudging me to put to practical use the French she'd tried to teach me in her classroom—a subtle attempt at rescue that failed.

"She's my cousin," Richard said, which, I guess, explained why she discussed my grades with him. "If you need some extra help, just ask her. She wants to help you."

"I don't need any extra help, man," I snapped, looking around to see if any of the other caddies had overheard Richard's words.

"Okay," Richard said as he turned to walk away. "If that's the way you want it."

That wasn't the way I wanted it. Inside, I was crying out for help. But I wasn't about to let my defensive shield down to allow Richard inside my secret world.

By midsemester I was failing miserably. Not just French, but all of my academic courses. I got a 40 in geometry and 55s in English, biology, and French. I don't remember which came first, the truancy or the bad grades, but they fed on each other. The worse I did in class, the less I went to school. Instead, I went to Woodholme.

But as fall gave way to winter, fewer and fewer club members came out to play golf and home became my retreat from school. At home there was no pressure on me to go to school. André left early each day for his classes at Morgan and came home late. And it didn't matter much to Rodney that I hooked school. Like me, he had a lot of psychological scar tissue from the deaths of our parents, more, in fact, than I did.

Even though we lived in the same house—and shared a bedroom—Rodney seldom had much to say to me. It was as though we were boarders brought together by a common need for shelter, but strangers when it came to all of the other things that mattered. We almost never talked to each other. Not because I didn't want to, but because I couldn't get more than a couple of words out of him at a time. It had been that way for years.

With my grades in free fall and no one at home to push me to go to school, my absences increased sharply. By the end of the semester I'd missed forty-four days of school. My midterm grades showed it. They ranged from a 30 in geometry to a 42 in French. Why I even bothered to return to school to pick up my report card is something I can't explain. As it turned out, I should have stayed home.

My homeroom teacher was a white man named Long. His first name has slipped from my memory. A retired naval officer, Mr. Long commanded his students about as if they were seamen aboard a ship at sea. "Close the port," he called out whenever he spotted an open door. "Batten the hatches," he'd always say when he wanted the windows shut. I got seasick just walking into his classroom.

"Well, what do we have here, an AWOL student?" Mr. Long called out to me as I entered his class.

"You talkin' to me?" I asked, with a hint of attitude in my voice.

"Yes, I'm 'talk-ing' to you, boy. Unless you have a note from your mother, you have been absent without official leave—that's AWOL," he said. Without responding, I made my way to my seat and started to sit down. But Mr. Long was persistent. He moved quickly toward me with a pointer wedged beneath his arm like a swagger stick.

"Don't sit down," he snapped. "Because if you don't have a note from your mother, you need to go home and get one."

What a jerk, I thought. I'd been in this guy's homeroom class for an entire semester and he didn't even know my mother was dead, something he could have easily found out had he ever bothered to look at my school records. I didn't know what to do—or say. Everybody was looking at the two of us standing there in the middle of the room staring at each other.

"Man, fuck you."

The words were mine all right, though I could hardly believe I'd spoken them. Blame it on a moment's rage, or a need to lash out at this man who wouldn't stop pressing me for something I could not produce. But in a strange way I hadn't actually lost self-control when I opened my mouth and let those three words escape—I'd gained it. Now no longer was Mr. Long pressing me for a note I could never give him. And no longer did I feel like the object of my classmates' scorn.

For that fleeting moment, at least, I had seized control of the situation by frightening the hell out of everyone around me. It was a short-lived victory.

"Get out of my class," the retired naval officer said in a quivering voice that made me think he would rattle easily in battle. "And march yourself straight to the office."

It didn't take long for school officials to match my bad grades with my bad attitude and decide that I didn't belong at City College. That morning I was told to use the Christmas break to find another high school to attend. Nobody bothered to call my home or send a letter to the address on my school records. They just hurried me out the front door of the prestigious high school and told me not to come back.

It was weeks before my brothers found out I had been expelled. Rodney's reaction—or lack of one—was predictable. André, on the other hand, was really upset. He wanted to know what had happened, but I didn't say much. I couldn't. By now he, too, was on the outside.

With no school to attend, I started spending more time at Woodholme. The club's complement of caddies shrank to about a dozen "regulars" when school was in session. A "regular" caddie was someone who worked at the country club year-round. Pop Henry was a regular. So were Reggie Shellington, Sugar Ray, John Henry and Willie Poole, an older white caddie who always seemed to make out better than the rest of us when it came to getting good bags.

There were two basic benefits that accrued to regular caddies. First, in the summer when play was heaviest, regular caddies got all the extra work they could handle. It was the caddie master's way of rewarding them for showing up during the slow months of the year. Second, they got to attend the Christmas party the Jewish club threw every year for its employees. The party was a real role reversal. It was held in the clubhouse, where members became servants for a day as Woodholme's waiters, parking lot and locker room attendants, and regular caddies partied the night away. I never went to the Christmas party. Despite all the good intentions that went into putting it on, I couldn't get excited about this "queen for a day" routine. I'd deluded myself about a lot of things, but never about my role and place at Woodholme.

My return to the country club in the middle of the school year went largely without notice by club officials and most members. As much as I could, I avoided contact with Richard. That was easy. Unlike me, he spent the winter and spring of 1962 in school. I did see him occasionally on weekends. But aside from once mentioning that his cousin told him I no longer attended City College, Richard avoided talking to me about anything having to do with education, which was understandable given the way I'd responded to his earlier attempt to do so. And as for the report he'd gotten from his cousin, I lied and told him I transferred to another high school.

On a good winter day I could make as much as twelve dollars at the golf course. But there weren't a lot of good days in the early months of 1962. Most days I was happy to make half as much in a workday that started late and ended early because of the shortness of daylight and the chill in the air. Some days I went home with just two dollars' worth of caddie welfare in my pocket.

Winter golf is a lot different from the game that's played in the summer. The rules are the same, except for a few minor changes meant to speed up play in cold weather, but people's approach to the game varies greatly. First of all, only the most devout golfers play the game after the frost arrives. They show up dressed in layers of clothing, a lot of which is shed as their bodies heat up during play.

In the warm months of the year, a round of golf is both a sports outing and a social event. But in the cold, wet air of winter, the golfers who showed up at Woodholme played with great dispatch—and little conversation. Caddies, too, were expected to quickstep about the course with a sort of military precision.

One day in late March, I got the bags of two men who

said they came out "to play a quick nine holes." They showed up right around noon on a bright but chilly day. Most of the caddies were already on the course working. A new guy, who sat bundled in a corner of the caddie house waiting for his first job, and I were the only exceptions.

"DeWayne, get up here," Mannion called out to me just as I was about to go into the bathroom to urinate.

"Give me a couple of minutes," I answered.

"Hey, they're ready to go. You want to walk, or should I give this job to the new man?" Mannion pressed me.

"I'm on my way," I said, deciding that I could hold my water for a couple of hours. As it turned out, it took only ninety minutes to finish the nine-hole round. But by the time I returned the golf bags to the pro shop and pointed myself in the direction of the caddie shack my bladder felt as if it were about to explode.

I jumped over the cinder-block wall and jogged through the open doorway of the caddie shack and into the bathroom. The door was partially closed as I brushed against it on my way in. Damn. Someone was standing over the toilet bowl with his back to me.

"Move over," I yelled.

Given that we had only one toilet in the caddie shack, it wasn't unusual for more than one caddie to use it for a urinal at the same time. As the guy stepped around the bowl to make room for me, I froze. It was John Henry, b-i-g John Henry, and from what I could see, the talk about his being well endowed was more than true, it was an understatement. There was no way I was going to drop my zipper and bare myself to him after what I'd just seen. No way.

"Whoa. E-x-c-u-s-e me, man," I blurted with a wide-eyed look before retreating out the back door of the caddie shack. Once on the patio, I jumped the railing and made a beeline for a bank of trees a few yards away, as my bladder screamed for the relief that almost came too late.

Gambling was a big part of a caddie's life at Woodholme. During the summer months when play on the golf course was heavy and caddies were in great abundance, the caddie shack had the look of a casino. The dice and card games went on almost nonstop from morning until the last caddies left in the late evening. On the patio out back, younger caddies pitched pennies—for quarters. The bets were held by a non-player, who was often called upon to settle arguments over which coins landed closest to the wall.

In the mornings, with only what remained of the previous day's earnings in their pockets, caddies didn't wager much. Small change mostly. But as the day progressed, so, too, did the betting. By afternoon, when most caddies had walked at least once, the crap game was going full blast.

In the summer, gambling was something most caddies did just to fill in the time between jobs. In the winter, it was what regular caddies did in hopes of making lean workdays more profitable. A caddie who got lucky one cold winter day might win ten or twenty dollars in the crap game to go along with the few bucks he made on the golf course. Those who lost didn't lose much, since they usually didn't have that much to begin with. But even a small loss could be devastating on those days when there was little opportunity of recouping it on the golf course.

One day, early in the spring of 1962, I'd hung around the golf course for hours before getting two bags to carry for a nine-hole outing. I returned to the caddie shack late in the afternoon with four dollars in my pocket and no chance of getting any more work that day.

"Come on over here and let that money you just made go to work for you," Reggie called out the moment I walked back into the caddie shack.

In his left hand, Reggie held a small wad of bills. In the right one, hidden from sight by the fingers of the fist he wrapped loosely around them, were a pair of dice. With his hand hoisted high near his ear, Reggie stood there shaking the dice as though he were waiting for some kind of a signal before rolling them across the bumpy floor.

"Roll the goddamn dice, Reggie," Jitter said, with about as much emotion as he could muster. That wasn't much. Jitter never seemed to do anything with much emotion. The heroin he was addicted to saw to that. Jitter was always laid back—even when his money was on the line.

"I don't know why you rushing me. The faster I roll, the quicker I'm gonna take yo' money," Reggie answered, without looking away from me.

"You better get a piece of me now, chump, while I'm trying to make this here nine," he taunted me.

Of all the numbers—or points—that a crapshooter has to make, nine is one of the most difficult. That's because there are only two combinations on the dice that add up to nine: five and four, or six and three.

"C'mon, Reggie, turn 'em loose," someone else hollered.

"Well, if you ain't gonna git in this, then I'm just gonna have to take these boys' money," Reggie said, before tossing the dice across the floor with a casual flip of his wrist.

Five. And four. The numbers appeared on top of the two cubes as the dice came to a stop. Nine. He made his point.

"What's that, sucker?" Reggie said, finally looking in the direction of Jitter. "Five and four. How much is that? C'mon now, somebody help this ol' country boy add up them numbers. How much is it? Huh? Huh?"

Nobody spoke. Not one of the guys huddled in a circle around the dice said anything as Reggie bent down to pick up his winnings.

"Well, if you can't add, maybe you can count," Reggie said defiantly. "The bet's two dollars, ante up," he said, dropping two dollar bills on the ground before picking up the dice and shaking them again.

"I'll take it," I said, a bit breathlessly. And with that I stepped forward and dropped two of my four dollars on top of his.

"Anybody else feel lucky?" Reggie asked.

Again, silence. Reggie was hot and no one else wanted to take him on. Then Jitter dropped a ball of crumpled bills on the ground.

"I've got five dollars that says you don't win," Jitter said softly.

With that icebreaker, some other guys came up with bets of varying amounts. Reggie matched each one dollar for dollar—and then rolled the dice.

Six. And five. In the game of craps a shooter who rolls seven or eleven on the first roll wins.

"Eleven," Reggie shouted. The wad of money in his hand had just gotten fatter.

"Bet again," Reggie said, throwing two dollars at my feet. Without saying a word, I matched his bet with the last of the money I'd just earned on the golf course. And with Jitter leading the way, the others also found the courage to bet against Reggie, again.

"Ah, sookie, sookie, now." Reggie beamed as the money piled high on the caddie shack floor. "Gimme some room," he said, flinging his arms wide to shed the full-length black leather coat he wore. Then, after one more shake of the dice, Reggie rubbed them against his crotch "for good luck," he said, and let them roll.

Four. And three. He rolled a seven. Another winner.

"Damn, this nigga's hot as a pistol," somebody yelled.

"Hot as your mamma," Reggie shot back with a big grin. "That how hot I am."

Too hot for me. I walked out of the caddie shack to get a deep breath of fresh air to calm my thumping heart.

"Boy, you oughtta have your dumb ass in school, 'cause you just got took," I heard someone behind me say. It was the unmistakable raspy voice of Pop Henry.

"Took, how?" I asked as I turned to face him.

"Them dice is loaded. Reggie and Jitter is partners. One sucks you in and the other keeps everybody bettin'. They probably in dere splittin' up the money right now," the old man said. "The next time you lucky enough to git some bags, you betta keep what money you make in yo' pants."

Pop Henry was no good Samaritan. In fact, rumor had it that he'd "palmed" the dice a time or two himself. "Palming" is a term used to describe how crapshooters switch dice right before your eyes. They pick up a regular pair of dice and, with everybody watching, somehow manage to exchange them for loaded ones.

"You should have told me that before I lost my money," I snapped.

"Young boy like you oughtta to be in school somewhere gittin' an education," Pop Henry said, ignoring what I'd just said. "This ain't no place for you."

"Yeah, well, this is where I am, Pop. And this is where I'm gonna be," I answered, trying hard to get him off the subject—and off my back.

"Ain't no future in this kind of work, boy. Leastwise, no future that anybody wit good sense would want," Pop Henry shot back. "I'm just tryin' to help yo' ol' dumb ass."

"Hey, if you're so worried about my future," I said, "lend me a dollar till tomorrow so I can get home."

He did.

Most days, the only future I looked forward to was the time I spent hanging out with my friends in the apartment my older brothers all but ceded to me. Danny and Chester were regulars. They'd come around in the evening, after they got out of school and I returned from Woodholme. We'd sit around for hours talking about the two things that interested us most: sports and sex. Occasionally Danny would bring one of his father's *Playboy* magazines over and we'd spend the evening eating cheese steak subs and Neapolitan ice cream while ogling the pictures. Like most guys our age, we were terribly macho. André was not.

People talked about my oldest brother, behind his back, of course, and mine, too. But that didn't stop me from hearing the ugly names they called him.

Queer. Punk. Faggot.

André was different from Rodney and me. Compared to him, we were the street-wise, athletic type. He sang on the church choir, cleaned house, and cooked us big dinners on Sundays. He made sure the rent and heating bills were paid —and held us together as a family. Sure, André was different, but that didn't make him one of "them," I used to tell myself. I don't know why it made such a difference to me. I really didn't know any homosexual men then—at least any who would admit it to me. I guess more than anything else I just gave in to peer pressure.

One evening during the spring of 1962, Danny and I were sitting in the living room of the town house watching television when André came in with a male friend. They were laughing and talking loudly. Right away I was embarrassed because it was obvious André had been drinking, something he almost never did. They went straight upstairs. There were three rooms on the second floor of our town house, a bathroom and two bedrooms. Rodney and I slept in one. The other belonged to André.

"Where are they going?" Danny asked with a shocked look on his face.

"Where does it look like they're going?" I answered defensively.

"For what?" Danny pressed me.

"How the hell do I know," I snapped. "What you trying to say, man?"

"Nothing. I ain't trying to say nothing," Danny answered.

It was an awkward moment. The two of us sat there stiffly. We were no longer watching the television. It was watching us. Our eyes were fixed on the small black-and-white screen, but our ears were finely tuned to the ceiling above. Sound traveled through our federally subsidized apartment like a fish through water.

Thump, thump . . . thump, thump.

"What was that?" Danny asked about what was unmistakably the sound of shoes dropping to the floor. I didn't answer him. I didn't have to. Within moments André's old wooden bed began to squeak. At first slowly. Then faster. And faster.

"What are they doing up there?" Danny squealed, his voice now pitched high with excitement. "Do you hear that?"

I did. But God knows I didn't want to. I didn't want to know what was going on in André's bedroom. I refused to let my mind connect the sound of the dropping shoes with those of the squeaking bed. If there was a conclusion to be drawn from what we heard, I would leave it to Danny to reach it. I just withdrew into myself until the noise stopped and André's friend bounced down the stairs and out the front door. André came downstairs a few minutes later, a lot more sober than when he had gone up them.

In our small town house, the couch sat against one wall of the living room and the television was pushed against the other. André walked casually between us and the TV on his way to the kitchen.

"DeWayne, I thought I asked you to wash the dishes," he called out to me from the other room.

"I'm gonna wash 'em," I answered him.

"When?"

"When I get ready."

Each time I spoke, my tone became harsher, my words sharper.

"What is wrong with you?" André stepped from the kitchen to ask me.

"Nothin'," I answered in a voice that was downright hostile.

"Well, then please act like it," André said. I think the word "please" was meant as a peace overture, but I wasn't ready to declare a truce.

"Faggot," I said.

I spoke the word in a low voice after he turned his back and disappeared into the kitchen. It struck him with the force of a rock hurled at the back of his head. I meant to inflict pain. But as soon as I spoke the word, I regretted that he had heard it.

André rushed from the kitchen and, instinctively, I jumped to my feet to meet him. Our bodies crashed together in the middle of the room, tumbling to the floor as we punched wildly at each other. I tried to scramble to my feet, but André landed a punch to the side of my head that brought me back down. As I fell to the floor he started choking me.

Danny called out to us to stop, but otherwise kept his

distance. I fought my way onto my knees and then threw myself at André as he tried to get up, toppling the coffee table in the process. A glass bowl on top of it crashed to the floor and broke into pieces.

By now Danny was shrieking, "Stop it. C'mon, stop it. Y'all gonna kill each other."

But it was our exhaustion, not Danny's warning, that ended our fight. We fought to a draw. Bruised and bloodied, we picked ourselves slowly off the floor. André retreated upstairs and I fell limply onto the couch. After Danny helped me put the furniture in order he went home, leaving me alone downstairs.

Emotionally, I was a basket case. I hated the man who had gone to bed with my brother. Over and over, I kept thinking, "I can't stand that faggot." But I couldn't think of André in that way. Sure, in my moment of rage I called him a faggot, but I just couldn't allow myself to think of him like that for very long. He was my brother and I loved him, even if I didn't know how to show it.

I didn't get any sleep that night. Instead, I just lay in my bed, reliving every moment of what had happened. Over and over again. I had goaded André into a fight because I wanted to hurt him, just as I had been hurt by the sounds that came from his bedroom. But I was proud of how fiercely he had battled me. Proud he had shown Danny that he could fight like a man.

I tossed and turned in my bed all night, worrying about how what I said must have hurt André. It was the lowest point of my life. I'd hit rock bottom. Expelled from high school, I spent my days in Woodholme's caddie shack with drug users, winos, and hustlers—and my nights glued to the television set while my mind atrophied.

If I had anything going for me at all, it was the one great advantage known by all those whose lives bottom out: the sick

comfort that comes from knowing that your skid through life
has ended, because you cannot fall off the floor.

André never owned up to his homosexuality. I wish he had.
The double life he tried to lead was really hard on him. Occasionally women from the Baptist church he attended came
over for Sunday dinner or stopped by in the evening to pay
him a visit. He'd go to parties and other social functions with
them, but only his male friends got as far as his bedroom.

The rest of the family was in denial, too, about André's
sexual orientation. None of us had the stomach—or the
heart—to confront him. It was just so much easier to act as
though he had us fooled. We didn't even talk about his homosexuality among ourselves. After the fight he and I had the
day I called him a faggot, I tried to ignore André's secret life.
But I couldn't.

The town house we shared was his sanctuary from the
heterosexual life he wanted people to believe he led. Inside it,
behind his bedroom door, André often let his guard down. I
hated getting up in the morning to find one of his lovers still
in the house. They made my skin crawl. They all put up such
a big front about being straight when my friends and I were
around. I blamed them for the things that went on in my
brother's bedroom. Somehow I thought that if it weren't for
them, André would be different.

I treated the guys André slept with as if they were the
scum of the earth. If they called when he wasn't home, I
intentionally didn't pass along the phone message. When they
spoke to me during their visits to our apartment, I usually
ignored them. If I saw them on the street, I acted as if I didn't
know them.

I was mad with André—but I took it out on them.

One day when André wasn't home one of his lovers stopped by the house looking for him.

"Let me ask you a question," he said after I cracked the front door just wide enough to tell him that André wasn't in. "Why don't you like me?"

"Who said I don't like you?" I answered, trying to duck the showdown that was about to occur.

"I can tell by the way you treat me that you don't like me, but I don't know the reason why."

"You don't, huh?" I said as I opened wide the door I'd been standing behind.

"No, I don't."

"Well, you ought to."

"What do you mean by that?"

"I mean you come in here and you sleep with my brother and you don't know why I don't like you?"

"Oh, so that's it."

"Yeah, that's it, all right. Why don't you just take your ass home at night and leave us alone."

"Is that what you want me to do?"

"No, what I want you to do is go away and never come back. That's what I want you to do."

He did. At least for a while. But when André found out what I had said to his friend he was really pissed off. He came to me with this long speech about how he put up with my friends and I should do the same with the people he brought into the house. At times what he had to say was angry talk; at times his words pleaded for compromise and understanding. In the end, I agreed to be more tolerant of his friends—a concession that actually settled little. Throughout the entire conversation we both avoided any mention of André's sexuality. It was a golden opportunity for one of us to bring it up. But he stayed hidden in the closet, and I was afraid to open the door.

CHAPTER 10

Long before they arrived at Woodholme, Putty and Bertha Butch had a job hauling bags. Grocery bags.

Weekdays after school, and on weekends, they joined the small army of boys, most of them too young to work legally, who massed in the parking lot outside of Cherry Hill's A & P with their motley collection of homemade wagons— the unmistakable tool of their trade.

They were called "grocery boys," and their wagons were a testament to the ingenuity of these poor kids. The bodies were built of wood, just about any kind of wood the boys could lay their hands on. Anything that could be fastened together and made to sit atop wheels was used. Wood scrounged from the dump. Wooden pallets stolen from the small steel plant on the front edge of Cherry Hill, or the warehouse across the street.

Once the main body of the wagon was built, a "tongue" was added. Usually a two-by-four, it protruded out from the center of the wagon's underbody. Attached to it was a smaller cross-board that held the wagon's front wheels. A rope, tied to both ends of the cross-board, was used to turn it from side to side and give the wagon its maneuverability.

Just about any kind of wheels were used to put these wagons into motion. Some were taken from grocery carts. Others came from baby carriages. But the wheels favored by most guys came off street skates, usually Union Ball Bearings No. 5, the kind a lot of kids in Cherry Hill got as Christmas presents.

The biggest advantage of these wagons was their size. They were much larger than the metal ones sold at the hardware store—big enough, in fact, to carry a dozen or more fully packed bags of food. With one of these wagons, a grocery boy could haul the bags of two or three customers at one time. Depending upon the distance to be traveled, and the size of the load, a grocery boy could earn from fifty cents to a dollar and a half per trip.

"Can I carry your bags, miss?" the boys would all chant in a singsong voice as shoppers made their way into the food store. The women had to navigate their way through the knot of young boys who all asked the same question: "Can I carry your bags, miss?"

Some of the boys turned these words into a sad, wide-eyed appeal for a chance to earn a few quarters. Others made them a bold pitch for work, meant as much to scare off their competition as to land the job.

Fridays and Saturdays were the grocery boys' best days. That's when most women in Cherry Hill did their shopping. A kid who got lucky could make enough runs to earn twenty to thirty dollars over the two days. After that, business fell off sharply until the next weekend rolled around—a loss of work that caused some grocery boys, eventually, to switch from hauling food bags to golf bags.

Lawrence Hawkins, Jr., was barely twelve years old the first time he showed up outside the A & P with his wagon— and his younger brother, Joey—in tow. A scrawny kid with a sandy-brown complexion, he was the oldest of eight children Lawrence and Bertha Hawkins had at the time. Two more would be born to them a few years later.

A postal worker, Lawrence Senior was an active member of St. Veronica's Catholic Church and Baltimore's fledgling civil rights movement. Bertha was a housewife who found temporary work at the post office every year around Christmas, when extra help was needed to handle the crush of holiday mail.

In the years following my arrival in Cherry Hill the number of two-parent families declined sharply. Hard times and joblessness having stripped them of their self-esteem, many of the community's black men just began to disappear. Lawrence Senior was one of those dads who didn't. In fact, he became a surrogate father to a lot of other kids in the neighborhood that surrounded the small four-bedroom public-housing unit his family was crowded into on Berea Road. His son, Lawrence Junior, was called Butch. And so were a lot of other boys in the neighborhood. So many, it turned out, that people started using the names of their parents as a prefix to distinguish one from the other. There was Jean's Butch. Vernon's Butch. Luby's Butch. And Lawrence Hawkins, Jr., whom everybody called Bertha's Butch. Over time, Bertha's Butch became simply Bertha Butch.

Felix Greene lived on Slater Road, just around the corner from Bertha Butch. He was the oldest of Bessye and Woodreau Greene's six children—four boys and two girls. Felix was called Putty, a name someone gave him after his nose was smashed in a pickup basketball game. The injury left it flattened and pushed slightly to the side of his face, like a nose that might have belonged to a hapless prizefighter whose head got in the way of too many brutal punches. His nose, somebody said shortly after the accident, looked like it was made of putty— and his nickname was born.

Putty was barely a teenager when his parents separated. But he was old enough to understand that he had to go to work to help take care of himself—and his family. So he built an oversized wagon and became a grocery boy.

He quickly gained a loyal following of regular customers —women who were smitten by his big, friendly smile and the gentleness with which he went about his work. He was soft-spoken, mannerly, and always neatly dressed, qualities that distinguished him from many of the other grocery kids.

The money Putty made was a big help to his mother, who struggled mightily to keep her family afloat. But it wasn't enough. So Bessye Greene went on welfare to ensure that the rent got paid and her kids would have something to eat. The first of each month, Putty and his mother rode two buses to get to the corner where Greenmount and North Avenues intersected. From that point, they walked south along Greenmount several blocks to Oliver Street. There, inside the city's Department of Social Services building, they picked up the family's monthly allotment of surplus government food: powdered eggs and milk, cornmeal, cheese, flour, butter, and lard, the processed hog fat that was used for cooking oil.

Putty hated these trips.

He was ashamed to be seen on the No. 37 carrying bags loaded with welfare food. The eyes of every passenger on the bus were trained on him, Putty was convinced, that one day of every month he was made to perform this embarrassing duty.

Putty and Bertha Butch were part of the second wave of people from Cherry Hill to descend upon Woodholme. The first was made up mostly of guys—like Reggie Shellington, the Ward brothers, John Henry, and Iney and Homer Gray —who were in their late teens and early twenties. Most of those who came in the second wave that brought me to Woodholme were younger and a lot more curious about what went on at the country club.

My first summer at Woodholme, caddies stayed pretty much out of sight until called on to work. We kept to the caddie shack, or lounged on the small patio out back. Instinctively, the older caddies knew it was best not to be seen, or heard, until Mannion called upon them to work.

The guys in the second wave—among them Putty, Bertha Butch, Ronald and Donald Small, Richard Banks, Kenneth Chapman, William Cross, and Julius McLaughlin—had different instincts. They'd all spent the better part of their lives in Cherry Hill, not only isolated but also insulated from the white world outside. While their parents knew how black folks were expected to act around white people, these young boys didn't have a clue when most of them first arrived at Woodholme in the spring of 1962.

Many of them routinely sat atop the cinder-block wall that separated the pro shop from the caddie shack to watch the comings and goings of the club's golfers, whose flashy clothes captured their attention. And they often stood near the practice tee, gawking—and sometimes snickering a bit too loudly— at some of the players who went there to work the kinks out of their golf game.

Woodholme, to these young black caddies, was a fascinating new world, a place they were anxious to get to know. Mannion, on the other hand, was determined to maintain order, if not the status quo. One day he told Pop Henry to send the new arrivals "round back." He never had to issue such an order to the older black caddies; they knew their place. But the new guys, younger and less compliant, had to be told how to behave.

"The Man say git round back," Pop Henry said to those of us who were seated on the wall. He repeated the order to the others, huddled near the practice tee, a few feet away. At first his words only caused us to shift positions. We rose up off the wall. The others pulled back from the edge of the practice tee. But no one went inside the caddie shack.

"What about them?" Bertha Butch, who had been seated next to me on the wall, wanted to know. His finger was pointed in the direction of two white caddies standing on the other side of the wall we'd just left.

The number of white caddies at Woodholme started to decline the moment blacks began working there in the mid-1950s. By the early 1960s only a few of them still bothered to show up there. The rest deserted Woodholme for those private country clubs around Baltimore which still considered caddying as a job "for whites only." The white caddies who remained at Woodholme enjoyed a special status, kind of like that of white sharecroppers during slavery—a step or two above black slaves and a world apart from the white plantation owners.

"Dey ain't none of yo' business," Pop snapped in answer to Bertha Butch's question. "Y'all wanna stay round here, you betta do as yo' told, or the Man gonna send you down the road wit no money in yo' pocket."

The threat of being sent home worked. One after the other, we quickly made our way into the caddie shack. Everyone, that is, except Bertha Butch.

Challenging the prerogatives of white folks was nothing new to Bertha Butch, who was one of the Cherry Hill schoolchildren sent to integrate P.S. 225 in September 1955.

"Go on back to Cherry Hill," yelled the white adults who crowded the sidewalks outside of Westport Elementary School the first day the buses full of black kids showed up there.

"We don't want any niggers here," came the refrain.

Aside from the shouting of ugly words and a bit of pushing

and shoving, the integration of Westport's school happened
without the kind of widespread violence that caught the nation's attention two years later when federal troops were called
in to protect the black students who desegregated Central High
School in Little Rock, Arkansas.

There were a lot of minor racial skirmishes at P.S. 225—
fistfights mostly—and Bertha Butch, who spent four years
there, had more than his share. It took him a while to warm
up to the challenge. At first he just cried a lot when the white
kids called him names and pushed him around. But eventually
he found the courage to fight back. Sometimes with words.
Other times with his fists.

By the time he graduated from Westport Elementary School
in 1958, Bertha Butch had developed a healthy disdain for
the special privileges that racism bestows upon white people
in this country.

"Get round back," Mannion snapped at Bertha Butch as he
stood alone arguing with Pop Henry, after the rest of us had
disappeared inside the caddie shack. "The next person I catch
standin' round front will be barred for a week."

There are times to fight and times to avoid a battle. Bertha
Butch knew this was his time to retreat. Without saying a
word, he turned and headed for the doorway of the caddie
shack. The point he was trying to make just wasn't worth
losing out on the money he'd come to Woodholme to earn.

There was another group of boys from Cherry Hill who came
to Woodholme around this time. They lived in a small cluster
of privately owned homes—red-brick row houses with small
plots of grass in front of and behind each building—located

in a tidy little neighborhood to the rear of the shopping center. Unlike just about everyone else in Cherry Hill, most of the people who lived in these houses were homeowners—a distinction that put them at the top of the community's social strata.

There were few broken families in this part of Cherry Hill, and virtually no pressing need for the teenage boys who lived there to go to work. They came to Woodholme, not as a matter of survival, but simply to earn spending money.

Still, there was no class conflict between them and us; the common bond of being from Cherry Hill eliminated any chance of that. But there was a major difference between those of us who came out of the projects and the guys who didn't. We were desperate for the money we earned. They were not. Most of us arrived at Woodholme early each day and stayed late. Most of them didn't. We were more inclined to take some grief from people at Woodholme. They seldom did.

Once while Julius McLaughlin and John Henry were caddying together during a Calcutta tournament, one of the golfers they were working for hit a bad shot. Angry, the man threw his club wildly in their direction. It slammed against John Henry's legs.

John Henry the former Marine.

John Henry the knockout artist.

John Henry, who tried to tear a hole in the chest of a guy he caught joking about his oversized penis.

Bad-ass John Henry.

Right away, Julius wanted to storm off the golf course in protest, leaving the four men to carry their own bags the rest of the way. But John Henry squelched that idea.

"Don't worry about it, man. I'm okay," he said softly, more concerned about the money such a show of rage would cost him than the damage done to his pride.

John Rhines never made such a concession. He was a tall, dark, good-looking guy with a deep voice, the kind girls swoon over. He lived behind the shopping center—and Woodholme was not his meal ticket.

One day a golfer John was caddying for knocked his ball into a pond—far enough from its edge that it could be retrieved only if someone waded into the water to get it. And that's just what the golfer asked John to do.

In a deep booming voice that left no doubt about the finality of his decision, he refused. There was no way John was going to walk knee-deep into the water to recover a fifty-cent ball and then spend the rest of the day sloshing about the golf course in wet clothes. No way he was going to drown his pride to make some cheapskate happy. His decision angered the golfer and cost him a tip—but not his self-respect.

One of the caddies, I don't remember who, hacked out a winding path through the underbrush behind the caddie shack. It wrapped around a few trees and laced through the bushes that covered much of the ground. Dug into the crusty earth at different points along the path were holes, a few inches deep and nearly as wide. Eighteen of them in all. It was the beginning of caddie golf.

More than a game to while away the time between "walking," caddie golf was a merger between the game of golf and the culture of the caddie shack. Our game was played with sticks, instead of expensive golf clubs, for the most obvious reason: we didn't have any clubs. The balls we used were stolen from the bags of unsuspecting golfers. Not new balls. Most members kept a fairly good count of them. But the old, beat-up ones that wouldn't be missed—the balls the faint-of-heart golfers pulled out whenever there was the slightest chance they might hit their next shot into a water hole. We used a stick or tree branch to bat the balls across the ground toward each hole, just as in miniature golf. And of course we played for money.

Occasionally some of Woodholme's young members—Richard Kress, Jimmy Molofsky, or Jack Applefeld—would slip around back of the caddie shack and challenge one of us to a game of caddie golf. Nobody was better at this game than Ronald Small, who took great pleasure in taking their money.

Out on Woodholme's golf course, with golf bags hanging off each shoulder, Ronald looked overmatched. He was nearly a half foot shorter than most other guys our age, but what he lacked in size he more than made up for in heart. During pickup football games in Cherry Hill, Ronald earned a reputation for being a fearless player who threw himself into the middle of every play. People said he had a lot of guts to play so hard against boys twice his size. It wasn't long before someone started calling him "Hog."

Hog guts—the pig's stomach and intestines, known as hog maws and chitterlings—are a delicacy to many blacks. Boiled in a big pot of water with flakes of hot pepper, a dash of vinegar, and several large slices of Bermuda onion to draw off the fat and reduce the smell, "maws and chitlins" are a fatty addition to the menus of many cash-poor black families.

Ronald had an awful lot of guts—just like a hog—and so the nickname stuck.

When it came to caddie golf, Hog was the best. Maybe his advantage came from being so short—so close to the ground every time he bent over to strike the golf ball. Or maybe it just naturally evolved from his fierce competitiveness. Whatever his advantage, Hog used it well. He played that bumpy, twisting dirt patch as no one else could. And more often than not, he beat all comers at a game I eventually convinced myself

was no game at all. It wasn't really golf. Anybody can paddle
a golf ball across the ground. Hitting it into the air—and
getting it to land where you want—now, that's golf. That's
the game I really wanted to play.

So I gave up caddie golf. Actually, I had to. Hog was too
good, and losing to him was costing me too much money.
Besides, the athlete in me wanted to experience the real thing.

My first chance to do that came during a twilight tournament, a lighthearted competition that always starts in the
late afternoon. It's the country club's equivalent of the company
picnic. The people who turn out for it are far more interested
in having fun than in playing golf. The twilight tournament
was one of the few coed golf events at Woodholme. Each team
was made up of a mix of women and men.

In most golf tournaments, the players all begin on the first
hole with about a five-minute interval between groups. By the
time the last group tees off, the first is nearly done playing
all eighteen holes. In a twilight tournament, the teams each
begin play on different holes to allow them to start and finish
at about the same time.

Mannion gave Richard Banks and me each two bags and
sent us to the thirteenth hole to await the arrival of our players,
who were in the clubhouse sipping cocktails. The thirteenth
hole, a short par-three, requires golfers to hit their balls from
a hilltop to a putting green a little more than a hundred yards
away. Around the hole were a small pond and a couple of sand
traps.

Since arriving at Woodholme, I'd watched hundreds of
golfers hit balls off that tee. Knocking a ball straight from
the tee to the putting green looked easy enough, but most
players couldn't do it with any regularity. It was more likely
they'd end up hitting their ball into the water or one of the
sand traps.

I'd never hit a golf ball with anything other than the stick I used to paddle them about the ground behind the caddie shack, but I just knew I could. I mean, how hard could it be?

From the grassy mound behind the tee, you can see people approaching the thirteenth hole from the direction of the club-house before they can get a glimpse of you.

"Get up there and let me know if anyone's coming," I said to Richard.

"Why, what are you gonna do?" he asked.

"I'm gonna take a couple of swings," I said matter-of-factly as I reached into one of the two golf bags Mannion had given me and pulled out a club.

"Man, you must be crazy," Richard said, looking over his shoulder to see if anyone was headed our way.

"Anybody coming?" I asked while digging into a pocket of one of the bags in search of a golf ball.

"No."

"Good, because I'm gonna hit this sucker right into the middle of that green."

This was the chance I'd been waiting for. An opportunity to do what I had done so many times before—in my mind. I dropped the ball to the ground and used the end of the golf club to prop it atop a clump of grass—just like I'd seen Richard Kress do so many times. Then I took a few practice swings.

"You betta hurry up," Richard Banks warned.

I wasn't going to be rushed. I took another practice swing. Then I stepped up to the ball, took a deep breath, and swung. I jerked the club back in a spastic motion and then quickly propelled it forward. As it hit the ball, I heard a familiar sound. Not the "click" that comes with a good golf shot, but the "clang" that announces a bad one.

Instead of flying straight at the putting green, the ball

took to the air like a boomerang. It arced to the right and landed far from the thirteenth green.

"Oh, shit. You betta get that ball before they come," Richard said.

"I'm gonna hit another one," I answered, anxious to prove that my first shot was a fluke. Again I reached into the bag, pulled out a golf ball, and dropped it to the ground. This time I didn't bother with a practice swing.

Clang.

The ball lurched up into the air in an out-of-control spiral before falling to the ground like a wounded bird.

Splash.

It landed in the water. Four more times I tried—and failed—to hit a ball to the putting green. I did, however, manage to knock three of them into the water and scatter three more wildly about the golf course.

"Here they come," Richard shouted, moments before the golfers we'd been waiting for appeared over the rise behind me. I barely had time to stuff the golf club back into the bag before they were upon us. No one noticed my panicky movements.

My heart was pounding as though I had just committed a crime—and gotten away with it. The guy whose club I'd used paid no attention to the clumps of dirt and grass clinging to it as he reached into his bag and grabbed a different one. He'd obviously had more than one cocktail. They all had. The four of them—two men and two women—were juiced.

"Give me a ball, caddie," the man called to me as he stepped on the tee to hit his first shot. I shoved my hand into a pocket of his golf bag—the one I'd gone into for the six balls I hit—and felt nothing. I tried another pocket. Nothing. Not a one. The guy had only six balls in his bag, and I'd just hit them all away.

"You, ah . . . you don't have any, sir," I said, as innocently as I could. Richard looked at me as though the sky were about to fall on us.

"Damn," the guy said with an embarrassed grin as he turned to face the other golfers. "Can you believe this? I forgot to bring some balls."

Nobody said a word.

"Come on, now, somebody let me have a couple until we get back to the clubhouse."

More silence.

"Ah, come on, you guys, give me a break," he begged.

"All right, all right," one of the women said, breaking the silence. She tossed him a package containing three golf balls. "But when we finish, the drinks are on you."

With that, they all laughed and I let go a big sigh of relief.

I never hit a golf ball at Woodholme again. It wasn't necessary. Caddie golf took root in Cherry Hill. Not the game played behind the caddie shack with sticks and tree limbs, but something a lot closer to the one enjoyed by Woodholme's members.

Next to P.S. 160, on a large athletic field the elementary school shared with Cherry Hill Junior High, several caddies from behind the shopping center fashioned a three-hole golf course that was quickly dubbed Cherry Hill Country Club. The place didn't have any putting greens, or fairways. No roughs, or tees from which to start each hole. Just three stretches of overgrown grass that substituted for Woodholme's well-manicured golf course.

And behind Slater Road, along the railroad track that was Cherry Hill's western boundary, the caddies who came out of the nearby public housing project built a makeshift golf course that became a neighborhood attraction.

"Give me that club," Lawrence Hawkins, Sr., ordered his

son one day after watching Bertha Butch muddle through an effort to teach his mother how to hit a golf ball. "Let me show y'all how to do that," he said with a big grin, to the obvious delight of the swarm of neighborhood children who cheered him on.

Armed with the golf club, Bertha Butch's father swung at the little white ball with a force so great the earth beneath it gave way. Grass and dirt exploded into the air, but the ball barely moved. It rolled just a few feet and stopped.

The children screamed with laughter.

His wife just shook her head.

And Lawrence Hawkins, Sr., never heard the last of it.

For all of the pleasure it brought us, caddie golf was only a caricature of the real thing. A poor man's version of a rich man's game. A crude imitation of the life we'd discovered at Woodholme Country Club.

CHAPTER 11

My second summer at Woodholme was very different from the first. The country club was just a job my first year there. A good job, to be sure, but just a job. At fourteen, I was a lot younger than the other caddies when I first arrived at Woodholme. And while most of the guys befriended me, I felt like a cabin boy on a ship full of crusty old sailors.

The summer of 1962 was different. The arrival of a lot of new caddies from Cherry Hill, most of them boys my age, or younger, who looked upon me as a veteran elevated my status in the caddie shack.

The caddie class that I'd taken my first week at Woodholme was an irregular event at the country club. It was held whenever the spirit moved the golf pro, or one of his assistants, to convene one. This presented a problem for the newcomers because Mannion was reluctant to send untrained and inexperienced caddies out onto the golf course to work. To get around his objection, new caddies depended on the old-timers in the caddie shack to teach them the job. Their training amounted to some quick words of advice and the instruction to lie when Mannion asked them if they'd had any experience caddying.

"You ever caddie before?" Mannion asked a new guy standing next to me one summer morning.

"Sure," he answered.

"Where?" Mannion wanted to know.

"At Carroll Park," he responded smartly.

Carroll Park was an understandable but much overused answer. It was a public golf course with only nine holes, one of which ran along the backside of the Montgomery Ward warehouse where Rodney worked. To the south of Carroll Park's golf course was the black community of Mount Winans. Pigtown, a neighborhood of poor whites, was to the east.

In social terms, Carroll Park was about as far away from Woodholme as Mercury is from Pluto. It was a safe bet that no one at Woodholme would bother to check the references of any would-be caddie who claimed to have worked at Carroll Park. Still, Mannion was not easily fooled.

"Do you know what a putter is?" Mannion quizzed the new guy.

"Yeah, it's what you use on the putting green to hit the ball," he answered.

"And a driver, what is that used for?" Mannion asked in rapid-fire fashion.

"To tee off with," came the answer, which, like the others, had been force-fed to the new guy by a couple of Woodholme's veteran caddies in anticipation of just this moment.

So far so good.

Mannion turned away and started toward the pro shop. The would-be caddie smiled broadly. He'd passed the test and fooled Mannion into believing that he was an experienced caddie. It was time for celebration: a cocky nod of the head to some friends standing nearby, a quick shuffle of the feet, and a pirouette à la James Brown. Just as he finished his spin, Mannion did one of his own, turning back to face him.

"Do you know what a spoon is?" he asked, nonchalantly.

"A spoon?" the teenager said, answering the question with a question—and a look of befuddlement.

"Yeah, a spoon?" Mannion said. "What's a spoon?"

"Something you eat soup with?" he guessed aloud.

"Is that what they use spoons for at Carroll Park?" Mannion asked with a cynic's smile, before disappearing into the pro shop.

A spoon is a golf club. Like the driver, it's one of those clubs used to hit golf balls great distances. The name fell out of common usage long ago. Most golfers now call the club a 3-wood. But in a game of one-upmanship, it becomes a golf trivia question to ask: "What's a spoon?" Only the most devout followers of the sport would know the answer. Mannion knew that, but his instincts told him he was being hustled by someone who knew a lot less about the game of golf.

As it turned out, Mannion never turned away anyone who wanted to work because he had never caddied. He was too dependent on a steady supply of guys showing up in the caddie shack to meet the demands of club members. His questions were just meant to ensure that first-time caddies were not sent out onto the golf course to work before going to caddie class, or being paired with someone who was experienced enough to show them what to do. Still, most new caddies tried to avoid being labeled as such because it limited the money they could earn. Without experience, the new arrivals had to start out as "B" caddies and work their way up to the "A" caddie status. Moving up through the ranks that way was central to the meritocracy that governed the limited opportunities for advancement Woodholme's black caddies enjoyed. Nobody had to tell us that a black caddie couldn't work his way up to become Woodholme's caddie master. We knew instinctively that was not a real option.

There were just three steps on our ladder of opportunity:

"B" caddie, "A" caddie, and "regular" caddie. Beyond that, there were really no opportunities for Woodholme's black caddies to move up. By the summer of 1962 I was on the top rung of that short ladder.

Woodholme had a lot of vices, but none of them took hold of so many of its caddies as did gambling. Reggie quickly sucked the newcomers into the daily crap game. There was some lightweight drug dealing in the caddie shack: marijuana and occasionally a little heroin. The guys who were into that stuff kept a low profile. Once in a while one of them would duck into the woods behind the caddie shack to steal a swig from a half-pint of "knotty head"—the street name for Seagram's gin. Occasionally someone showed up at the country club with a carload of hot stuff to sell—clothes, food, small appliances, whatever the black market in stolen goods produced the night before. But for the most part, our vice was limited to illegal gaming.

Woodholme's crap game took on new life with the arrival of a new crop of caddies from Cherry Hill in the summer of 1962. Unlike the older guys who manned the game the summer before, the new arrivals brought a lot of energy into the caddie shack. For most of them, craps was more than a simple game of chance. It was their bar mitzvah—a coming of age that announced their early arrival into manhood. They gave the game a carnival atmosphere. They yelled and screamed at every roll of the dice, turning the once-tranquil crap game into a noisy sideshow that quickly drew Mannion's attention.

"Keep the noise down. They can hear you all the way out front," Mannion rushed into the caddie shack one day to complain. We had to have been making an awful lot of noise for him to venture into the caddie shack. The more heavily populated the place became with new faces, the less he came around. But he had no choice this day because the "they" he was talking about were Woodholme's members, who were being disturbed by the wafting sounds of laughter and street talk coming from our crap game.

"Listen, I don't care what you all do down here, as long as you keep it quiet," Mannion said. "Just hold it down, goddamnit, before I have to send somebody down the road." As usual, the threat of being barred from Woodholme was all that was needed to bring us in line—at least for the moment. But it just wasn't possible to turn one of our crap games into a wake. Not after Bertha Butch caught the fever.

Getting the fever is what happened to those caddies who came to Woodholme as much for the action in the caddie shack as for a chance to make money out on the golf course. It didn't start out that way with Bertha Butch, but it wasn't long before gambling became an obsession with him. He wasn't the only one who caught the fever. I had it bad for a while. So did Chester and Putty. But no one got it quite as bad as Bertha Butch.

He loved to gamble. Dice. Cards. Pitching pennies. It really didn't matter what the game was as long as he was in it. Like everybody else, he wanted to win. But winning wasn't nearly as important to him as the rush he got just from being part of the action. It was the action that got his juices to flowing—the heart-thumping excitement that came with every roll of the dice, every turn of the cards or toss of the penny.

Some days, Bertha Butch would go home with a pocket full of winnings piled on top of the money he earned caddying. And then there were times when, after a full day of caddying, he'd go home broke—having gambled away all of the money he made walking the golf course. The more hooked Bertha Butch got on gambling, the more reckless he became. Once he lost an entire day's earnings shooting dice with Julius McLaughlin. Then he begged Julius to lend the money back to him so he could get back into the crap game, only to lose it all again, doubling his debt. A few days later, as Bertha Butch was leaving a downtown store with a new pair of shoes under his arm he bumped into Julius, who demanded the money he was owed. After some quick curbside negotiations, Julius agreed to accept Bertha Butch's new shoes as payment of the debt. The next week, Bertha Butch—who bought the shoes to wear to a school dance—had to borrow them back from Julius to wear to the affair.

On the days that he went home broke, Bertha Butch would lie to his parents. He'd tell them he spent the entire day at Woodholme without getting any work. His mother often wondered aloud why he stayed at the country club all day if there was no work for him to do. But his father wasn't fooled. One day he pulled his wife aside and told her what his instincts told him: that their son "was probably gambling away his money."

The biggest gamble I took that summer was not made in a crap game on the floor of Woodholme's caddie shack. It came on a street corner, late one Saturday afternoon. As usual, I had ridden the No. 7 bus from just south of Woodholme all the way down Reisterstown Road to the point where it merges into Pennsylvania Avenue. I was headed for Luigi's restaurant when something caused me to do what I had studiously avoided doing before.

Instead of getting off the bus and making a beeline straight for the soul-food restaurant on Fulton Avenue, I headed south on Pennsylvania Avenue a few steps to Isidor Cooper's clothing store. At first I approached it from the other side of the street. I stared at the sign, COOPER'S WEARING APPAREL, for a few minutes before I found the courage to head for the store's entrance. As I crossed the street, I could feel my heart throbbing inside my chest. With each step my heart beat faster and harder than before. By the time I stepped through the front door of the clothing store, my heartbeat had become a drone. The shop looked much smaller—longer, narrower, and a lot more cluttered, too—than I remembered. Nervously I summoned the words to announce my presence.

"Anybody home?" I called out.

Aunt Mary Louise, who was waiting on a customer, was the first to notice me. She smiled broadly.

"Well, now to what do we owe this surprise?" she asked me.

"I was just in the area, so I thought I'd stop by," I said.

Actually, I'd been in the neighborhood many times before without ever stopping by Mr. Cooper's store. Like so many other things in my life, his shop was something I was running away from. For more than a year, I had ridden the No. 7 bus to the same intersection, gotten off, and headed straight to Luigi's without so much as a single glance in the direction of the store I hadn't been inside of since the afternoon of December 16, 1954. There were just too many memories there. Too much of the life I'd lost was inside that building for me ever to go back. At least, that is what I had thought.

But there was something pulling at me that day—something that drew me to Mr. Cooper's store just as surely as I once had been drawn there every day after school. Whatever the force, it had me standing awkwardly in the middle of the clothing store, as my mind flashed back to the last time I was there.

"Mr. Cooper, do you know who this is?" my aunt called out to her boss, who was at the back of the store fussing over some newly arrived stock.

"Sure I do," Isidor Cooper said after taking a couple of

steps in my direction. "You're Sylvia's boy, aren't you?" he said with a big smile.

"That's DeWayne," Aunt Mary Louise said to remind him of my name.

"Oh, I know that," he gushed. "How can I forget him, huh?

"How are you doing, young man?" he said, his trembling hand reaching out to grab my shoulder.

"I'm okay," I answered.

"You're sure?" he asked.

"Yeah, I'm fine," I said.

"Well, come over here and let me see you," Mr. Cooper said, guiding me toward the light streaming through the glass pane in the front door of his store. As we moved away from her, Aunt Mary Louise went back to the customer she'd been helping.

"Your aunt tells me that you're not in school," Mr. Cooper said in a low voice. Behind him, I could see my aunt stealing a glance at us.

"What happened?" he asked.

"Nothin' . . . nothin' happened," I answered him.

"Nothing? If nothing happened, then you should be in school," Mr. Cooper said. "Your mother was a good woman. She worked hard for her children. Everything she did, she did to make things better for you and the others."

Mr. Cooper's right hand, those trembling fingers that had always seemed so unsteady, dug deep into my shoulder. His grip, strong and sure, punctuated his point. "It would break her heart—may she rest in peace—to know that you didn't finish school.

"You think about that," Mr. Cooper said as I walked out from under the arm he had draped around my shoulder, and out the door. "You think about it."

I thought long and hard about what Mr. Cooper said, but I wasn't ready to go back to school and give up the life of a "regular" caddie. The money was good. I was pulling in a hundred dollars or more a week, tax free, in the summer, and about half as much during the winter months. There was no clock to punch and little chance of layoffs. If I wanted to, I could spend the rest of my working life at Woodholme, where a strong back—not a high school degree—was the passport to success.

A few days after my visit to Mr. Cooper's shop, I was standing with two other caddies under the tree that served as a loading zone for caddies trying to leave Woodholme, when a car pulled to the curb. Inside were two young club members. One of them was Richard Kress.

"You want a ride?" Richard leaned out the passenger side of the front seat to ask.

"Sure," Lonnie Howard, the lanky guy standing next to me, answered him.

It was a blistering hot day and Lonnie had decided early on that the heat and humidity were more than he could stand. He'd been hovering under the tree for more than an hour waiting for someone to come by and offer him a ride to the bus stop. I'd just arrived there after walking eighteen holes with two bags. I was wet with perspiration and dog-tired.

The heat kept most of Woodholme's members off the golf course that day. Many of them were holed up in the air-conditioned clubhouse waiting for the sun to go down before venturing out for some golf or tennis. Even the swimming pool behind the clubhouse was nearly empty. Richard and his friend had spent some time on the practice tee hitting balls, but even they decided it was too hot to play golf.

"C'mon, get in," Richard said.

"How far you goin'?" Lonnie asked as he and the other caddie climbed quickly into the backseat of the two-door car. After a moment of hesitation, I followed them into the car.

"All the way into town," the driver answered.

"You can let us off at the No. 7 bus stop," I said.

It was only a ten-minute drive to the bus stop, down the winding road that led away from the country club and then south along Reisterstown Road into Pikesville, a mostly Jewish suburb that butted up against the northwestern edge of Baltimore. The section of Reisterstown Road that ran through Pikesville was heavily traveled and usually pretty congested with cars. As our car approached the intersection of Reisterstown and Old Court Roads, we could see ahead of us a No. 7 bus weaving its way through traffic.

"There's the bus," Lonnie blurted out.

"Don't worry, we'll catch it," the driver said as he surged forward. But almost as quickly, he slammed on the brakes. The traffic was stop-and-go. Cars were bobbing back and forth between lanes in a frantic effort to speed their passage through Pikesville's small business district. Our chances of catching the bus didn't look good.

"Can you catch it?" Richard asked the driver.

"Sure," the driver exclaimed, just as he tried, unsuccessfully, to change lanes. Horns honked. Tires screeched. And the car jerked back across the broken white line in the road that divided the narrow lanes. Ahead of us was a traffic signal. The light went from green to yellow just as the No. 7 bus passed under it.

Suddenly the lane in front of us was now open all the way to the traffic light. The car sped forward with everyone inside playfully urging it on. On the other side of the intersection, the bus stopped to pick up several passengers as the light in front of us turned red.

"Go, go, go," we chanted. Again the driver accelerated the car and then quickly slammed on the brakes.

"You could have made it," Lonnie complained, as the traffic on Reisterstown Road gave way to cars coming into the intersection from a side street.

"I don't think so," the driver said, pointing off to his left to a state police car pulling through the intersection. A few feet away, set back from Reisterstown Road about thirty yards, was the walled entrance to the Maryland State Police headquarters, the place where we likely would have spent some time that afternoon had our car run that light.

As we sat there pondering the fate we'd just escaped, the bus disappeared down Reisterstown Road. By the time the light turned green, it was out of sight.

"You guys wanna have some fun?" the driver asked, as if to salve our disappointment.

"What kind of fun?" Lonnie asked.

"We're going to Gwynn Oak Park. Why don't you guys come with us?"

"What do you think?" Lonnie asked me and the other caddie.

"Okay with me," the guy said.

"What about you, DeWayne?" Lonnie pressed me.

"C'mon," Richard said, adding his voice to the chorus of those now urging me to go to the amusement park.

"Okay . . . why not?" I answered with a weak shrug of my shoulders.

Why not, indeed.

The Gwynn Oak Amusement Park sat on sixty-four acres of low land at the southwestern tip of Woodlawn, a largely rural community that intersected with Baltimore along Gwynns Falls creek. The park, which opened in 1894, was a local landmark that attracted thousands of daily visitors during the spring and summer months. Open-air trolley cars used to ferry city residents to within a couple of blocks of the place, discharging them onto the grassy shoulders of the road for the short walk to the amusement park's entrance. Others would come by car from more distant locations and park along the stretch of Gwynn Oak Avenue that bent lazily past the park's front.

Inside, beyond the large archway that served as a gate, there was a carousel, miniature cars, and a wide assortment of rides and booths, from which barkers tried to lure visitors to the games of chance that lined the midway. There were ponies to ride and goats to pet. And at the rear of the park there was a pond, where boats and canoes were available for rent.

On occasion, Gwynn Oak Park closed to the public when businesses rented the entire complex for a company outing. But most days it was open to all comers—with one very important exception.

It was dusk when our car pulled to a stop along Gwynn Oak Avenue. The amusement park's lights were on and the sounds of music and laughter rippled through the muggy air. Richard and his friend crossed the street ahead of us and headed straight for the entrance to the amusement park. We followed a few yards behind. I could see the rotating carousel, full of people, young and old, at the center of the park's packed midway.

We were just a few steps inside the arched entrance, just short of the admission booths, when whistles began to blow. People all around us started yelling—though I couldn't make out a word they were saying—and dogs began to bark. Several uniformed security guards, some with snarling dogs, came running toward us. Instinctively, Lonnie and I turned and ran as fast as we could back through the archway toward the street. The other caddie was right on our heels. When we hit the roadway, Lonnie and I headed east toward the city line, the other guy ran west in the direction of a waiting line of public buses. In all the excitement, I caught a glimpse of Richard and his friend, bent over with laughter as we ran away.

For much of the spring and summer of 1962, Gwynn Oak Amusement Park had been the target of an interracial group of protesters bent on ending its whites-only admission policy. Pickets showed up outside the park from time to time carrying signs and chanting slogans. Each time they did, the park's owners responded by beefing up their private security force and calling in the county police to keep the demonstrators at bay. There were no violent clashes—and no Bull Connor–type police chief who loosed vicious dogs and baton-swinging cops upon unarmed protesters—just the unrelenting demands of civil rights protesters for change.

Until the very moment I was chased from the segregated amusement park, I had no idea what had been going on there. How could I have? I was a high school dropout who read only the sports pages of newspapers. Television news, what little there was of it, didn't interest me. My life revolved around the golf course, where I worked seven days a week, and the Cherry Hill shopping center, to which I went most days after work to hang out. Up until that very moment I had been blissfully ignorant of what was going on at the amusement park.

Lonnie and I didn't stop running until we reached Liberty Heights Avenue, a good two miles from Gwynn Oak Park. We waited there for a bus—any bus—to come along. The first to arrive was a No. 37. It had been one of the buses parked just west of the park's entrance as we made our escape. But in our hurry to get away, Lonnie and I didn't notice it. The other guy with us did. He was slumped low in a seat near the rear of the bus when we got on. Lonnie sat in the seat across the aisle from him. I slid into one right behind him.

"They don't let no niggas in there, man," the guy turned to me and said. "That's what the bus driver says."

"You think they set us up?" Lonnie asked me.

"Who?" I wondered aloud.

"Your boy, Richard, and his friend," Lonnie said in a tone that demanded to know who else he might be talking about.

"I don't know, Lonnie . . . What do you think?" I replied, shifting the burden of answering the question I wasn't ready to deal with back to him.

"I don't know either. But if I find out they did," Lonnie said, "I'm gonna kick their little white asses all over that golf course."

"Sure you are, Lonnie," the guy seated across from him said. "And then where you gonna work? Huh?"

Lonnie and the other guy got off downtown and transferred to buses that took them to their homes in other parts of the city. I stayed on the No. 37 until it came to a halt at the bus stop just around the corner from my home in Cherry Hill—a home I had never been happier to see.

The next day, Richard came to me and apologized. He said he hadn't known that the amusement park was segregated. He said he was really sorry about what happened—especially sorry that he had laughed when we were chased from the park by the security guards. His apology seemed genuine enough, but I found it hard to connect with his feelings. I wasn't angry with Richard and his friend. It didn't matter to me at that point if he was telling the truth or pulling my leg. I was angry with myself.

How could I have been so stupid to walk into the middle of a segregated amusement park in my own hometown without knowing of its whites-only admission policy? How could someone who thought he was so damn smart, I asked myself over and over again, do something so dumb?

CHAPTER 1 2

All summer André pressed me to go back to school in September. He'd help me find a school that would accept me, he said. After our fight, you'd think he would have washed his hands of me, but he didn't. In fact, he was more determined than before to help me get my life in order. But as badly as I needed help, I wasn't ready for his support. It was my life, and my responsibility to get it back on track. If I was going to go back to school and repeat the tenth grade, when and where I chose to do so was a decision that had to be mine—and mine alone.

I had gone to City College because André went there. I never told him that. I didn't know how to tell him how proud I was of the name he had made for himself there. I remember seeing his report cards—the ones where he had nearly perfect scores for semester grades in every one of his subjects. I thought that simply by following in his footsteps I could do just as well. That was a mistake I was determined not to repeat.

This time I'd go to a school where I'd be comfortable—and one that I was certain would be comfortable with me. I decided to enroll in Carver Vocational Technical High School. Chester had just completed his first year at Carver, where he was majoring in tailoring. Carver was the school Rodney had attended, but I convinced myself that he was not the reason I chose to go to his alma mater.

Like Chester, I decided to take up tailoring. Rodney had been a star half-miler on the school's track team. In fact, he was the best half-miler in the city his senior year and would have won the scholastic championship had it not been for a pretty nasty fall he took during the title meet. I planned to play football and basketball at Carver.

I had another connection to the school. "The murder-suicide" that took the lives of my parents, the *Afro-American* had reported eight years earlier, occurred "at the site of the vocational school now under construction"—Carver High.

Having failed to make it at André's alma mater, I decided to give Rodney's a try. I got a provisional acceptance into Carver the week before summer football practice started there. My class assignment, one of the school's counselors told me, would have to await the arrival of my records from City College.

The provisional acceptance was all I needed to try out for Carver's football team. I got to the school's practice field early, and this time there was no doubt in my mind what position I wanted to play.

I wanted to be a quarterback.

Black kids in Baltimore had only three chances of becoming a high-school quarterback. They could enroll in either Dunbar, Douglass, or Carver, the city's black high schools. At the city's other high schools the job of quarterback was pretty much reserved for the white kids. Being a quarterback was not an option for me at City College, but it was at Carver.

There were no long lines of guys to compete with for a spot on Carver's team. In a way, going out for Carver's football team was just like playing on the field at the end of Cherryland Road. Everybody who showed up was black—and all the equipment was second-rate. The helmets and pads they gave me were older and more frayed than what I was given to wear the year before when I tried out for City College's junior varsity. But while the setting seemed familiar, my chances of making Carver's squad turned out to be no better than the year before at City College.

Two things worked against me. One was that the team had a lot of good players back from the previous season. And the other was Dr. Benjamin Whitten.

On the football field I had plenty of raw talent, but no high school experience. From the beginning of practice, that was a disadvantage that plagued me. Still, I managed to survive the first two cuts. Then, with just a few days to go before school started, I found myself one of four guys competing for the team's three quarterback slots. As it turned out, one of the other guys and I were fighting for the third-string job, a decision the coach told us one Wednesday morning he'd make the following day.

That afternoon I got called into the office of Benjamin Whitten, Carver's vice principal. Dr. Whitten was a lean man with a taut face that no doubt had been drawn tight by his many unpleasant encounters with the troublemakers it was his job to handle. He wasted little time with me.

"You had a brother who went here a couple of years ago, didn't you?" he asked as I sank into a wooden chair across from his desk.

"Yes, sir," I answered.

"He was a track man, right?" he said.

"Yeah, he ran the half mile," I responded, wondering all the while why he had summoned me.

"Well, it's too bad you didn't follow in his footsteps and come here first," the vice principal said, lowering the boom before I knew what hit me. "I've looked at your record from City College and I'm sorry to tell you there's no place for you here at Carver."

Just like that, I was gone. Kicked out of Carver before I'd even gotten the chance to attend a single class. I don't know what the people at City College said about me, but it must have been awfully bad—bad enough to convince Dr. Whitten that there was no hope of saving me.

The very next day, I tried to enroll in Edmondson High School. Rise was about to start the tenth grade there. Edmondson was a newly built, integrated school in the Edmondson Village section of west Baltimore. The student body was mostly white. But black students from as far away as Cherry Hill were being admitted.

Before our parents died, Rise and I were nearly inseparable. When the time came for me to attend kindergarten, my sister cried so badly when I left home to go to school that my mother didn't take me back to class the next day. I didn't go back to school until the following year when it was time for me to go to the first grade and Rise was old enough for kindergarten. We walked together to and from school every day that year. If I could get into Edmondson High, the chances seemed pretty good that we'd end up in the same class.

As it turned out, my stay at Edmondson was brief. Two days after I arrived at the school my records showed up. The next day I was gone. They didn't want anyone at Edmondson, I was summarily told, with your "history of disruptive behavior."

Somehow that one four-letter word I shouted at Mr. Long had become more than just a single uncivil act. It had been stretched and pulled, massaged and inflated, until it was distorted into a far greater offense: a disqualifying pattern of behavior that was causing school doors to slam shut in my face.

Essie Meade Hughes didn't shut school doors, she opened them. A small woman with a king-size heart, she was the last of Marshall and Mary Hughes's eight children. Essie was born in 1908 and raised in the house on Asquith Street her parents had settled into thirteen years earlier after moving to Maryland from rural Beaver Dam, Virginia.

In September of 1921, she dropped three cents into the fare box of a trolley car for the ride across town to the Daley Building, half a block from the intersection of Pennsylvania Avenue and Dolphin Street. It was there that members of Douglass High School's freshman class took their entrance exam. In the room with Essie that day was a teenager from west Baltimore named Thurgood Marshall. Essie and Thurgood scored well on the exam and ended up in the same homeroom class. Eventually the two of them joined Douglass's debating team. Thurgood was on the first team, Essie was on the second. They also took Gough McDaniels's class together.

McDaniels, who was a history teacher and coach of Douglass's debating team, had gone off to fight in World War I with the enthusiasm tens of thousands of black American soldiers carried into battle before him. He thought that by fighting for the freedom of people abroad, he would ultimately win it for himself and other blacks at home. But all he got for his troubles was a whiff of mustard gas—and the low, guttural sound that was all his singed vocal cords could produce from then on.

One day McDaniels came to class outraged by something H. L. Mencken had written in the *American Mercury*. It was a fleeting reference to the failure of blacks to think for themselves. Mencken's charge that too many blacks continued to act and think like slaves had enraged McDaniels.

"Thurgood, you ought to go down there and challenge him," McDaniels said in an effort to get his top debater to go to the south Baltimore home of Mencken, a man who had already earned a national reputation as a sharp-tongued columnist and social commentator. But instead it was Essie

Hughes and her friend DeVera Boston who took up the challenge. The two of them walked about twenty blocks to the Hollins Street house Mencken shared with his brother, and got a brief audience with the man many called the "Sage of Baltimore." Mencken listened patiently as the two girls stood in the vestibule of his home and voiced their objections to the magazine article. The whole thing lasted just a few minutes. When it was over, Mencken, obviously moved by their words, thanked them for coming.

"I'm glad I said something to make you think," he replied with a big smile.

After high school, Essie Hughes went on to college at Morgan and then from there to a teaching career that eventually landed her a job as a vice principal at Douglass High in September 1961. A year later, she got a call from George Moore, a junior high school language instructor who had done his student teaching under her supervision.

As Miss Hughes had been a mentor to Mr. Moore, he performed the same service for André, whom he encouraged to major in foreign languages and pursue a teaching certificate at Morgan.

Mr. Moore told Miss Hughes about me. Not a lot. Just enough to pique her interest. He said I'd lost my mother at an early age, but made no mention of my father's death. He said I was a bright kid who had gotten into trouble at City College. He told her how I had tried on my own—and failed—to get into Carver and Edmondson. And then he asked if she would help me get a second chance at Douglass.

For nearly half a century Frederick Douglass High School had been the pride of Baltimore's black community. Until 1940 it was the only full-fledged academic public high school blacks could attend. The school moved in 1925 from the cramped space of the building on the corner of Pennsylvania and Dolphin to a larger facility at the intersection of Carey and Baker Streets, a few blocks away. And then in 1954 Douglass moved again, this time to the sprawling three-story structure on Gwynns Falls Parkway.

It was an impressive-looking school. A driveway looped past one end of the building, near the promenade that led over to the top row of stadium seats on the hillside overlooking the school's track and football field. At the rear of the school were acres of athletic fields and a baseball diamond, where several of Douglass's teams practiced. Along the front of the building, the tree-lined parkway gave the inner-city school the look of a suburban campus.

As you enter the building from the circular driveway, the auditorium sits on the right; the locker rooms for the second-floor gym are to the left. Straight ahead, up a small flight of steps, are the administrative offices. On the left, those belonging to the school's counselors; and across the hall, a suite of offices that house the school's principal, vice principals, and administrative staff. It was there that I met Essie Meade Hughes.

We sat in her office for several hours one afternoon in September of 1962, talking about an awful lot of things. She never came right at me with her questions. Instead of asking why I had been expelled from City College, she wanted to know what interested me. I remember her asking if I'd "read any good books lately."

I told her about a couple of biographies I'd read that summer between caddying assignments. One was the story of Theodore Roosevelt. The other was about Zachary Taylor, the old Indian fighter who became president in 1849. They weren't heavy, just some quick reads that I'd gotten from Cherry Hill's makeshift library, but still I think she was impressed.

"Come back and see me tomorrow morning," she said,

satisfied that I was worth the effort it would take her to open up some doors. "And bring a notebook," she called out behind me as I left her office.

In the hallway outside the school's office I ran into Danny. He was in his second year at Douglass, having gone there the year before straight from Cherry Hill Junior High. Every school has a guy like Danny. He knew everybody and almost everyone knew—and liked—him. The thugs. Honor students. Hustlers. Members of the student government. The stickup artists. Athletes and girls. He knew them all.

"Hey, Sweet Wick," Danny called out to me, using the nickname I'd earned on the basketball courts of Cherry Hill's playgrounds where my jump shot, quick hands, and spinning moves got me nearly as much attention as my big mouth. Every time I stepped onto one of Cherry Hill's basketball courts I would start talking trash. It got my juices flowing and made me a better player. When I tauntingly told someone that they couldn't stop me, it was more than hype. I really believed it—and over time, so did many of my opponents. Talking trash to opposing players pumped me up and often broke the spirits of a lot of guys I faced on the other teams. It wasn't long before some of the guys who hung around Cherry Hill's basketball courts started saying I had a "sweet game." Before I knew it, they were calling me "Sweet Wick."

"What you doing here," Danny asked from the center of a crowd of boys huddled just outside the school's office.

"I'm thinking about going to Douglass," I answered, giving him the clear, though misleading, impression that the decision whether I would attend the school was mine to make.

Danny was happy to know that we might hook up again in school, something we hadn't done since the eighth grade. Only Aunt Annette's move out of Cherry Hill kept me from being in his ninth-grade class. When the time came to pick high schools, Danny, for reasons I never understood, chose Douglass, a liberal arts high school that seemed best suited for students who planned to attend college. Danny had no such plans. His only real goal in life was to hang out and have a good time.

"It's gonna be just like old times," Danny bragged to the guys around him about the possibility of my enrolling in Douglass. "Me and my boy, Sweet Wick, will be back together again."

The next morning I arrived in the school's office at 8 a.m. with a brand-new loose-leaf notebook in hand. Classes didn't start for another hour, but I wanted to make a good impression on Miss Hughes. Besides, I figured it would take her some time to do whatever paperwork was needed to get me registered and assigned to a homeroom.

The office was a lot busier that morning than it had been the afternoon before. Teachers rushed in and out, pausing just long enough to sign in and check their mailboxes. Students, some with parents, were there to solve problems that needed to be taken care of before the school day got under way. One secretary stood over mimeograph machines running off copies while another bounced back and forth between a telephone that wouldn't stop ringing and the counter that stretched the length of the office's waiting area. On the other side of the counter a short line of people waited for a chance to talk to her. Just as I stepped to the rear of the line, Miss Hughes came out of her office and pulled me aside. She told me she had to work out a few things with the school's principal, a no-nonsense former English teacher named Lillian Murphy. In the meantime, Miss Hughes told me to take a seat on one of the wooden benches on either side of the office door and to "be on your best behavior until I get back to you."

I sat there all day. With the exception of the time I spent

in the cafeteria eating lunch, I tossed and turned on that bench until the bell rang at the end of the school day. Several times during the day Miss Hughes came out of her office to offer me a few words of encouragement and a warning not to cause any problems. But she didn't say a word about the battle she was waging behind closed doors with Mrs. Murphy to get me into Douglass.

From the beginning, Mrs. Murphy didn't want me in her school—and she told Miss Hughes as much. According to the record she received from City College, I'd been absent ninety-three days the previous year, and when I did come to school my conduct was unsatisfactory. How did forty-four absences become ninety-three? My old homeroom teacher marked me absent forty-nine days and late once during the spring semester, even though I was expelled from City on the last day of the fall semester. I guess that was his revenge for the grief I'd caused him.

For five straight days, I reported to Douglass's office each morning, only to sit all day on those wooden benches while Miss Hughes and her boss argued my fate. From time to time, Mrs. Murphy would come out of her office, scowl at me, and then disappear behind her door. Almost as often, Miss Hughes would appear, smile softly, and tell me to "sit still, keep quiet, and stay out of trouble." On the fourth day, Miss Hughes arranged for me to see one of the school's counselors.

"I want you to be on your best behavior," she said before sending me on my way.

My meeting with the counselor lasted most of the afternoon. I was so happy to get off that hard bench that my time in the counselor's office seemed to fly. She asked me a lot of questions and took numerous notes. At one point she asked about my parents. I told her they had died in a car accident. It was the best I could come up with off the top of my head.

It didn't seem like a very big lie at the time. They died in a car—and to my warped way of thinking, what happened to them was some kind of freak accident. Anyway, the counselor mumbled something about how sorry she was to hear of my parents' misfortune and quickly moved on to other things. At one point during the interview she scribbled down the words "very intelligent" and "inclined toward nervousness" on my personnel record. She also wrote that I was "interested in journalism."

Miss Hughes's unrelenting push to get me into Douglass —and the counselor's favorable report—paid off. Late the next day I was told to report to Mrs. Ashe's homeroom class on Monday morning. But as a concession to Mrs. Murphy, I had to stop in the office every morning before classes started to pick up a sign-in sheet. Each of my teachers had to sign the form to prove that I had been to their class that day and— most important—to grade my conduct.

All things considered, I had no complaints. After weeks of frustrating effort, I'd finally found a school that was willing to give me a second chance. My up-again, down-again life was once more on the upswing.

On Saturday I spent the day caddying at Woodholme. Late in the afternoon I headed for Luigi's with Bertha Butch and a couple of other guys who were ready to make the pilgrimage back to Cherry Hill. It felt like springtime to me, even if it was fall and the grass was starting to lose its color. The flowers were fading and the birds had already started their southern migration. But Monday would be a day of new beginnings for me: my first official day back in school.

When the bus stopped to let us off at the corner of Pennsylvania and Fulton, Bertha Butch and the others headed straight toward the restaurant. I told them I needed to check out something, and went off in the opposite direction toward Mr. Cooper's store.

He was in the window adjusting one of the displays when I approached. I just stood outside watching him work until he noticed me. Moments later he was standing next to me on the sidewalk.

"What are you doing out here? Come in and see your aunt," he said.

"No, I got some friends waiting for me," I said, backing away from the window so no one inside the store could see me. "I just came by to tell you that I'm back in school."

"Where?"

"Douglass. I start on Monday."

"Good. Good. Does your aunt know?"

"Not yet."

"Well, come on in and tell her the good news."

"I've got some friends waiting for me in Luigi's. I'll tell her later. I just wanted to thank you . . ."

"For what?"

"For what you said to me about school the last time I was here."

"Don't thank me. Thank your mother. She always wanted so much for you and the others. I just said what I know she would have told you."

CHAPTER 13

"Who was that coon I saw you with?" Thelma Bush asked her daughter Ruth one October day in 1962 after the two of them scrambled off different ends of the same crowded No. 37 bus.

Ruth Frederick was one of five children born to the woman just about everybody, including her children, called Nanny. She was a sharp-tongued girl with short hair and a disarming smile. Ruth had a walnut-colored complexion and the cute look of a tomboy about to blossom into womanhood.

She lived with her mother and a younger sister and brother on the top floor of a three-story public housing apartment building across the street from Cherry Hill's Community Building. Ruth was born after her mother's marriage to Joe Bush ended. Her father, Robert Briscoe, was a postal worker by day and a professional gambler by night who hung out in the illegal gaming halls that operated in the back rooms and upstairs parlors of Pennsylvania Avenue businesses. He never got around to marrying Nanny. So when Ruth was born, her mother scribbled her maiden name on the birth certificate in the space that asked for the child's last name.

Ruth spent much of the summer of 1962 in Brooklyn, New York, with two older sisters who shared an apartment in an area called Brownsville. She returned home just in time for the start of her junior year at Eastern High School. Although Ruth had been in my third-grade class at P.S. 159, I lost track of her after I was bused to the school in Mount Winans the next year. She surfaced again in my life when we ended up in the same seventh-grade homeroom class at Cherry Hill Junior High. By then she had become a cute and sassy twelve-year-old girl who kept boys at bay with her wicked verbal jabs. At the time I didn't give her much notice. Girls were still off the scope for me. I mean, I liked them in an abstract way, but I wasn't ready for a relationship—or even a date, for that matter. Besides, Ruth had this annoying habit of calling me "Dee-Wayne." Everybody else pronounced my name "Dwayne," as if the first "e" in its spelling of D-e-W-a-y-n-e didn't exist. But not Ruth. She knew it rubbed me raw to be called "Dee-Wayne," but she did it anyway, just to pluck my nerves.

During the one semester I spent at City College, I saw Ruth and her girlfriend Landoria McDougal on the No. 3 bus a couple of times. The first time they got real giddy, like comedians who stumble upon a really good joke. I was standing near the back door. Ruth and Landoria were seated a couple of rows ahead of me, although I didn't notice them until the bus reached Thirty-third Street. That's when I heard the voice.

"E-x-cuse me. E-x-cuse me," I heard someone say moments before Ruth, followed by Landoria, plowed through the crowd of people standing between them and the rear door of the bus. I was hanging on to a rail by the door when they spotted me.

"Where are you going, Dee-Wayne?" asked Ruth in a way that only she could.

"To school," I answered in a voice meant to hide any sign of my irritation with her question.

"What school?" Landoria chimed in.

"City," I said. "Somethin' wrong with that?"

"No, I guess they let anybody in there now," Ruth said as the bus pulled to a stop in front of Eastern High and the rear door opened.

" 'Bye, Dee-Wayne," Ruth said as the two of them left the bus.

It was that way every time I ran into them on the No. 3 bus. They would thrust. I would parry. If there was any advantage in getting expelled from City College, it was that I wouldn't be riding the bus to school with those two anymore.

Danny lived on Carver Road, two stops away from where I boarded the bus each morning for the ride to Douglass. I'd call him just as I was leaving the house so that the two of us would end up on the same bus. My first day of classes at Douglass, I grabbed a seat at the back of the bus and dropped my notebook into the empty space next to me until Danny got on to claim it.

He was right. It was just like old times, the two of us together on the way to school. At first it didn't matter to me that he was headed to the eleventh grade and I was on my way to repeating the tenth. I was too happy to be with one of my boys to worry much about that. As hard as it was for me to get into Douglass, I was sure this black school would not give me the bum's rush the first time I got into trouble, the way white folks had at City College.

By the time the No. 28 bus stopped across from the Community Building the morning of my first day of classes at Douglass, it was already full of passengers—women on their way to jobs in the homes of white families and students headed for school. When the bus doors sprang open, more people got on.

"Well, hello, Dee-Wayne," Ruth said as the bus turned the corner and lumbered down a hill toward the last two stops in Cherry Hill. She and Landoria had gotten on at the Community Building and snaked their way to the back of the bus.

"Do you still go to City?" Ruth asked, squinching her face so as to punctuate her question with a look of doubt.

"I transferred to Douglass," I said without making eye contact.

"So I guess that means the two of you are going to give us your seats, right?"

"Yeah, Donald, get up," said Landoria, who always called Danny by his given name.

"C'mon, give us those seats. We get off downtown to transfer to the No. 3. You ride this bus all the way to Douglass. You can have your seats back when we get off," Ruth reasoned.

Danny gave in first. With a silly grin all over his face, he slid out of his seat and offered it to Landoria.

"W-e-l-l?" Ruth said to me.

Reluctantly, I got up, too. As I did, Ruth smiled a big smile and then shoved her books into my arms.

"Be a gentleman and hold these," she said before plopping down into the window seat I'd just forsaken.

"Donald, are you going to hold my books?" Landoria said to Danny, sounding hurt that she had to ask.

"Sure," he answered with an even sillier grin.

That's how we got started, Ruth and me. From that day on, our paths just kept crossing. At first by chance. And then by design. We'd meet on the No. 28 bus leaving Cherry Hill each morning. After school, Danny and I would catch the eastbound No. 13 to the corner of North and Park Avenues. Ruth and Landoria would ride the No. 3 to North Avenue and then take the westbound No. 13 over to meet us. Then together we would climb aboard the No. 37 for the forty-minute ride to Cherry Hill. It was during one of those trips home that Nanny got on the bus one afternoon after a day of domestic work and spotted me and her daughter sitting together at the back of the bus.

Ruth couldn't wait to tell me what Nanny said. She

thought it was funny that her mother called me a "coon." That night she telephoned to tell me all about their conversation. I was surprised to hear from her because I hadn't gotten around to giving Ruth my phone number. Things hadn't progressed that far between us. When I asked how she got the number, Ruth became defensive.

"What does that matter? You don't want to talk to me?" I did, of course. I just didn't know what to say. On the bus, most of our conversations were playful. We talked about anything and everything, except what was happening between us. We battled each other with words every time we were together. But each time we did, the edges on our words got softer— and the look in our eyes warmer. It wasn't long before Danny, who was hopelessly hooked on Landoria, started teasing me about Ruth being my girlfriend.

I denied it. A friend, yes. My girlfriend? No way. Ruth had a well-earned reputation of being hard on boys. She could chew you up and spit you out with a few sharp words and a menacing stare. But she never used profanity. Not a single curse word. She didn't need the help. Ruth could turn the most innocent of words into a deadly weapon just like Katharina, the unwilling bride in Shakespeare's *Taming of the Shrew*. No, we were just friends, I told Danny. But he knew better.

There never came a time that I asked Ruth to be my girlfriend. Things between us just seemed to progress to that stage without the official notice that asking the question brings. It wasn't long before I stopped calling Danny before going to the bus stop, and I started calling Ruth instead.

One weekend, about a month after we got close, I ran into Ruth at the shopping center and she invited me home with her. Up until this point I hadn't met Nanny, or anyone else in Ruth's family. When we got there, Ruth opened the door and pushed me in ahead of her.

"Nanny," she called out behind me, "I've got somebody for you to meet."

The little shove I got from her left me standing a few feet inside the apartment's living room, facing the kitchen. Ahead of me, a woman with an awful scowl on her face stood tending some pots on the small stove. In the center of the room, under the kitchen table, a man lay on his back, dressed neatly in a suit and tie. His arms were wrapped firmly around a half-gallon bottle of White Horse scotch that rested atop his ample gut. The woman was Ruth's mother. The man was John Lucy, her boyfriend. As was his habit most weekends, John Lucy had drunk himself into a stupor. He was out cold. When Ruth saw him, she ran crying into her bedroom. That was the first time I really saw her soft side.

A few weeks later, Ruth and I went to the Hill Theater one Saturday night to see a movie. By this time our relationship had only progressed to the hand-holding stage, but neither one of us had any doubt that we were in love. Throughout the movie I sat next to Ruth with my arm draped over her shoulder. I wanted to kiss her, but I wasn't sure how to do it, since I'd never kissed a girl before. I just couldn't figure out how to get into the right position for a kiss when the two of us were sitting side by side.

After about thirty minutes of false starts—at one point I faked being asleep and tried to toss and turn my head into the right position for a kiss—I slipped away to the bathroom.

The bathrooms in the Hill Theater were on either side of the candy counter. The women's room was to the left, the one for the men on the right. Inside the men's room there was a single urinal and toilet. A sink and mirror hung on the wall just inside the door. When I walked in the bathroom there was a guy at the urinal and another standing nervously behind him waiting for a chance to relieve himself. There was also someone inside the booth that held the toilet.

I got in the line for the urinal. By the time the man in front of me had finished, the guy in the toilet booth came out. In another minute they were all gone—and I was alone in the bathroom.

Quickly I slid over to the mirror and raised the back of my hand to within an inch of my mouth, looked at it sensuously for a few seconds, and then planted my lips firmly against it. The first couple of times I kissed it with a pucker. Then I kissed it with an open mouth and a probing tongue, just as I had once seen a passionate kiss described in one of those *Playboy* magazines Danny was always stealing from his father. How hard could kissing be, right? A couple of more practice pecks and I could get back to my seat and confidently plant my first real kiss right on Ruth's lips.

After some practice kisses with my eyes open to observe my technique, I did one more with my eyes closed, the way all truly passionate kissing is done.

I don't know which sound I heard first, the door opening or the guy's voice.

"Man, what the hell is wrong with you," someone yelled.

My eyes opened wide and the passionate kiss I was practicing gave way to an overacted gnawing.

"Damn splinter," I said, shaking my hand to relieve the imaginary pain.

"A splinter," he echoed me with a trace of doubt in his voice.

"Yeah, a splinter. It's a damn shame, man, I come in to take a leak and get a big-ass splinter in my hand."

"A splinter," he said again as he looked around for the wood that might have caused my injury.

"Hey, be careful, man, it's rough in there," I said, pointing to the wooden booth that surrounded the toilet as I hurried out of the movie's bathroom.

Having dodged that bullet, I rushed back into the theater ready now for the real thing. But something was wrong. The movie was still running, but the lights—the ones that burned dimly throughout the picture show—seemed brighter than before. All of a sudden, I could see everyone. And everyone, I was certain, could see me.

There was no way I was going to kiss a girl for the first time with everybody in the theater gawking at us.

"What's wrong with you?" Ruth asked me as we left the movies later that night holding hands. In the weeks we had been together she'd gotten me to open up a little. I'd talked to her about being put out of City and the troubles that drove me from Aunt Annette's house. But there was still a lot that I kept hidden from her. Any talk of my parents or André's homosexuality was off limits. She once asked me "what happened" to my parents, and I told her the lie about their dying in a car accident. And once when she started talking about one of her neighbor's "queer" friends, I abruptly changed the subject.

Ruth sensed my mood change after I returned from the bathroom. Instead of putting an arm back around her shoulder, I folded both of them across my chest and sank low in the seat. But instead of saying something then, she waited until after the movie was over and we had left the theater.

I wanted to tell her about the kiss that never happened— to say how I had gone into the bathroom to build up my courage and then came out and lost my nerve. Just thinking about telling her all of this made me feel good. It also made me realize that there was a lot more I wanted to tell her. I had gone too long with no one to talk to. Nobody to tell how abandoned I felt after my parents died. No one to talk with about the torture I inflicted on myself by thinking it was my school pictures—the ones my mother told me we couldn't afford just hours before her death—that might have triggered what had happened. I wanted to let all the stuff bottled inside me pour out that night as I walked Ruth home, but before I could we ran into Keno.

"Damn, boy, what you doing with a cute little thing like that?" he said.

Ever since Keno snatched that soda from my hands I had successfully avoided getting caught again in his wake of terror. Alone, I could have walked away from this Neanderthal bully. But with Ruth at my side, I had no choice but to stand my ground—and defend it, if it came to that. But before I was faced with that choice, Ruth went on the attack.

"Thing? Who are you calling a thing?" she said, getting up in his face before I could react. "Do I look like some kind of thing to you?"

Every time she spoke, the decibel level of her words rose.

"Aw right now, don't git in my face, girl," Keno said as he backed up a couple of steps.

"Well, then don't call me a thing," Ruth said, matching his steps backward with some forward steps of her own.

"Hey, boy, you better check your girlfriend," Keno said to me in what almost sounded like a pleading voice.

"Get out of my way," Ruth said, moving Keno aside with a half-playful swipe of her arm. He fell back against the pool hall door, feigning injury, as Ruth walked by him. Before I could follow, Keno jumped in front of me, bobbing and weaving his head and jabbing his fists in the air like a shadow boxer. I lamely raised my hands to a defensive position and backed into the parking lot to get around him.

"She don't know who she's messing with, man, 'cause I'll

hurt her," Keno yelled as we walked away. "I'll hurt her."

But the only thing he really hurt was my pride. I don't know how what happened that night played in Ruth's mind, but as far as I was concerned she had just saved me from an ass-whipping at the hands of a maniac. Instead of baring my heart to her, I spent the rest of that night choking on all of the pride Keno made me swallow.

CHAPTER 14

Between school and Ruth, I started spending a lot less time at Woodholme. I went there on the weekends to earn what I could. Without the money I made caddying, I had no consistent way of coming up with the bus fare and lunch money I needed for school. So as long as the weather permitted, I spent my weekends at Woodholme. But my weekdays I spent in school.

Pop Henry flashed a snaggletooth grin at me every time our paths crossed the day he found out I had gone back to school. As quickly as he'd do that, I would hustle off in the opposite direction. I just couldn't figure him out. At times Pop Henry seemed like an old foot-shuffling nigger, obsessed with guarding the privileges of white folks. Then at other times he'd display the black pride of Marcus Garvey. I didn't know which one was the real Pop Henry.

"Come here, boy," Pop called to me late on the day he found out. "Why ya duckin' me, huh?" he asked, his raspy voice sounding a bit playful.

Then, more seriously, he said, "I hear ya back in school. Is dat right?"

"Yeah, Pop, I'm back in school," I answered him with a sigh and a frown, hoping to avoid a long conversation with him on the subject. But he would not leave it alone.

"You think I like dis here work?" Pop said in angry reaction to my dismissive attitude. "You think dis is what I wanna be doin'? Boy, I'm old a'nuff to be yo' grandfather. I oughtta be retired somewhere, me and my wife. Sittin' by a creek fishin', or travelin' round the world like these here Jews do, vacationin' and stuff. That's what a man my age oughtta be doin', not caddyin'.

"But I never had no schoolin'—leastwise not a'nuff to do more than work wit my hands all my life. I come out here because I don't have no choice. But you a young boy with mo' life in front of you than behind ya. You know what I'm sayin'?" Pop asked me.

"No, Pop, I don't have the slightest idea what you're sayin'," I said sarcastically.

"What I'm sayin', boy, is don't be stupid. Keep yo' ol' young ass in school and git yo'self an education. It's hard 'nuff out here for a black man who got an education to make it. But it's a lot worse for niggas who don't.

"That's all I've been tryin' to tell ya', boy," Pop said as he turned to walk away. "You can do a lot betta than dis—if ya want to."

Pop Henry wasn't the only one in the caddie shack who was concerned about my return to school. In their own way, a lot of the older guys were glad that I had gone back. It was as though many of them were investing a bit of themselves in my troubled life. Although nobody came right out and said it, they were rooting for me to succeed in a part of life where they had all failed. But what they wanted from me was more than I was ready to give them.

Not long after classes started at Douglass, my biology teacher became ill. At first she just missed a day here and there. But soon her absences lasted longer and occurred more often. It wasn't long before Miss Hughes came to our class one day to tell us that the woman would not be back. Then she introduced us to her replacement, a substitute teacher named Lawrence Parker.

Mr. Parker was just a year or two out of Morgan when his substitute-teaching job turned into a full-time position at Douglass. He was lucky. He lacked the certification needed under normal circumstances to teach a high-school science course, but these weren't normal times. Douglass was short one science teacher, and Mr. Parker was in the right place at the right time. I wasn't. His good fortune turned into a disaster for me. Right from the beginning, he and I didn't get along for two reasons.

First, because he was a dandy. A male peacock in a building full of boys who dressed more like crows. But it wasn't just that he was always fashionably dressed; he flaunted it so it rubbed me and a lot of other guys the wrong way. The girls, on the other hand, loved to see him and cooed every time he came into the classroom—which did nothing to improve his relations with most of the guys.

The second reason was that he didn't know jack about science. When it came to teaching, Mr. Parker was a big phony. He didn't teach science so much as he just read it to us from the textbook. I don't think he knew a Bunsen burner from a Sterno stove.

On both counts, I gave Mr. Parker a hard time. When the girls cooed at him, so did I. Every time he made mention of his designer shoes or high-fashion clothes (and he did it often), I would have something negative to say. Once, after a girl in my class complimented him on a really nice shirt he was wearing, Mr. Parker responded by saying he had gotten it in New York.

"Pop Kelly's got the same shirt for five dollars," I blurted out to the obvious delight of the other guys in my class. Pop

Kelly's was a men's clothing store on Pennsylvania Avenue that carried a lot of knockoff imitation designer clothes.

"You ought to know," he shot back. This time it was the girls' turn to laugh.

My biology class met every day right after lunch. Most days I'd grab a quick bite to eat and then beat a path outside to find the crap game. It usually could be found out behind the shop building. Unlike the guys in Woodholme's caddie shack, the students who shot dice at Douglass played for coins, not dollar bills. Mostly they bet nickels. But the game didn't lack for excitement. Not with James Spencer always in hot pursuit of it.

Mr. Spencer was Douglass's other vice principal, the one responsible for keeping up with the school's boys. After I first met with Miss Hughes, who was Douglass's vice principal for girls, she went to Mr. Spencer to discuss my case. He took one look at my record and reminded her that because I was sixteen I could legally quit school.

"Yes, but just because he can doesn't mean he should," Miss Hughes responded.

No amount of talk convinced Mr. Spencer to take up my cause with the principal. After much discussion, he told Miss Hughes that he didn't feel comfortable pleading my case with Mrs. Murphy—but if she wanted to, she could.

Mr. Spencer was always sneaking about the school trying to catch up with our floating crap game. But as soon as he'd get a fix on it, we'd change locations. The best—and for us, safest—spot for the crap game was at the backside of the shop building. There were only two approaches Mr. Spencer could take to get there, and we had them both covered with lookouts. What we didn't anticipate was that he would climb atop the school's roof with a pair of binoculars to try and identify which students were gambling so that he could call us into his office one by one rather than risk confronting all of us at one time.

One day when a lookout spotted the vice principal on the school's roof with his binoculars in hand, he sounded the alarm. We scattered. Dice and money were left on the ground as we all took off in different directions. I ran toward the Warwick Avenue end of the school building, turned the corner, and ducked quickly into a little-used service area where one of the shop teachers usually parked his car so that school officials couldn't keep track of his comings and goings. And there, squeezed in behind the teacher's station wagon, was a small sports car, inside of which sat my science teacher, smoking a joint.

We saw each other at about the same moment. I was obviously in flight from something, or someone—and he was caught red-handed smoking marijuana on school property. It turned out to be the defining moment of our relationship.

The next day I sat in the back of the class mocking Mr. Parker. With my hands to my mouth as if I were pinching a joint, I mimicked taking several deep drags. By the end of class, Mr. Parker had seen enough. He pulled me aside and said he didn't like me and it was obvious I didn't like him. Then he made me an offer I couldn't refuse.

"If you keep your mouth shut and don't come back into my class, I'll give you a passing grade."

As it turned out, it was a deal I was too stupid to turn down. I forgot about Mr. Parker's illegal drug use and he kept his end of the bargain. After a little more than a month of tenth-grade biology, I spent the rest of the school year hooking Mr. Parker's class, with his permission. Every day he marked me present and gave me a satisfactory grade for conduct. And at the end of each semester he gave me a passing grade.

It was obvious, by then, that I had gone to Douglass for all the wrong reasons.

Getting a high-school degree was the farthest thing from

my mind. I really didn't think it would make my life any better. How could it? I didn't know of a single adult in Cherry Hill who brought home more money than I could in a good week at Woodholme. And most of the guys from the Hill who stayed in school long enough to get their diploma didn't go on to college. André was the exception. Rodney was the rule. The odds were that most guys in my neighborhood who finished high school would end up working in some low-end, backbreaking job that had no greater chance for advancement—and a lot less income potential—than did a caddie at Woodholme.

Plain and simple, I went back to school because I wanted to get people off my back, and because I was lonely.

I couldn't go home without André bugging me about going back to school. And I couldn't go to Woodholme without Pop Henry constantly pointing out how dumb I was, a finding of stupidity he always linked to my decision to drop out of high school. Mr. Cooper put the squeeze on me as well when he said it would break my mother's heart if I didn't finish high school.

All of that amounted to a lot of pressure. But an even stronger motivation for me to return to school was my loneliness. As much as I wanted to prove my manhood by making my own way in the world, I missed that part of growing up which my friends in high school were experiencing. They all seemed to be having so much fun, while I was spending most of my time sitting around Woodholme's caddie shack with a bunch of misfits. That, in a nutshell, was the reason I went back to school.

One of the things I decided to do was to go out for the basketball team. Ever since the legendary Frank James left Douglass a few years earlier, the school's basketball fortunes had been on the decline. Integration was partly to blame for this. As the old all-white high schools started opening up their doors to black students, a lot of the best black athletes were among the first to break the color barrier. Their departure put the athletic programs at the still all-black schools in free fall. Another reason for Douglass's decline was Mack Payne, the team's aging basketball coach and athletic director.

Like an old general who uses the tactics of the last war to fight the next one, Coach Payne was wedded to the past. His favorite offensive weapon was the figure eight, a play that most coaches ripped out of their playbook before I got out of elementary school. Every time he jumped to his feet during a game and ordered his players into the figure eight, fans from the opposing school would begin to laugh and Douglass students would hiss their disapproval. None of this fazed Coach Payne. He was stuck in his ways, like refusing to let tenth graders try out for his varsity basketball team, which meant I could try out only for the junior varsity squad.

Douglass's JV basketball team was coached by Roy Cragway, a burly man with a fair complexion and pockmarked face, who was a good twenty years younger than Coach Payne. Coach Cragway's first love was golf, a game he played better than most of Woodholme's members. In the spring he coached varsity golf. But in the fall he took charge of the school's junior varsity basketball team.

When I told Danny that I was going out for the basketball team he decided to come along. It would be like old times, he said, the two of us running ball together again. But that wasn't to be. Danny was cut after the first practice. On the fifth day of practice, Coach Cragway posted the names of the twenty players who made the team. My name was at the top of the list. But I soon found out that the position of my name on the list was nothing more than the luck of the draw.

I may have been one of Coach Cragway's early favorites to

be in his starting lineup, but it didn't take me long to change his mind about that. The thing that made me such a celebrity on the basketball courts of Cherry Hill worked against me at Douglass. I was a hot dog. A show-off. A loner in a team sport. Every time I got my hands on the ball, all I thought about was scoring a basket. As far as I was concerned, everyone else on the floor was my supporting cast. Playing like that made me a local hero in Cherry Hill. At Douglass it turned me into a benchwarmer.

I spent most of the season sitting on the bench watching guys with less talent play basketball. But even without me in the starting lineup Douglass's JV team was one of the best in its league that year—which made it easy for Coach Cragway to keep me on the bench. As a result, most of my playing time came in the last few minutes of each game, after the final outcome seemed certain.

Our toughest opponent that year was Mount St. Joseph, an all-white Catholic team that played in the public schools league. St. Joe drew most of its students from working-class white neighborhoods on the city's southwest side. At its home games, the stands would be packed with white people—many of them adults—who came to cheer the St. Joe team on to victory. The first of our two games with St. Joe that year was played at the Catholic school. It was close from start to finish. With just a couple of minutes left in the game and our team leading by six points, the St. Joe coach called a time-out. Looking dejected, the St. Joe players returned to their bench.

"We're not going to let these niggers beat us, are we?" one of the St. Joe players yelled to his teammates.

The scorer's table separated the bench holding the St. Joe players from the one assigned to the visiting team. But the guy's words sounded as though they had been spoken in our huddle, not his.

"If we don't win the game, we'll win the fight," one of

my teammates said in reaction to what we'd all heard so clearly.

"Don't start that mess," Coach Cragway snapped. "We came here to win the game and that's just what we're going to do. Beating them is the way we get even."

We didn't. They came from behind to snatch the victory away from us. It was a humiliating defeat, made all the worse by the ugly words that rallied the St. Joe team.

Our next game with the Catholic school team was played at Douglass several weeks later. Coach Cragway didn't say it, but the game meant a lot to him. He worked us hard at practice the week leading up to the game and brought us to the gym a couple of hours early on game day to get our juices flowing. Word about what happened at St. Joe had spread and a large crowd—maybe twice the size for a junior varsity game— showed up to cheer us on.

This time, as before, the game was close. Too close for Coach Cragway's comfort. With things going badly early in the game, he decided to take a big chance in an effort to turn things around.

"W-i-c-k-h-a-m." He called my name. It was just minutes into the first quarter in a four-quarter game and already he was calling for me. My teammates looked at him as though something was wrong. Maybe the pressure had gotten to him. The game was on the line and he was about to send the team's biggest hot dog into the game.

"W-i-c-k-h-a-m," he called my name again, this time look-ing quickly down the bench to see what was keeping me.

"DeWayne, Coach wants you," one of my teammates called out to me under his breath.

It was too late. By then Coach Cragway had spotted me sitting three rows deep in the stands with his young son, a crayon in one hand and his boy's coloring book in the other. He turned away and quickly called for someone else to go into the game. I think the only thing which kept Coach Cragway from kicking me off the team that day is that we won. After the game he called me to his office.

"The next time I look up and find you in the stands," he said angrily, "that's where you'll spend the rest of the season. Do you hear what I'm saying?"

"Yeah, Coach, I hear ya."

I stayed out of the stands, but whatever chance I had of getting off the bench and into the game in anything other than a mop-up role had all but vanished.

Basketball kept me busy after school, but not having to go to my biology class put a hole in my school day that wasn't easy to fill. It's one thing to cut a class once in a while, but quite another to stay away for most of the semester. At first I just found places to hang out around the school building. In the gym. The cafeteria. The stadium. On occasion I'd even go to the school library and pretend I had been sent there to work on a project. Imagine the irony of that, huh? Cutting class in the library.

But it didn't take long for me to run out of things to do and places to go around the school when I should have been in my biology class. What I thought was a blessing fast became a curse. At Douglass, students caught outside of a classroom during school had to have a pass. Any boy who got caught roaming around without one ended up in Mr. Spencer's office. I couldn't afford that kind of trouble. So when I ran out of things to do in the school when I should have been in Mr. Parker's class, I left the building.

Most days I'd cut out after lunch. That was pretty easy to get away with because I had only two classes after my lunch period. The first was biology. The other was actually two classes, physical education and music, which I took at the same time on alternate days. Because I was on the basketball team, my music teacher was understanding when I didn't show up for class. She thought I was in the gym practicing. My phys ed teacher usually let the basketball players use our time in the gym to do whatever was needed to prepare for our next game. Sometimes that meant spending the time shooting baskets. Sometimes it meant going outside to jog. Other times it meant spending the period in the weight room or the pool working on a nagging injury. With all those possibilities, keeping up with us was next to impossible.

Once again I had managed to get myself out on one of life's slippery slopes. To cover my tracks, I began forging my teachers' signatures on the daily attendance sheet I was made to carry.

One day, instead of going to school, I met Chester at a pool hall at the corner of Fulton Avenue and Baker Street. It was about a ten- or fifteen-minute walk from the house I used to live in on Whittier Avenue. The place was a real joint, full of bad dudes—and bad goings-on. Everything was for sale there: drugs, guns, and sex. Chester brought along two of his friends from Carver High, and the four of us spent the entire day there shooting pool and otherwise just hanging out.

From then on, I used the pool hall as my hideaway from school. Most days I'd take a book along with me. Not a textbook, but usually something I picked up in the school library. My favorite was *My Darling Rachel*, the story of Andrew Jackson and the woman he loved and married. I loved to read about historical figures. It was an interest of mine which my teachers never tapped—and which I didn't put to very good use.

"What cha readin', professa?" a man in a dingy plaid car coat asked me one winter day early in 1963 as I sat alone at the back of the pool hall with a book in my hands.

"Just a book," I answered guardedly while closing it gently and pressing the front cover against my lap.

"What's it about?" he persisted.

"Nothin' special."

"It's about somebody famous—and dead—ain't it?"

"How'd you know that?"

"You're John Wickham's boy, ain't cha? You look just like 'im."

The question stopped me cold. I didn't respond. I couldn't respond. I wanted to get up and run out of the pool hall, away from this man who was about to open up that door in my life I had tried so hard to keep shut.

"Your dad and I drove for the same cab company," the man said just as I got up to make my escape. "He was always readin', or talkin', 'bout famous dead people."

Still, I couldn't manage to say a word.

"Sit down, boy, I ain't gonna bite cha."

And then for nearly an hour he sat there telling me things about my father I didn't know or had long forgotten. He talked about how he liked going to boxing matches and stock car races—and how he would visit Civil War battlefields and come back to work talking about what had happened there. Not once did he mention what was for me the unmentionable. Not a word about how my parents' lives came to an end.

"You know, I still got some pictures of your dad," he said as he got up to leave. "If you wanna see 'em, I'll bring 'em by tomorrow, 'bout this time, if you gonna be here."

"Yeah, I'll be here," I said, my mind anxiously racing ahead to the next day. I wanted to see the pictures. It had been more than eight years since my father's death and the memory of what he looked like had become a dim, fuzzy image. No photos of him made the trip with me from Whittier Avenue to Cherry Hill. Seldom was his name ever mentioned in my aunt's house after Rodney and I moved in. Not since the night I saw his image against my bedroom wall had I allowed myself to see him in any way. But now I wanted to put a face to all the memories this man had just shared with me.

The tomorrow he promised couldn't come soon enough.

The following day I had a good reason for hooking school. I went straight from home to the pool hall, not bothering to spend the first half of the school day in class. And I waited. But the man didn't show. Finally I asked the manager about the guy I'd been sitting with the day before.

"You mean Reds, that ol' drunk? He comes in here once in a while. He's one crazy nigga. All that jungle juice he's been drinkin' done pickled his brain. Gawd knows the next time he'll come round here agin."

I went back the next day—and a couple of times after that—hoping to run across him, but without any luck. After a while I gave up looking for him and stopped going to the pool hall as well. The weather was warming up, and if I was going to cut class away from the school building, I figured I might as well do it at Woodholme.

CHAPTER 15

The spring of 1963 brought new demonstrations at the Gwynn Oak Amusement Park. Busloads of people—black and white—some of them famous, most of them not, started showing up there to protest its refusal to admit blacks. Many came from as far away as New York and Philadelphia, but the people in charge were local religious leaders and civil rights activists whom *The Baltimore Sun* called "integrationists." At first they went to the amusement park in small interracial groups and staged sit-ins in front of the entrance. Each time county police showed up to cart the demonstrators away, television cameras recorded the event for the evening news.

By now I was painfully aware of what was going on at the amusement park. Every day I got the newspaper and went straight to the local coverage (instead of the sports section) to keep up with events. After what had happened to me the year before, I felt as if I had a personal stake in the outcome even though I refused to take part in the demonstrations and knew I would never, ever, set foot in the park again.

The leaders of the movement to desegregate Gwynn Oak Amusement Park were members of a group called the Goon Squad, a mix of local ministers and activists, including Parren Mitchell, who years later would become Maryland's first black congressman. The Goon Squad was the straw that stirred the drink when it came to keeping the pressure on the owners of the amusement park to end their discriminatory admissions policy. They rallied local demonstrators, helped coordinate the involvement of people from out of state, and generally kept the story alive.

By summer, the demonstrations outside the amusement park really heated up. Civil rights activists from across the country poured into Baltimore to join the local "Freedom Seekers" outside the park's gates.

"Let's go to Gwynn Oak Park tomorrow," Lonnie said as he cornered me on the patio out back of the caddie shack one hot summer day. "C'mon and go with me."

"For what? To get our asses chased up Gwynn Oak Avenue again?"

"No, there's going to be a big protest there tomorrow—hundreds, maybe thousands of people."

"Man, are you crazy? Tomorrow is the Fourth of July. You know how much money we'd be missin' here if we were there?"

"Some things are more important than money."

"Like what?"

"Like pride."

"Hey, well, you try eating some pride the next time you get hungry, okay?"

"C'mon, DeWayne, you gotta go."

"No, I don't gotta go, man. I ain't ever goin' back to that damn place."

"Not even if they desegregate it?"

"There ain't nothin' they can do to that place to make me go back there. Not a damn thing!"

"I hear you," Lonnie said dejectedly. "I hear you."

The next day hundreds of civil rights protesters descended upon Gwynn Oak Amusement Park to challenge its whites-only admission policy. People poured into Baltimore from all over the nation for the protest march. Even Marlon Brando was on his way to join the picket lines when he was hospitalized with a kidney ailment.

To make sure that the protest didn't spark a race riot, Spiro Agnew, the Baltimore County executive, sent scores of police to the amusement park with orders to use no force or police dogs in arresting demonstrators. Local officials didn't want a replay of the violence that occurred in Birmingham, Alabama, a few months earlier when Bull Connor used high-powered fire hoses and snarling police dogs to rout civil rights demonstrators.

In all, police arrested 283 people during the Fourth of July protest at Gwynn Oak Amusement Park. Three days later, when a second wave of marchers showed up, a hundred more arrests were made. Lonnie was there both days. Though he didn't get arrested, he did get his revenge. After the second mass demonstration the park's owners began negotiating secretly with protest leaders to end their whites-only admission policy.

Ruth spent the Fourth of July in Brooklyn. In fact, she spent the entire summer of 1963 there. We'd been seeing each other for nearly eight months when she left for New York. Up until then our relationship had been primarily platonic. Aside from some hand-holding, nothing happened. I was almost seventeen and still hadn't found the courage to kiss her. So, understandably, I was a little relieved when she went away for the summer. We needed a break, and I needed an escape from all the pressure I was under, a lot of which came from friends like Chester and Danny who were constantly pressing me to find out if Ruth and I had "done it" yet. But most of it I brought on myself.

For years, the favorite subjects of conversation when I got together with Danny and Chester were sports and sex. As we got older we began to talk about both more from the perspective of participants rather than spectators. By the summer of 1963, sex overtook sports as the topic of conversation. But there was just one problem with that; I hadn't had any sexual experiences. Danny and Chester claimed they had, but when pressed to talk about it they were pretty thin on the details of what happened—and with whom. Deep down, I doubted that either one of them had scored, but I hardly knew enough about sex to challenge their stories. So instead, I matched them with lies of my own.

I never actually told them that Ruth and I had slept together, but I did imply as much. That was enough to convince them that I was no chump when it came to women, even though the lie I told made me feel like one.

By early August I was love-sick. Ruth and I had talked several times a week by telephone, but I was dying to see her. My chance came when Chester told me about a charter bus trip from Cherry Hill to Coney Island, the oceanside amusement park in Brooklyn. The bus was scheduled to leave early on a Saturday morning for the four-hour drive to New York City and leave late in the afternoon for the return trip to Baltimore. Chester and I bought tickets. Then I called Ruth and told her when we would be arriving. She agreed to meet us at Coney Island, near the parachute drop.

When we got to the ride Ruth and her sister Vicky were there waiting for us. For the next few hours we hung out at the amusement park, going on rides and stuffing ourselves with food. Then as the time neared for me and Chester to get on the bus for the trip home, Ruth popped the question.

"Why don't you and Chester spend the night with us?" she asked. "Nanny and John Lucy are here. You can ride back with them tomorrow."

I didn't need much persuading to accept her invitation. The day had gone better than I thought it would. There were a lot of funky vibes bouncing back and forth between me and Ruth. My mind was racing ahead of her invitation and my libido was in fourth gear. Chester, on the other hand, was reluctant. His mother would be expecting him home that night. If he spent the night, he'd have to do a lot of fast talking when he did get home to keep her off his butt. Eventually, Vicky and Ruth convinced Chester to stay. Moments later we were on a subway train headed for Brownsville.

Ruth and her sisters lived in an apartment above a Laundromat at 431 Stone Avenue, between Sutter and Belmont. Across the street was a Carvel ice cream shop. Down on the corner of Stone and Sutter was Nate's, a delicatessen that filled the crowded streets with the smell of hot corned beef and knishes. Throughout the subway ride Ruth and I sat holding hands. I could feel her leg against mine, and I sensed something exciting was going to happen that night.

But when I entered the apartment, what I saw hit me like a cold shower. The place was packed with people. There was Ruth's oldest sister, Lorsie, and her three kids, Vicky and her two children, plus Nanny and John Lucy. In all, counting Chester and me, twelve people would be spending the night in the two-bedroom apartment. The females got the bedrooms while the males jockeyed for sleeping space in the living room. That night I curled up in a tattered living room chair and went to sleep. Ruth slept in a bedroom down the hall—and my fantasies ended up being just that.

The next day Chester and I hopped into the backseat of John Lucy's 1954 Cadillac for the ride back to Baltimore. Ruth and I said our goodbyes at curbside with what seemed like the whole world looking on. I went home without so much as a peck on the cheek. When Chester got home his mother was furious. She had roamed the streets looking for him the night before until someone who had been on our bus trip told her he'd decided to spend the night in New York with my girl-friend and me.

Not long after Chester and I got back from New York, Bertha Butch had a big run-in with his father. It happened one night when Lawrence Hawkins, Sr., asked his son to go with him to a civil rights demonstration that he and some other postal workers planned to attend the next morning. The following day, a Wednesday, was supposed to be a good day for the caddies at Woodholme. There was a special golf outing sched-uled and work for caddies would be plentiful. Bertha Butch didn't want to miss out on the money he could make.

There was another reason for his unwillingness to miss work that day. Mannion always rewarded the caddies he could de-pend on—those who worked at least six days a week during the summer months—by seeing to it that they got as much work as they could handle. Those who missed some of the golf club's busier days found it harder to get bags when they did show up. Bertha Butch didn't want that to happen to him. Besides, he was only sixteen, and the idea of giving up a day's pay to attend a civil rights demonstration really didn't appeal to him.

At first Bertha Butch's father tried to reason with him. But when reason failed, Lawrence Hawkins, Sr., told his son he had no choice but to go with him.

"You'll go with me tomorrow," he said, "or you ain't going nowhere at all."

The next day, Bertha Butch and his dad climbed aboard a chartered bus for the forty-five-minute ride from Baltimore to Washington, D.C. It was the morning of August 28, and they were two of the hundreds of thousands of people who went to the nation's capital that day for the March on Washington.

Lonnie didn't show up at Woodholme that day either.

Instead he went back to the Gwynn Oak Amusement Park—this time not as a protester but as a patron. After months of picketing and ugly confrontation, the owners of the amusement park agreed to open it up to people of all races for the first time on the very day millions of Americans sat glued to their television sets as Dr. Martin Luther King, Jr., delivered his "I Have a Dream" speech.

For me, August 28, 1963, was just another day at the office. I arrived at Woodholme early that day and, as usual, stayed late.

The civil rights movement didn't pass Woodholme by; it just arrived in Baltimore too late to have much of an impact there.

The year 1963 was a big one for the civil rights movement. It was the one hundredth anniversary of the Emancipation Proclamation, Abraham Lincoln's executive order that has been wrongly credited with freeing the nation's slaves. Actually, Lincoln's order applied only to slaves in those parts of the nation that were "in rebellion against the United States." In other words, he freed slaves in areas not under his control and left enslaved those in places that were. It wasn't until the Thirteenth Amendment was ratified nearly three years later that slavery in America was ended. Still, in a symbolic way, the one hundredth anniversary of the Emancipation Proclamation made 1963 an important year for black civil rights activists and their supporters. But even with that, the year could hardly have gotten off to a worse start.

In January, George Wallace was sworn in as Alabama's

governor and immediately promised, "Segregation now. Segregation tomorrow. Segregation forever."

The open resistance of Wallace and Mississippi governor Ross Barnett to integration and desegregation efforts gave license to the brutality of Bull Connor and Byron de la Beckwith. It was Connor who turned high-powered fire hoses and snarling police dogs on black children during a Birmingham desegregation march in May of 1963. The next month, de la Beckwith shot Medgar Evers in the back late one night as the NAACP Mississippi field secretary was returning home. Afterward he bragged to friends about the murder he had committed. It was in the wake of these two events that more than 200,000 people took part in the March on Washington.

Speaker after speaker that day called upon federal officials to do something to protect the rights and ensure the well-being of the black people who were feeling the brunt of America's racism. And when Martin Luther King, Jr., spoke that day he moved an awful lot of people—black and white—to take notice of the civil rights struggle, which until then was concentrated largely in the South. But if his words won sympathy among some for his cause, they also drew the contempt of others. Less than three weeks after he spoke, segregationists set off a bomb in Birmingham's Sixteenth Street Baptist Church while a group of black children was gathered there for a Sunday School class, killing four young girls.

Maryland also wound up in the civil rights spotlight that year. Not because of the campaign to desegregate the Gwynn Oak Amusement Park, but because of the actions of Gloria Richardson, a black housewife who lived in the small Eastern Shore town of Cambridge, Maryland. In March of 1963, she led a desegregation campaign on Maryland's Eastern Shore that dragged that largely rural area of the state kicking and screaming onto center stage when the National Guard was called out and a state of martial law was declared to control outbreaks of violence there.

Resistance to Richardson's efforts was at times mean-spirited. A fifteen-year-old black girl who knelt down and prayed outside a segregated bowling alley in Cambridge was arrested and held without bond. Eventually she was given an indeterminate sentence in a state correctional school for juveniles.

When Richardson pleaded with Attorney General Robert Kennedy to investigate violations of black protesters' constitutional rights and to help end the violence occurring on the Eastern Shore, he reacted by blaming her for what had transpired. After some hesitation, Kennedy did intervene, and the movement Richardson led won major concessions from local government officials, including the integration of all of the county's schools and hospitals.

Woodholme was largely insulated from the civil rights movement that swirled all around it that year. As a private country club, it had legal immunity from the charge of racial discrimination. Besides, by the standards of the day, it was ahead of the times. From the beginning, Woodholme had black employees. The first was Sam Watkins, who, along with his wife and two other helpers, maintained the clubhouse and prepared lunches for club members from 1926 to 1929. When the country club opened a full-fledged dining room in 1930, Watkins was named co-chef, a job he held until 1952. It wasn't long after he left the club that the first black caddies came to Woodholme. Just one or two of them in the beginning, but their numbers grew quickly. By the end of the decade, blacks were a majority of the club's caddies.

The closest thing to a civil rights demonstration at Woodholme occurred in the summer of 1963, nearly two years after Dick Whetzle became club pro. Whetzle was a likable Texan with a cocky walk who had been an assistant to Carroll McMasters, the crusty old golf pro who treated caddies like sedan chair carriers. News of the change of command raised expectations among caddies that the conditions we worked under would improve. But there were few improvements after Whetzle became the country club's head pro, and over time the condition of Woodholme's caddie shack worsened.

The spark that set things off was toilet paper—actually, the lack of toilet paper. At best the supply of toilet paper to the caddie shack's bathroom had been erratic. Some caddies brought their own personal stash from home and carried it around with them until it was needed. Others waited until they got home to relieve themselves. Those who couldn't simply made do with whatever substitutes they could find. Of all the stuff that caddies griped about, no toilet paper in the bathroom was the thing that pushed us over the brink after somebody went into the bathroom one morning and belatedly discovered there was none. When we heard a voice in the bathroom pleading for toilet paper, Bertha Butch and I cracked up.

"Dat shit ain't funny," said Bad Feet Willie, an older black caddie whose flat feet and hobbled walk earned him his nickname. "Dat ain't funny at all."

Of course he was right, but that didn't stop us from doubling over with laughter as the guy inside the bathroom begged for someone to find him some paper—any paper. But our mood changed quickly as other veteran caddies stepped forward to complain about conditions in the caddie shack.

"Man, fa-fa-fuck this shit," Iney said. "My faa-mily might be poor, ba-ba-but we keep toilet paper in our ba-ba-ba-bathroom."

"They treat us worse than slaves," Sugar Ray snapped. The anger in his voice spread through the caddie shack like a flash flood. People started talking about a job action. Somebody suggested picketing the clubhouse. That idea was quickly rejected as too extreme. Nobody wanted to piss off Woodholme's members. No, our beef was with the club pro, it was decided. He was the one responsible for conditions in the caddie shack, we thought. If things were going to get fixed, Woodholme's golf pro would have to see that they got done. And until that happened, we weren't going to work. Word was sent to Mannion that we would not take any bags until we'd had a meeting with Dick Whetzle.

"What's the problem?" Whetzle asked the moment he stepped through the caddie shack's front door.

"Toilet paper," Sugar Ray said, speaking up quickly.

"Toilet paper?" Whetzle repeated Sugar Ray's words.

"Yeah, we don't have any. There's never any toilet paper in the bathroom," someone else jumped in.

"I'll take care of that," Whetzle responded with an is-that-what-this-is-about look on his face. "Anything else?"

"Yeah," another person spoke up. "This place is filthy, especially the bathroom. It needs a good cleaning."

"I'll get you some cleaning supplies. It's your bathroom, so you'll have to keep it clean. Fair enough?"

That answer produced some grumbling. Nobody wanted to take on the job of cleaning the caddie shack's bathroom. The place was worse than filthy. The toilet bowl and seat were badly stained. The sink was discolored by layers of greasy dirt and partially clogged. And there were no soap and towels to wash and dry our hands. After some negotiations, Whetzle promised to see that the bathroom got a thorough cleaning before turning over the maintenance duties to the caddies. He also said he'd see to it that we got regular supplies.

And with that it was all over.

Our work stoppage lasted the better part of fifteen minutes. Afterward Whetzle kept the promises he made. He brought in someone to clean the bathroom and saw to it that we had toilet paper, soap, and paper towels. Pop Henry was given the responsibility for making sure the caddie shack bathroom was well stocked.

After the meeting with Whetzle, there was talk in the caddie shack about getting some other things done, like installation of a water fountain, lockers, and possibly a shower, but nothing ever came of it. Whetzle's quick acceptance of our bathroom demands stripped too many caddies of their rage.

There was another reason why our rage fizzled out so fast: daddies. Several of the caddies had them. I'm not talking about their biological fathers, but the ones Woodholme's paternalism produced. To the country club's caddies, a daddy was a member who became their protector. I don't think the club members who took on this role actually knew we called them "daddies," but it's hard to imagine they didn't understand that their relationship with these caddies reeked of paternalism. First and foremost, a daddy was someone who made you his personal caddie. Whenever he played, you were expected to carry his golf bag. Both the golfer and the caddie benefited from this feature of the relationship. The caddie got a steady source of income and the golfer got a caddie of predictable ability.

But there was more to having a daddy than this. When John Henry landed in jail one night, Bill Adelson, a Woodholme golfer with close political ties to Mayor Theodore McKeldin, got him out. Adelson was John Henry's daddy. Pop Henry caddied regularly for William Kress, and the dentist rewarded him not only with money but with hundreds of dollars' worth of free dental work. One winter, Putty's golf daddy put him to work in his company to tide him over until

play at the golf course picked up. Most caddies didn't have
daddies at Woodholme, but those who did weren't about to
risk losing them for the sake of a water fountain, a shower,
or a few lockers. Those things didn't put money in their pockets
or keep others off their backs. But their Woodholme daddies
often did.

A lot of club members treated caddies, regardless of their
age, like children. I suspect this was in part because of the
subservient manner of some caddies. But more than anything
else, I think it resulted from an unspoken belief among more
than a few Woodholme members that black people were both
hopelessly immature and intellectually inferior. I don't think
they thought we were capable of thinking and acting like
adults, at least not in the same way that they did. For the
most part, this perception was not intentionally mean-spirited
or racist, although it was hurtful nonetheless. But it was
condescending and patronizing in the way that many white
liberals then thought of, and acted toward, black people.

To them we were not depraved and inhuman, as bigots
claimed, but we weren't their equals, either. No one ever said
as much, but there were those who certainly implied it.

One day, as Putty was being driven to the bus stop by
Gabe Paul, a Woodholme member with a reputation among
caddies for decency, he was stung by a question the man put
to him.

"Why don't your people vote?" he asked.

"I don't know," Putty answered with a shrug and a look
of embarrassment.

It was a question seemingly meant more to shame Putty
than to evoke a thoughtful answer from a teenager who was
himself years away from being able to vote.

Once a member asked me if I knew Charlie Sifford. After
a moment's hesitation, I said I didn't. My answer produced

a look of amazement on the man's face—and then laughter.

"Can you believe that?" he said to no one in particular as we stood among a crowd of club members and caddies near the first tee. "He doesn't know Charlie Sifford."

I was embarrassed, although I really didn't know why. I'd never heard of the man, but I could tell by all of the head shaking and snickers among the white people around me that they thought I should have. Later I learned Sifford was one of the first black players to distinguish himself on the professional golf circuit.

Incidents like these caused most black caddies to keep their guard up around club members. We'd be friendly, but never very revealing of ourselves or our families. That's the way most of us preferred it. Being pleasant with club members often got caddies a nice tip. But getting too close to them, we feared, could exact a big emotional price from a caddie. Still, there was a lot more Jew envy going on in the caddie shack than Jew-bashing.

Every day there was talk about Jews and their possessions. The new car a club member bought, the expensive clothes of another, or the wealth they all were mistakenly rumored to have. But the thing I remember best is all the talk among caddies about how Woodholme's Jews stuck together.

"I'll give them this," Sugar Ray used to say, "they really take care of their own."

I don't know how true it was, but that's what most of us came to believe. And every time he'd say it, his words had the effect of pulling the black caddies together—as if to show that we, too, could take care of our own.

I guess that's the reason I never had a Woodholme daddy. I easily could have. For a while my relationship with Richard Kress came close to that. But I didn't want that kind of relationship with any of the country club's members. There were a lot of fine people at Woodholme. But there were also more than a few people who were paternalistic in their dealings with the club's black caddies. I didn't want another daddy. Not while I was still haunted by the memory of my real father.

CHAPTER 16

Just before school reopened, I went to the Royal Theater with Danny to see a big Labor Day show. Martha and the Vandellas and Tommy Hunt, the former lead singer for the Flamingos, were the big attractions. The other acts on the show were the Flamingos, Dionne Warwick, the Supremes, and a local group called the Royalettes.

Martha and the Vandellas got top billing because they'd had a string of big hits. Tommy Hunt shared it with them because he was such a big hit with women. They turned out in droves every time his name showed up on the Royal's marquee. Women really thought he was fine. I don't know about that, but the guy could really blow. He had one of those big masculine voices—like Teddy Pendergrass—that made women crazy with emotion every time he cut loose. And when he sang "Human," his signature song, women treated him as if he were the only man on a lost island with a thousand sisters. And in return, Tommy Hunt would give them their money's worth every time he came on stage.

He sang that song whenever he played the Royal. And every time he did, Tommy Hunt blew the women away. That's why the line outside the theater stretched for about a block down Pennsylvania Avenue that day. Women from all over town turned out for the show.

I think Danny knew half the people in line. The two of us jumped off the bus at the corner of Pennsylvania and Lafayette Avenues, almost right in front of the Royal's box office. As we headed for the back of the line, Danny kept stopping to greet people he knew. In between a lot of glad-handing with the guys and posturing with the girls, he'd ask me if I knew this person, or that one. When I said I didn't, Danny would laugh and then introduce me to them. Later on he told me they all attended Douglass and that he was surprised I didn't know them. But as much as I cut classes and hooked school, I didn't even know half the people in my class.

Near the end of the line, Danny introduced me to several girls who had been in his class the last school year. One of them took an immediate liking to me. That wasn't hard for me to figure out. No matter who was talking, her eyes kept darting off in my direction. Once or twice, when our eyes met, she gave me a big, wet smile. Finally, when she got up the nerve to speak, she asked what school I attended. When I told her Douglass, she looked surprised.

She said, "Who's your homeroom teacher?"

"Mrs. Warrington," I answered, giving her the name of the homeroom teacher I would report to when school opened for the fall semester.

"No, not last year," she shot back. "I mean whose homeroom will you be in this year?"

"Mrs. Warrington," I said again.

"But she's got the eleventh grade?"

"Yeah, I know. Something wrong with that?"

"No, I just thought . . ."

"What?"

"That you were a senior, like us."

Up until that very moment, I really hadn't given much thought to being a year behind other students my age. I had escaped most of the embarrassment that usually comes with failing a grade in high school by transferring from City to Douglass. At Douglass, only Danny and a few other friends of mine knew I was actually repeating the tenth grade—and they spared me the embarrassment of having to talk with them about that.

When the girl found out that I was only a junior, her attitude changed. I don't know if she thought I was a year younger, or if she figured out I had failed a year and in her mind branded me an idiot. Whatever the reason, the twinkle I'd spotted in her eyes moments earlier was gone, replaced by a nervous flutter. After that, our conversation stiffened and she became a lot more interested in what Danny and her friends were saying—and a lot less interested in me. I was more hurt by the obvious put-down than the loss of her interest in me.

Ruth was my girl, and I knew she'd be home soon. As it turned out, she came home from New York a couple of days after Danny and I went to the show. I was really glad to see her. In a lot of ways I think my attachment to Ruth was much stronger than hers was to me. I couldn't have gone away for the summer and left her behind, as she had done with me. The emotions I was feeling for her were too strong. But for Ruth, her decision to spend the summer in New York with her sisters hardly seemed heart-wrenching. That's the way it was the whole time we were together. I always felt I cared for her much more than she cared for me. Eventually that emotional imbalance destroyed our relationship. But back then I needed whatever it was we had too much to start questioning Ruth about how strong her feelings were for me.

Danny, on the other hand, had no choice but to question Landoria about her commitment to him. Their relationship had more ups and downs than a roller coaster. One moment they were together, the next they were not. I think Danny's drinking had a lot to do with making their relationship so stormy. When sober, he was pretty even-tempered and mild-mannered. But when he got juiced, Danny would fight at the drop of a hat. Almost any insult, real or perceived, would set him off. But that wasn't all of it. More often than not, Danny would drink himself into a stupor on the weekend. I mean, he would get pissy drunk and that made Landoria really mad. When she couldn't take it anymore, she'd break off their relationship and start seeing someone else.

On one occasion she quit Danny and hooked up with a slick little dude named Ronnie Bushrod. Now, this was a classic case of jumping out of the pan and into the fire. Bushrod was what we called a jitterbug. Some jitterbugs were defined by their dress: they wore long pointed-toed shoes, baggy pleated pants, fly-collar shirts, and "Big Apple" caps. More than a few of them had flashy gold teeth in their mouths. Jitterbugs were also defined by their behavior. Many of them were thugs. Bushrod easily met both definitions. A slender weasel of a guy, he always traveled with his partner, Smiley.

One night a group of us were hanging out in the parking lot outside the apartment where Ruth lived. Danny, Chester, Ruben, Lionel—a friend who lived near my old home at the bottom of Cherryland Road—and I were sitting on the brick wall at the back of the parking lot talking trash. The guys had a jug of wine and Danny was drinking more than his share. All of a sudden he leaped to the ground.

"There's that motherfucker," Danny said, pointing to two guys walking off in the distance along Spelman Road. It was Bushrod and Smiley.

"I'm gonna kick his ass if he don't stop messing with Lannie," Danny said, his voice jumping up a couple of octaves.

"Sit down, nigga," Chester said with a laugh. "Landoria ain't thinking 'bout you."

"Naw, man, you're wrong. That's my girl. She loves me," he shot back.

"Nigga, that's that wine talkin'," Chester responded.

"Hey, Danny, I think they're headed for Landoria's apartment," Ruben said with an instigator's grin. "They gonna run a train on her."

Danny lunged for Ruben and wrestled him to the ground, heaving and grunting like a sumo. Ruben was a lot bigger. But what Danny lacked in size he made up for with reckless courage. He was all over Ruben, squirming and kicking and groping for an advantage. They weren't fighting. Neither one of them threw a punch. They were just tussling.

"He's kicking your butt, Danny," I said, picking up with the instigating where Ruben left off. Chester and Lionel laughed. Finally Ruben broke free of Danny's grip and the two of them scrambled back to their feet.

"While y'all were down there playing grab-ass, them niggas are probably all over Landoria," Chester teased Danny.

"Yeah, well, I'm gonna find out," Danny said, taking off across the parking lot, setting off another wave of laughter with his long Groucho Marx–like strides.

"Where you goin', Danny?" Ruben asked.

"I'm goin' to see what them niggas are up to," he answered.

"By yourself?" Ruben said.

Danny stopped and turned back toward Ruben.

"Yeah, unless you got the heart to go with me."

With that, Ruben had to go. Danny was daring him. We all knew he didn't want to go. Ruben was a big guy with a lot of mouth and a pea-sized heart. But he didn't want to chump down in front of us, either.

"Yeah, I'll go," Ruben said halfheartedly.

It didn't take long for Danny and Ruben to reach the

apartment building where Landoria lived, which was just a block away. Once the two of them got there, they checked out the area around the building and didn't see any traces of Bushrod and Smiley—which came as a big relief to Ruben, who immediately wanted to beat a path back to us. But Danny had other ideas. He wanted to go upstairs and find out "what Lannie sees in that nigga." Reluctantly Ruben followed him into the building. They were barely inside when Bushrod and Smiley came walking down the steps.

Bushrod gave Danny one look and asked, "Where you goin'?"

"To see Lannie," Danny answered defiantly.

"I don't think so," Bushrod said coolly, as Smiley positioned himself a few steps to the side of where Danny was standing. Instead of stepping up to cover Danny's flank, Ruben turned and broke for the door.

"I'll be back, Danny. I'm gonna get some help," he shouted.

By the time Ruben returned with us, Bushrod and Smiley were gone. They split after a man passing by saw what was about to go down and intervened. When Danny saw Ruben he went ballistic, pulled out a knife, and took off after him. Chump that he was, Ruben tried to beat a quick retreat. Danny pulled up and let the knife fly. It struck Ruben in the leg, causing just a superficial cut. Ruben fell to the ground as if he'd been brought down by an elephant gun. A few minutes later, we were all back on the wall outside Ruth's apartment, laughing and joking about everything that happened. A few days later, Danny and Landoria were dating again.

The grades I got my first year at Douglass weren't great. They weren't even good. But they were high enough to get me into the eleventh grade, which meant they were a big improvement over what I got at City. I wanted to do better in the eleventh grade. If I just stayed out of trouble—and stayed in school— getting decent grades wouldn't be a problem. That was easy enough for most students, but conduct and attendance always seemed to be my undoing.

The first day back at school I went straight to Miss Hughes's office to pick up the attendance sheet I had to carry to all of my classes in the tenth grade. Much to my surprise, the vice principal said I would no longer have to get a daily report on my conduct and attendance from each of my teachers. I had proved last year that I could be trusted, she said. I was glad to be out from under that yoke, but at the same time I felt like a real jerk, given all the times I had cut class or hooked school during my first year at Douglass. If it hadn't been for Miss Hughes, I wouldn't be attending Douglass—or even in school, for that matter. She really had gone out on a limb for me, and while I had certainly exceeded Mrs. Murphy's shallow expectations of me, I hadn't come close to doing what I could to make Miss Hughes really proud. As I left her office I made a promise to myself to do better.

To begin with, doing better meant not giving Mrs. Warrington, my homeroom teacher, a hard time as so many others before me had. The woman's nerves were badly frayed by too many years in the trenches of Baltimore's public school system, leaving her in only minimal control of my eleventh-grade homeroom class. When I walked into her classroom the first day of school, the place looked just like a scene out of *The Blackboard Jungle*, the 1955 movie that gave Sidney Poitier one of his first roles in a major film. Once the bell sounded for the start of the homeroom period, Mrs. Warrington struggled mightily to get people into their seats—and vainly to keep them quiet. By the time the homeroom period ended, I was exhausted just from watching her. I figured the school really had to be shorthanded to have her as a teacher. She may have been a good teacher of willing students, but her homeroom had an oversupply of misfits, troublemakers, and underachievers, most of whom were determined to make her life as miserable as theirs must have been. Right away I figured that if I was going to be a better student in the eleventh grade, I had to keep my distance from that crowd.

I soon learned they weren't going to be my problem—but Lawrence Parker was. I got assigned to his eleventh-grade chemistry class. Talk about bad luck. The science teacher whom Mr. Parker had filled in for the previous school year was still out on medical leave, and so once again the pot-smoking substitute got her job. When I walked into his class later that day he stopped me before I could find a seat.

"Mr. Wickham, we've got the same deal, okay?" he said.

"That's fine with me," I said on my way out the door.

Cutting his chemistry class was a serious mistake. I knew that. It meant that every day for the rest of the school year I'd have to find some place to hide out when I was supposed to be in his class. As I had learned the previous year, it doesn't take long to run out of places to go and things to do when you're cutting the same class every day. What he offered me was a sucker's bet—just as Reggie Shellington had done in that crap game at Woodholme—and I couldn't resist it. There was some kind of testosterone thing going on between us that he was controlling. I knew he was a drug user and he figured me for a loser. It took me years to figure out that the deal he offered me was no deal at all. Not only did he get me out of his class and off his back, he also robbed me of a valuable piece of my education in the process.

It wasn't too long after Ruth returned from her summer in New York that we finally got around to that first kiss. By then I was seventeen. We had been dating for nearly a year and all of my buddies were convinced that I was scoring big with her. And while I did nothing to disabuse them of this idea, I was anxious to get something real going on between us.

One Friday night it just happened. We were sitting on her living room couch watching television. Nanny was upset that John Lucy hadn't come straight home from work, and had gone to bed early. There was a light on in the kitchen, but with the exception of the glow that came from the picture tube of the black-and-white TV we were staring into, the living room was dark.

I didn't give it a lot of thought. There was no plan for what happened. No rehearsal, as there had been during my dry run in the Hill Theater bathroom months earlier. One moment we were watching TV and the next we were kissing. Somewhere in between the two events there was a little head butt, as I led with my forehead instead of my lips the first time I tried to kiss Ruth. But I got over the pain the moment our lips connected. For the next couple of hours we sat there on the couch kissing nonstop. The longest break we took came when Nanny got up to make a trip to the bathroom. Except for that and the necessary pauses to accommodate some heavy breathing, we went at it pretty good until about midnight, when Nanny got up again and sent me home.

The next morning, Ruth called to tell me her lips were swollen. I'd heard of people's lips swelling up in an allergic reaction after eating pork that wasn't fully cooked, but never from kissing. She insisted that when she woke up, her lips were twice their normal size, a predicament that had not escaped Nanny's notice.

"What did she say?" I asked with nervous laughter.

"She said we better not give her any surprises," Ruth answered.

Nanny had been surprised twice before. Once when Lorsie, the first of her four daughters, gave birth to a son at the age of fourteen. And again when Vicky, who was next in line, had a daughter when she was seventeen. Ruth was the third of Nanny's four girls.

"I don't think she has to worry about that," I said.

"I know she doesn't," Ruth snapped.

Robert Frost once said that "love is an irresistible desire to be irresistibly desired." After my parents died there was nothing I wanted more than for someone to really make me feel loved. I knew what it was like to be pitied. I remember how this one woman in the neighborhood used to hug and squeeze me every time I got within arm's reach of her in the days after I moved in with Aunt Annette's family.

"You poor baby," she would always say, "come here and let me hold you."

Every time she did, the children I was playing with would all stop what they were doing and just stare at us as if wondering why she was singling me out for her affection. I hated those encounters. Finally, one day I'd had enough. She reached for me and I pulled back. As I did, I yelled, "Leave me alone," and ran away. It wasn't pity I was in need of, it was love—the love good parents give their children. What I wanted was to be hugged by my mother, or wrapped in the arms of my father. The last thing I wanted was pity.

Not long after our first kiss, I told Ruth that I loved her. Of course, I didn't know what I was talking about. I had no idea what love was—not in the way the children who grow up in loving homes, around loving parents, come to know it. But I knew I felt something real special—something I'd never felt before—so like a lot of teenagers whose libidos start kicking like wild horses, I just assumed it was love.

Like our first kiss, my confession of love required some

lead time. I gave a lot of thought to when and where to say those three words to her. Finally one night I decided to do it over the phone. After that our relationship became much more physical. There was a lot more groping when we kissed. And after first stopping me, Ruth started letting me kiss her when we were alone at my place. Before long I was out trying to buy some rubbers in anticipation of the big event.

Back then rubbers were not easy to get. In Cherry Hill's drugstore, for instance, they were kept behind the counter, out of view from customers. To purchase them you had to go to the cashier and ask for "a pack of prophylactics." Anyone my age who asked for rubbers, I thought, was too immature to purchase them. Getting the word right was the easy part; building up the courage to pop the question in a drugstore full of people was something else.

The day I went to buy some rubbers I foraged through the shelves of the drugstore while the line of customers at the cash register disappeared. As soon as the last person was out the door, I stepped up to the counter and asked the black woman on the other side for some prophylactics.

"You want what?" Miss Lena asked sharply.

"Some prophylactics," I said again.

"Ain't you the boy who's seeing Thelma Bush's girl?"

"Yes, ma'am."

"Boy, you betta git yo' butt outta here and hope I don't go tell her what you up to."

I did. Just as fast as I could. But getting chased out of the drugstore didn't stop me from trying to get some protection. It just sent me off in another direction. Some time ago, Ruben had shown me a rubber he was carrying in his wallet. And while I'd never seen it, Lionel, too, claimed to be packin' one. I went to both to see if I could scrounge up a rubber. Lionel said he had just used his. Ruben, too. So I didn't know what to do until he offered me some advice.

"Use some Vaseline," Ruben said. "It kills the sperm."

"Vaseline? Where'd you get that from?" I asked him.

"Mr. Brown told me," he answered.

George Brown was an elementary-school teacher with whom Ruben hung out. A couple of times I saw Ruben driving Mr. Brown's car, which I thought was strange, since he didn't have a license. Once when a girl Ruben dated off and on saw them together, Ruben told her Mr. Brown was his cousin. Danny said Ruben was "spiking" Mr. Brown for money, in which case he would've had a real need for some rubbers. I didn't know what to believe—about the Vaseline or Ruben's relationship with the elementary-school teacher. But I was getting desperate. And the more desperate I became, the more willing I was to think that Vaseline just might work.

The first time Ruth and I came close to having sex there wasn't a drop of Vaseline in my house, so at the last minute I backed down. But the next time we were alone in my place I had a jar of Vaseline at the ready and we went all the way. That was in October of 1963, a few weeks before basketball practice got under way at Douglass.

When basketball practice started that school year, Coach Payne invited all but a couple of the guys who played on the junior varsity team the year before to try out for the varsity squad. I was one of the guys who didn't get an invitation. I was too embarrassed to be visibly pissed off. Over the summer, I'd spent a lot of time after returning home each day from Woodholme playing basketball on the playground behind P.S. 159. I worked hard on being more of a team player. Setting picks. Passing the ball. Running the give-and-go—with special emphasis on the "give" part. Sometimes, when I got home after dark and there was no one else to play with, I'd practice shooting at the end of the basketball court where the glow from a nearby streetlight spilled over onto the playground. By the time basketball practice started at Douglass my game was really hot.

Coach Cragway noticed right away. The first day of junior varsity practice, I played like a veteran. I took charge in the scrimmages, directing the play so effectively that the coach left me on the floor as he rotated the other guys in and out of the practice sessions. By the end of the first week of practice, Coach Cragway told me I would be one of his starting guards. A week later, he named me team captain. He had a good squad that year. A lot better than the one he coached the year before. There were some really talented newcomers—tenth graders who were better than guys playing the same positions on the varsity—and he had me. The new and improved version.

It was something of a tradition at Douglass that the school's varsity and junior varsity basketball teams would scrimmage each other a couple of times in the final days before league play began and again during the Christmas break. The first game usually took place during a closed practice. The second was open to the student body.

Coach Cragway was never really fond of having his JV team scrimmage the varsity. His players usually got manhandled. And while such lopsided victories were good for the varsity players' self-esteem, they usually had the opposite effect on members of the junior varsity team. But this year he was anxious to have his players take on the varsity for the simple reason that he knew he had a better team. Coach Payne made a mistake not inviting me to his practice. And he erred in not letting Sam Cherry, Beverly Roberts, and Walter Green try out for the varsity. Man for man, we were all better basketball players than the guys in his starting lineup—and we proved it. Not once, but twice.

In the first scrimmage we battled back and forth with the

varsity team for three quarters. Then in the fourth quarter we started to pull away. That's when Coach Payne jumped up and called his favorite play: the figure eight. Immediately his players began bobbing and weaving across the width of the basketball court, running along an imaginary path that looked like a diagram of the number eight. But instead of chasing behind them, Coach Cragway told us to fall back near the basket in a zone defense.

The object of the figure-eight play was for all of the players on the team to move the ball in different directions until one of them got the chance to race toward the basket. When this happened, the player holding the ball would pass it to the player who had broken free for an easy layup. But for this play to succeed, the players on the opposing team had to chase after them. When we didn't, the varsity's chances of overtaking our lead disappeared. We ended up winning the game by about a dozen points.

The second scrimmage was held the Friday before the opening week of the season. This time both teams dressed in their game uniforms and students and faculty members were allowed into the gym to watch. During the warm-ups, Coach Payne barked orders to his team like a general about to lead an army into battle.

But when the game was over, the score wasn't even close. We took an early lead. By halftime we led by about 10 points. When the game ended, our lead was nearly twice that. That season the junior varsity won its conference title and lost the city championship to Carver in the last game of a best-of-three series. Coach Payne's varsity had a mediocre season, during which he decided to forgo the traditional Christmas break scrimmage game with the junior varsity.

CHAPTER 17

Two things happened in November 1963 that turned my life around. Ruth missed her period and Lee Harvey Oswald killed John Kennedy. It took weeks for me to find out about Ruth's pregnancy, but news of the President's death reached me not long after the President was shot on Friday, November 22, 1963.

I was in school that day, though not in class. Instead I was hiding out in a maze of hallways near the gym locker rooms —hooking class with a couple of other guys—when Mrs. Murphy announced on the intercom that the President had been shot. Right away, school came to a halt. Teachers and students began streaming into the hallways. Some of them were whimpering, but mostly people just looked shocked. I mingled with them, trying to look more concerned about the President's fate than relieved that this tragedy had given me an excuse to come out of hiding.

Then, as people started to return to their classes, Mrs. Murphy spoke on the intercom, and in a voice far more shaken than before, told us that President Kennedy was dead. Someone standing not far from me shrieked, "Oh, Jesus," as people all around me let go of their emotions. Some began to cry like babies. A guy from the football team cursed the unknown assassin, slamming his fist into one of the hallway lockers as he did. One of the teachers took charge and asked for a moment of silence. And then, as we stood there, one of the students began to recite the Lord's Prayer.

Later that day, Lyndon Baines Johnson was sworn in as president. Five months earlier, while still Vice President, he had delivered a Memorial Day address in Gettysburg. "To ask patience from our colored citizen is to ask him to give more of what he has already given enough," he said. "Until justice is blind to color, until education is unaware of race, until opportunity is unconcerned with the color of men's skins, emancipation will be a proclamation but not a fact."

The Vice President's address came just eleven days after President Kennedy sent to Congress a civil rights bill meant to open up public accommodations to blacks. The proposed legislation caused the President's popularity among blacks to soar—and heightened our sense of loss on his death.

The day President Kennedy was buried, I sat alone for hours in front of the TV watching the funeral. I had never seen a funeral before. Not once had I been to one. I never got to say that final farewell to my parents. They were just with me one day, and then gone the next. I knew they were dead because I had been told as much, but for years I couldn't accept this reality. For the longest time I treated them like a possession that had been misplaced. You know, like the sock whose match you've mislaid, or the favorite comb you always have trouble keeping up with? Deep inside I just knew that someday they'd turn up again in my life.

As I watched the burial of President Kennedy, I imagined what it was like when they put my father in the ground. Both men were military veterans. Both were buried in veterans' cemeteries. And while the President's funeral was a much bigger event, I imagined the basic ceremony—the flag-draped coffin, the military honor guard, the playing of taps, and the gun salute—was pretty much the same.

When I saw that large family of his standing together at

the President's graveside, I thought of what it must have been like the Sunday my mother was laid to rest in the small cemetery behind the Brooks AME church in the little town of Mutual, Maryland, with so many members of the Chase and Howe families gathered around. Watching the President's funeral, I let my thoughts linger for the first time on the deaths of my parents. The nation buried a president that day, and in the dark recesses of my mind I finally got around to burying my mother and father.

I don't know who Ruth told first that she was with child, but it wasn't me. And it certainly wasn't Nanny. The surprise Ruth's mother had warned us against came in the form of a diaper service. Somebody sent one to the apartment for Ruth. It was their way of blowing the whistle on the pregnancy. Nanny must have taken the news hard because Ruth was her favorite child, the one who she thought had the most promise. She was an excellent student and hadn't given her mother an ounce of trouble up until that very moment. If any of her children could look forward to a future that was better than the life Nanny had lived, it should have been Ruth.

I was really excited about spending Christmas of 1963 with Ruth and her family. Nanny had invited me to have Christmas dinner with them. That was fine with me. André and Rodney both had made plans to have dinner away from home. Rodney was going to be with his girlfriend, Paulette, and her family. André was having dinner with some friends who lived in one of the private homes behind Cherry Hill's shopping center. He'd offered to fix a meal for me if I planned to eat at home, but after I got the invitation from Nanny I told him not to bother.

Nanny's apartment was packed when I arrived there shortly

after noon on Christmas Day. Lorsie and Vicky had come down from New York with their children to spend the holiday with their mother. As usual, Nanny was sweating over a hot stove when I walked in. The turkey was still in the oven. A pot of kale sat atop one burner. Some sauerkraut with neck bones simmered next to it. Nanny's candied yams, which I first got a whiff of outside the apartment's door, were cooling down on a kitchen counter. And John Lucy, for a change, was sober.

I spent the entire day there, not leaving until around 8 p.m., when people started staking out a place to sleep in the tiny apartment. As soon as I got home, the phone rang. It was Ruth. She said she wanted to thank me for the gifts— two mohair sweaters—I'd given her. We talked for a while about some small stuff and then Ruth said she had something to tell me.

"I'm moving to New York," she said.

I didn't know what to say. My chest felt as if it had just collapsed against my lungs. The air rushed out of me, causing the first word I spoke to break up.

"Wha-hut? . . . What do you mean, moving to New York? When?"

"Next week, when Vicky and Lorsie go back."

"Why?"

"Well, Lorsie really needs some help with the kids, and . . ."

"What about school?"

"I'll finish the rest of the year up there."

She had an answer for all of my questions, but still I felt she wasn't telling me the real reason why she was leaving. For a time after that conversation, I thought there was someone else, somebody she had met in New York during the summer to whom she was returning. Then I went through a period of thinking that I had driven her away—that my "irresistible desire to be irresistibly desired" had caused her to leave. I was depressed for days, once she left for New York.

Vicky stayed on in Baltimore for a while to visit some friends after Ruth returned to New York with Lorsie and the kids. I went by Nanny's almost every day just to talk and to see if she'd heard from Ruth. By then it was too cold to find work at Woodholme and the money I'd saved from the summer was running out. I couldn't afford to call Ruth, so Nanny would often wait for me to come around so I could talk to her daughter when she put a call through to New York.

One day I stopped by Nanny's place and Vicky was there alone. I must have had a pretty sad look on my face because right away she asked me what was wrong. Her question opened the floodgates. I told her how much I missed Ruth and confessed my fears about her having gone to New York to be with someone else.

"She didn't go to New York to see some other guy," Vicky said incredulously.

"Then why did she go?" I wanted to know.

"Because she's pregnant, you dope," Vicky said. "You're gonna be a father."

I could have killed Ruben. Vaseline didn't kill my sperm. If anything, it must have helped it get where it was going. And I was pissed off with Miss Lena, too. If she hadn't run me out of the drugstore I wouldn't have been facing the prospect of being a seventeen-year-old father. But most of all, I was disgusted with myself. While it was easy to blame others for my mistake, I knew the fault was all mine. I couldn't just declare my manhood one moment and then abdicate it the next. I had been man enough to leave my aunt's home, man enough to feed and clothe myself, and man enough to get Ruth pregnant. Now I needed to be man enough to be a good father, a better father than my dad had been to me, if only I knew what that meant.

Ruth may have thought about getting an abortion, I don't know. If she did, she probably dismissed that idea pretty fast. First, because she was Catholic. And second, because she was too smart to put herself in Poosum's hands. Most abortions in Cherry Hill were performed illegally by a woman called Poosum. She was squat, at least 250 pounds, and her meaty arms looked as if they were stuffed full of Jell-O. People said Poosum could work the roots on a person, or get rid of a spell that someone else had cast. But what she was best known for was the abortions she performed—including a botched one that people said later cost Miss Lena her life.

Once Ruth decided to have the baby, I guess she also figured it would be easier on both her and Nanny if she stayed with Lorsie and Vicky until the child was born.

After she left town, it didn't take long for the word to get out that Ruth was pregnant. Whoever pulled the prank with the diaper service was probably having a good time leaking the news all over Cherry Hill. A few weeks after Ruth's departure, Danny came by my place and said he'd heard that Ruth was pregnant. We sat at the kitchen table with a half gallon of Neapolitan ice cream and a cheese steak sub. I took a large butcher's knife and sliced in half the paper containers holding the ice cream and the sub. Danny took one side of each. I took the other. Then we sat there eating and talking about the mess Ruth and I had gotten ourselves into.

Eventually, word of Ruth's pregnancy reached André. He came home one day and asked me if what he heard was true. When I told him it was, he looked real disappointed. Maybe "disgusted" is a better word.

"Well, what are you going to do?" he asked me.

"What do you mean?"

"What are you going to do about taking care of the baby?"

"I don't know."

"Well, I think you ought to start thinking about it," he said softly.

I didn't think there was much to think about. The baby was due in July. That was the height of Woodholme's golf season. By then I'd be swimming in money—at least for the summer. I could give Ruth enough then to stock up on diapers and milk to get the baby through my last year of school. After that—well, we'd just have to see.

No, I wasn't concerned about meeting the baby's financial needs, but privately I worried that I might not be able to give Ruth and our child the emotional support they required. I wasn't sure I knew how. There was little that I remembered about the way my parents raised me. Nothing that I could recall from the years I'd spent in Aunt Annette's house made me feel confident about handling the responsibilities of parenthood. Outwardly I was determined to be a good father. But just beneath the thin skin of my false face was a doubt I couldn't suppress.

Ruth's pregnancy came just as I was getting myself straightened out in school. Even with the dumb deal I'd struck with my chemistry teacher, I was doing better in school. My grades halfway through the eleventh grade were an improvement over what I'd earned the year before, though by any other standard they were unimpressive. My absences were down to a trickle. And most days when I cut Mr. Parker's class I spent the time in the school library, or study hall—instead of behind the shop building shooting craps. And I was starting to consider seriously the story I told my counselor about wanting to attend a college and about becoming a journalist.

More important, I was just beginning to break out of the

emotional and psychological web I had woven so tightly around myself for the past nine years. Ruth was someone I felt I could talk to—someone to whom I was slowly opening up. And there was a lot I needed to talk about. Up until the time we hooked up, I had lived my life like a person on the run from the cops, secretive and guarded about anything personal for fear that if I exposed a part, I'd open up a window onto the rest of my life.

The emotional barrier I had spent so much time constructing made cold and indifferent a heart that should have mourned. And it took away the memories, which, if allowed to remain, would have made the loss of my parents too hurtful for me to deny. But as I grew older, the shield that was supposed to protect me instead kept me from reaching out to others.

My relationship with Ruth had started to chip away at my defenses, and gradually I began to let her inside my world. But when I found out she had lied to me about her reason for moving to New York, a part of me began to push her away. As afraid as I was of being a seventeen-year-old father, I was even more frightened of Ruth's decision not to tell me of her pregnancy.

It was as though she had found me unfit to be a father even before I had a chance to be one. I wondered if she had somehow found out what my father had done to his wife— and his family. Maybe it happened when I first moved to Cherry Hill and transferred into her third-grade class when our teacher, Mrs. Foster, was supposed to keep that knowledge secret. Maybe she slipped up and said something in front of someone she shouldn't have. I don't know. What I do know is that there were people in Cherry Hill who knew too well what had happened and weren't at all reluctant to talk about it.

Not long after we moved there, Rise had gotten into an

argument with an elementary-school classmate, a verbal fight that turned ugly when the boy blurted out, "At least my father didn't kill my mother."

Maybe Ruth knew, too. You know what old folks say about an apple not falling far from the tree. Maybe she thought it would be better not to get any more deeply involved with me than she had already. Maybe she just wanted to make a clean break with me now that I had messed up her life. I thought about all of these things and a thousand other reasons why she might not want me to know she was carrying our child. But without asking her, I had no way of knowing the truth. So I decided to go to New York to see Ruth. The last thing I needed in my life at that time was a baby. But if I was going to be a father, I wanted to make sure my child got more out of life than my father gave me.

Before I could go trooping off to New York, I had to get my hands on some money—which, as usual, meant that I had to go back to Woodholme. During the first half of my eleventh-grade year, I went to the country club only on weekends, and then just until the first frost came. By that time I had enough money, if spent wisely, to get me through until the spring, when the work there for caddies picked up. But now, with a baby on the way, I couldn't wait that long to get my hands on some dough.

After several telephone conversations, Ruth and I decided that I would visit her during the spring break from school. I would go up on Good Friday and return to Baltimore on the day after Easter. In the meantime, I was determined to make as much money as I could. Which meant hooking school. To keep from failing again, I tried to come up with some formula for being out of school. I tried not to miss days when tests were scheduled, but with six classes a day, that proved impossible. For a while I went to Woodholme every Tuesday and Thursday—both good days for caddies to get work—and attended school on Mondays, Wednesdays, and Fridays. As the money I made at Woodholme went up, my grades went down.

But Woodholme was my lifeline and I couldn't let it go. To one degree or another, it had been that way ever since my first day there. Chester was able to cut it loose. He'd gotten a part-time job in a tailor shop downtown on Baltimore Street, working there after school and sometimes on the weekends. After that, he didn't come back to Woodholme very much.

And while Bertha Butch was hooked on gambling, he wasn't nearly as strung out on the golf course as I was. During the school year he came to Woodholme on weekends, but almost never hooked school to caddie. Bertha Butch had a profitable hustle at school. Like me, he started the tenth grade at City College. Unlike me, he stayed there long enough to graduate.

Most days after school, Bertha Butch would stake out a bus stop near City looking for students who needed to ride just one bus to get home. He convinced some of them to get a bus transfer from the driver anyway and toss it out the window to him. Transfers were free for students. But Bertha Butch sold the ones he collected at a discount to other bus riders, picking up some fast money every school day—money that kept him in school and away from Woodholme when classes were in session.

Like me, Putty found it harder to let Woodholme go. He often hooked his classes at Carver to go to the golf course to caddie. After his father left home, his mother began to have bouts of depression. They got so bad that she spent years going in and out of state mental institutions. When she was out, the welfare payments she received kept her family going. When she was in, a lot of the burden of taking care of his younger brothers and sisters fell on Putty's shoulders. To get away from some of the pressure, he started doing drugs.

Putty was fifteen the first time he smoked reefer. By the

time he was eighteen, he was getting high damn near every day on something. But Putty never got so wasted that he couldn't find his way to Woodholme. For both of us, there was something far more intoxicating about that place than any of the dope he was using.

The time was fast approaching when a lot of Woodholme's young caddies would have to make some tough decisions about what they wanted to do with their lives. The war in Vietnam was heating up, and so was the military draft at home. Eighteen was the magic number, and my eighteenth birthday would come in July of 1964, the same month my baby was due.

Being an unwed father was not always enough to keep you out of the service, but enrolling in college or getting married could. Guys who went to college got deferments that delayed their eligibility for the draft until after their graduation. Those who married were usually exempt from the draft.

The United States had 16,000 troops in Vietnam in 1963. That number increased to 23,000 in 1964. Many of them were blacks, young men too naïve to know how to milk a deferment out of the system, or too patriotic to try. I didn't want any part of that scene.

In the spring of 1964, a lot of the talk in Woodholme's caddie shack was about "the War." By then most of the guys knew of someone who was in "the Nam." But most of the stories we heard in the caddie shack were about love, not war. The Vietnamese women loved black men. Even prostitutes would give a brother some free of charge once in a while, just to get some good lovin'. At least, that's what we were hearing.

At the time, the planeloads of GIs in body bags hadn't started coming home yet, so people were still doing a lot of fantasizing about what was really happening over there. Older guys like Reggie Shellington and John Henry, who had spent time in the service, tried to tell the younger caddies what it would be like in Vietnam. Neither one of them had actually been there, but that didn't matter. They were ex-Marines. And to most of the guys from Cherry Hill, that meant they were something special. Many of us had this fascination with the Marine Corps. I think the uniforms had a lot to do with it. When someone showed up in the shopping center in those dress blues, the girls went crazy. It didn't take much more than that for a lot of us to decide then that one day we, too, would be Marines.

And if I needed any more incentive, there were all those war movies I'd seen at the Hill Theater. Films like *Bataan*, *To Hell and Back*, and *The Fighting Seabees*. Of all those shoot-'em-ups, my favorite was *Sands of Iwo Jima*. There's this one scene in the movie where an officer gives John Wayne and his men a pep talk just as they are about to storm an island stronghold held by Japanese soldiers.

"They're dug in and they're mean," the officer says. "They just as soon die as stick a nickel in a jukebox. But that's all right. Let the other guy die for his country, you'll live for yours."

I loved that little speech. I must have seen that movie a dozen times. And then afterward when I would go into the woods behind my house on Cherryland Road to play army with Ty and Roach, I would send them out on patrol against an imaginary enemy and tell them to "make sure it's the other guy who dies for his country." Over the years, I forgot about that line until the day I read a quote from H. L. Mencken about heroes.

"All heroes, at bottom, die in vain, whether in war or in peace," Mencken said. "The rewards of life go to those prudent enough to live on."

Most of the really tough guys who grew up in Cherry Hill with me—those who didn't end up dead or in jail—went into the Marine Corps. It was a kick-ass place and they were kick-ass kind of guys. A perfect match. So anything an ex-Marine had to say to us about war was believable stuff. Reggie Shellington told us that as long as the Army was in charge in Vietnam, things would get worse, not better. "But if they turn the Corps loose over there, that shit will be over with P.D.Q," Reggie said. And of course we took his word for that, too.

I wasn't the only one in the caddie shack who was fast approaching draft age. Bertha Butch, Putty, Julius McLaughlin, and Hog were all within a few months of their eighteenth birthday. The big debate among them was not whether they were going into the service but whether they would enlist or wait to be drafted. There were pluses and minuses to both. Draftees served less time on active duty. But with less time to learn a job skill, they were more likely to be put in a combat unit and sent off to the jungles of Vietnam. People who enlisted usually got better jobs. But they also spent more time in the military, which to my way of thinking meant there was even more chance of them ending up in Vietnam. Still, most of the guys said they would rather enlist than be drafted. Not me. Despite my love of the Marines, I said, the only way Uncle Sam was going to get me into a uniform and away from Woodholme was with a draft notice.

CHAPTER 18

In the weeks leading up to the spring break, I spent almost as much time caddying at Woodholme as I did going to my classes at Douglass. I was really riding the horns of a dilemma. I needed to get my grades up if I was going to have any chance of getting into college. Even community colleges had admission standards. But on the other hand, if I was going to show Ruth that I could be a good father, I needed to make some money so I could take care of my responsibilities. Juggling those balls was going to be tough enough, but when Coach Cragway pulled me aside one day to tell me his good news, my problems started to multiply.

"Coach Payne is retiring," he said. "I'm going to coach the varsity next season."

"Congratulations, Coach," I said.

"Yeah, well, get in shape," he said, "because I expect you to be a starter.

"And there's something else I want you to think about," Coach Cragway said. "I can't make any promises, but I might be able to get you a college scholarship. Nothing big, but I might be able to get you into a school like Virginia Union, or Norfolk State. Maybe Morgan. But you've got to get your grades up, okay."

I had to bite my lips to keep from smiling. Not only was

I finally going to play on the varsity team, but there was a chance that I could also get a scholarship to play college basketball.

"Don't worry, Coach," I said. "I'm already working on that."

Baltimore's Trailways bus station was a cramped space on Fayette Street, a narrow east–west thoroughfare that cut right through the heart of the city's downtown shopping district. Just inside the door, to the right, was a small cafeteria. Ahead to the left was the ticket counter. Fastened to the floor directly in front of the counter were about two dozen plastic chairs full of people waiting for the express bus to New York I was scheduled to board early on Good Friday.

The only other time I'd been to New York was when Chester and I rode the chartered bus to Coney Island. I didn't see much of New York then. Mostly just the amusement park and the block in Brooklyn where Ruth's sisters lived. This time would be different. Ruth gave me instructions for taking the subway to Brownsville from the bus station in Manhattan, a place she called the "Port Authority."

It was easy, she told me the night before I left for New York. All I had to do was get on the A train at the Forty-second Street station and ride it into Brooklyn to the Broad-way–East New York station and transfer to the Canarsie line, which I would then take to the overhead stop above Sutter Avenue. From there it was a quick walk to Stone Avenue. The whole trip, she said, wouldn't take more than thirty or forty minutes. That sounded easy enough to me.

The bus ride to New York took just under four hours. Once the Trailways bus came up out of the Lincoln Tunnel, it was only a matter of minutes before it pulled into the Port Authority Bus Terminal on Eighth Avenue. New York's bus station was huge. Trailways and Greyhound, the large interstate carriers, parked their buses on the lower level of the mammoth building, which stretched for a block in every direction. The ticket counters were on the first floor. Overhead were several floors of parking space for the regional and commuter buses that linked New York City to suburban communities in New Jersey, Connecticut, and upstate New York.

When I walked off the bus I stepped into a world I had never seen before, nor could hardly have imagined. Up until that moment, my world had been shaped largely by the two places in which I'd spent most of my time: Cherry Hill and Woodholme Country Club. One was almost all-black, the other was nearly all-Jewish. New York's bus terminal was a window onto a much larger world. The place bustled with people. Many of them spoke Spanish, though I had no idea who they were or where they'd come from. Others spoke languages I didn't recognize. There were people of every color and description imaginable.

Outside, Eighth Avenue was as crowded as Baltimore's Thirty-third Street on the opening day of the baseball season. I walked north, as Ruth had told me to do, and turned right as soon as I reached Forty-second Street. What I saw next was awesome. A line of movie marquees reached from one end of the block to the other. There were more movie theaters on this one block of Forty-second Street than could be found along the entire two-mile length of Baltimore's Pennsylvania Avenue. I walked from one end of the block to the other, looking at the billboards outside each theater. Between two theaters, a man with a heavy accent sold slices of pizza to people on the sidewalk from a window at the front of a pizza parlor. Awkwardly, I stepped up to the window and bought a slice topped with pepperoni, sausage, and a mound of cheese. Then, finding a spot of brick front near a store whose display windows were full of cameras and small electronic products, I leaned back against the wall to eat my pizza and think through what I wanted to say to Ruth about her decision not to tell me about her pregnancy.

More than an hour had passed since my bus arrived when I pushed away from the wall and started down some nearby steps that led to the subway station below Forty-second Street and climbed aboard an A train headed for Brooklyn.

By the time I rounded the corner of Sutter and Stone, I had been in New York for nearly two hours. Ruth was sitting on one of two milk crates outside a door bearing the numbers 4-3-1.

No. 431 Stone Avenue was an address shared by the two apartments that sat atop a Laundromat in the middle of the block. The one to the right at the top of the stairs was where Ruth lived with her sisters and their children. The apartment on the left was occupied by a woman in her twenties named Dora. She lived there with her two children and the Laundromat's owner, a surly old man who was almost twice her age.

Ruth was happy to see me, but she was also annoyed that I had not called to let her know I had arrived safely. When more than an hour passed after the time my bus was scheduled to arrive at the Port Authority terminal and she still hadn't heard from me, Ruth put on a coat and came downstairs to wait, as though that might speed up my arrival. She'd been sitting on the milk crate for about an hour when I finally got there.

"Where've you been?" she snapped only half-playfully as I plopped down on the other milk crate.

"Baltimore," I wisecracked.

My flippant answer set off some light verbal sparring that ended when both of us started laughing at how silly we were acting. I hadn't gone all that way to argue with Ruth about petty stuff. Especially when there was something a lot more important that had my gut churning. And she wasn't going to let the first time we'd been together in over three months turn into a pouting match, either.

After that rough beginning, our weekend together was actually a lot of fun. We acted like tourists and went to the top of the Empire State Building. We took in a movie on Forty-second Street, went shopping in Macy's huge department store on Thirty-fourth Street, and ate dinner at the Tad's steak house across the street.

Lorsie and Vicky introduced me to a lot of their friends, just about all of whom had migrated to New York from someplace else. A couple of them, Charlie Williams and Warren White, were from Baltimore. Charlie was a big guy with an even bigger mouth. He kept everyone laughing whenever he came around—which was often. When Charlie wasn't hanging around Lorsie's apartment, he drove a delivery truck whose route every day took him throughout Brooklyn, lower Manhattan, and a scattering of towns in northern New Jersey. Warren was a former Golden Gloves boxer whose wife, Tina, treated him as if he were her sparring partner. She used him for a punching bag. Whenever Warren was slow to do something she asked, Tina would start beating on him. It didn't matter much where they were, she'd pop him good a couple of times. Warren tried to dismiss these assaults with a few words of warning, but more often than not, Tina—a country girl from Georgia who loved eating eggs scrambled with pigs' brains—eventually got her way.

At first I backed away from talking to Ruth about her pregnancy. We were having so much fun I was reluctant to open up the discussion, or press her to explain why she left Baltimore without telling me the truth. It wasn't until late in the day on Easter Sunday that I decided to broach the subject. Charlie had come by the apartment and piled Ruth, Vicky, a couple of the kids, and me into his car for a trip to the White Castle, where they sold hamburgers so small that people often bought them by the dozen.

When we got back to the apartment, I convinced Ruth to sit outside with me while everyone else went inside. The night air was cool. We huddled together atop the milk crates, eating the tiny cheeseburgers and talking about nothing in particular until I got up the nerve to ask the question I'd come all the way to New York to get answered.

"How come you didn't want me to know about the baby?" I asked her as calmly as I could.

At first Ruth fumbled for an answer. But the more I prodded her, the closer I think she came to telling me the truth.

"I just thought you had too many problems of your own to deal with," she finally admitted.

I wasn't sure what she meant, but I knew I didn't like her answer. Instead of pressing her to explain, I tried to stay out of the bog I knew that discussion would lead us into.

"I can't believe you did that," I said softly, trying to ease our conversation past the excuse she'd just given me. "What were you thinking about?"

"You're not ready to be a father," Ruth said pointedly. "You have more than enough problems now just trying to take care of yourself."

"Yeah, and you're not ready to be a mother, either, but you will be soon. And I'm gonna be a father—a damn good father," I said.

Just how good I really wasn't sure, but I knew I'd be a better father to my child than my father had been to me. Of that I was certain. He had gone away and left me forever before I even got to know him. I didn't want to do that to my child. I didn't want to end up being just a dull, fuzzy memory to

the child I was bringing into the world—as my father had
become to me.

Before leaving the next day I gave Ruth most of the money
I'd made in the past weeks at Woodholme.
"What's this for?" she asked, sounding honestly surprised.
"It's for you—and the baby," I said.
"You don't have to do that," Ruth said, reaching out to
give back the money.
"I know I don't have to do it," I said, pushing her hand
away, "but I want to."
Ruth rode the subway with me to the Port Authority
terminal and hung around until I boarded the nonstop bus to
Baltimore and it pulled out of the station.
By the time the bus was on the New Jersey Turnpike, I
was reliving every moment of my weekend with Ruth and
wondering what I could do to convince her that despite all
my problems I was determined to be a good father to our
child.

I don't know how I managed it, but when the school year
ended I was passed to the twelfth grade. Given all the time I
missed from school during the spring semester, that news came
as a surprise to me. On the day report cards were handed out,
I ran into Coach Cragway in the hallway outside the school's
office. He asked me about my grades. I lied and said they
were pretty good. He didn't bother to ask to see my report
card. We both knew he'd eventually get around to going into
the office to check on the grades of all of his players. I was
banking on him doing that later rather than sooner, so that
by the time he found out that I had passed by the skin of my

teeth, school would be closed for summer recess. That way Coach Cragway would have three months to get over his disappointment with me.

The end of the 1964 school year brought a third wave of black caddies to Woodholme. Some of them came from Cherry Hill, but many of these new caddies were from other parts of Baltimore: the run-down east-side neighborhoods that surrounded the Johns Hopkins Hospital; the west-side black belt that fanned out from Walbrook Junction down North Avenue and then south toward Poplar Grove Street and Edmondson Avenue. Some of the new caddies came from the Murphy and Gilmor Homes, two west Baltimore public housing projects. The word had spread about the money to be made at Woodholme, and poor kids from all over the city who weren't afraid of hard work began flocking to the country club.

The veteran caddies were the lords of the caddie shack. The new guys clung to our every word in much the same way that people who flock to the tents of evangelists cling to what they have to say.

"Don't forget to ask him if he has his sand trap key," Bertha Butch advised one new arrival the first time Mannion called him to the front of the pro shop and gave him a golfer's bag to carry.

"What's that?" the kid asked.

"It's what they need to get their balls out of the sand trap. If they forget to take their sand trap key, you'll have to walk all the way back to the pro shop to get one. So be sure to ask the guy if he has one before he gets started.

"Yeah, I was all the way out there on the fourth hole one day when a guy I was caddying for hit his ball in a sand trap and didn't have his key," Richard Banks chimed in. "I had to come all the way back to the pro shop to get him one. That was a long walk."

"Damn, I didn't know nothin' 'bout no sand trap key," the new guy said as he left the caddie shack. "Thanks for tellin' me."

By the time he got to the first tee with the single bag draped awkwardly over one shoulder, most of the other veteran caddies and I were massed behind the cinder block wall waiting for this rookie to ask the question. There were three players on the tee. Bad Feet Willie carried the bags for two of them. The new guy had the other bag. When the man he was caddying for walked over to get a club, the new caddie straightened up, smiled, and asked the question.

"Excuse me, sir, but did you bring your sand trap key?" he asked confidently.

Startled, the man said, "My what?"

"Your sand trap key," the new caddie said smartly.

Behind the cinder block wall we began to snicker.

"What the hell is that?" the man asked, as our snickering turned into loud laughter.

I was really cracking up when Pop Henry broke the moment for me. "Boy, I hear you done gone and got yo'self in trouble," he said loudly. News of Ruth's pregnancy was slow in reaching Woodholme's caddie shack. That was largely because most of the guys who knew about it had been in school for the past six months. But as soon as they returned to Woodholme for the summer, the word got around the country club pretty fast.

"What do you mean, trouble?" I said as I wiped the tears of laughter from my face.

"I mean you been pokin' round where you shouldn't and now you got some girl knocked up."

"What's it to you, old man?" I snapped, my laughter now replaced by anger.

"It ain't nothin' to me. Question is, what's it to you? You gonna take care of dat girl and her baby?"

"Yeah, Pop, I'm gonna take care of 'em."

"And how you gonna do dat?"

"I got a job."

"Where?"

"Here."

"I told you befo' dis ain't no job for a young man. Maybe it was ten or twenty years ago, but things are changin' now. You can do betta than dis."

It annoyed the hell out of me that Pop Henry was always butting in on my life and giving me advice. Whenever Mannion or Dick Whetzle was around, he acted like just another house nigger who had long ago made his peace with white folks—one of those yaz'um, no'zum, foot-shuffling, handkerchief-head brothers who was always kissing up to the Man. Whenever the Man came around, Pop Henry would slouch a little lower and walk a little slower than when he was nowhere in sight. Sugar Ray could put on a Stepin Fetchit act when he wanted to, but everybody knew he was acting. Pop Henry's pandering didn't seem like an act. I never knew where he was coming from when he talked to me about leaving Woodholme. In the back of my head was the suspicion that he was just trying to get rid of one of the "ole po'-ass niggas" from Cherry Hill he feared were trying to take over Woodholme's caddie shack.

Two weeks before Ruth gave birth, the Civil Rights Act of 1964 was signed by President Lyndon Johnson. It was the most comprehensive antidiscrimination legislation in nearly a century. One of its provisions prohibited discrimination in hotels, restaurants, movies, and other places of public accommodations. Another created a federal commission to help end racial discrimination among employers.

The intent of the new law was to speed up the nation's sputtering movement toward integration. It came a decade after the Supreme Court ordered that racial segregation in public schools be ended "with all deliberate speed"—words that for too many were a brake rather than an accelerator for that change. One of the men who led the fight to win passage of the 1964 Civil Rights Act was Clarence Mitchell, Jr., the NAACP's Washington lobbyist whose tenacity in pursuit of this and other legislation caused people to call him the "101st Senator." Like Essie Hughes and Thurgood Marshall before him, Clarence Mitchell was a graduate of Douglass High School.

"We got a civil rights bill. We got a civil rights bill," Lonnie Howard shouted as he ran into the caddie shack in the early evening of July 2, 1964. He was too excited to make much sense of the news he'd just overheard some of Woodholme's members discussing.

Reggie Shellington, who as usual was presiding over a crap game, looked up and said, "So what?"

"So we can now go into any store we want. Go to any movies we want. Stay in any hotel we want. And eat anywhere we want," Lonnie answered.

"Is that right?" Reggie said contemptuously.

"Yep," Lonnie gushed.

"You sure?" Reggie asked.

"Yeah," Lonnie answered. "The President signed it today."

"Well then, I tell you what," Reggie said as he pulled a few dollars from the wad of bills he held in his left hand,

"Why don't you run up to the clubhouse and buy me something to eat?"

"This is a private club. It don't apply here," Lonnie explained.

"So then why are you so fuckin' happy?" Reggie said as he turned back to his crap game.

CHAPTER 19

Ruth's water broke while she was washing the dinner dishes around nine o'clock on the night of July 15. She was already several days past her due date when it happened. I had just arrived in New York that afternoon and was lounging in front of the television set in the Brownsville apartment when she screamed out the news, setting off a small panic. I started running about, bumping into people and things, in my confusion over what to do. Vicky, who was only slightly more in control of herself, managed to pick up the telephone and call Charlie, who had been on standby for several days to take Ruth to the hospital. In a matter of minutes, Charlie was on the street outside honking his horn.

Lorsie, who worked a night shift at the main post office on Eighth Avenue in Manhattan, was at work. So Vicky herded all the children together for the ride to the hospital while I helped Ruth out of the apartment and down the stairs. Once outside, I sat Ruth atop a milk crate and ran back into the building to get her overnight bag. When I stumbled back out the door moments later with the small bag under my arm, Vicky was loading the last of the children into the car. I hopped in the already crowded front seat and shouted, "Let's go." As Charlie eased his car out of the parking space, Ruth let go a loud, agonizing yell.

"Heeeeeey, come back here."

"Oh my God," Vicky screamed more in laughter than shock, "we left Ruth." In all the confusion, Ruth was still seated on the milk crate as the car pulled away from the curb.

"Where are you going without me?" she hollered.

Charlie slammed on the brakes and jerked his car into reverse. Before he could stop it, I jumped out and ran over to where Ruth was sitting. Everybody was laughing—everybody, that is, except Ruth.

"I'm the one who's pregnant," she complained as I helped her into the front seat of the car. "Where were y'all going without me? Can somebody tell me that, huh?"

Over and over again she asked variations of the same questions, each time sounding more annoyed than before. But the more Ruth pressed for an answer, the harder everyone else in the car laughed. By the time we got to the emergency room of Brooklyn Women's Hospital, the whole thing had become a running gag that had even Ruth wiping tears of laughter from her eyes.

Ruth spent most of the next day in labor while I waited out the final hours of her pregnancy at the apartment. She gave birth to a baby girl at 11:05 p.m. on the night of July 16. Long before the baby was born, we reached an agreement. If she had a boy, she would name him. If our baby turned out to be a girl, I would get the honors. When I got to the hospital the next morning, I named our daughter Vanessa Denise. Weeks later, the state of New York sent Ruth an official copy of Vanessa's birth certificate. In the space where the father's occupation was supposed to be listed someone had typed in the word "student."

I didn't want to be a father. Not at seventeen. I didn't want to be a father before I'd even had the chance to become a man. What I wanted out of life was to play basketball—at Douglass, in college if I was lucky, or just back on the playgrounds of Cherry Hill, where I was a star. And I wanted to return to Woodholme. Caddying was my job. I was good at it. It was the safety net that kept me from sliding into the pit of unemployment and despair that trapped so many other guys from Cherry Hill in a life of drug abuse and crime. More than anything else, I wanted to turn back the clock to the way my life had been before Ruth got pregnant.

But once I saw Vanessa cradled in her mother's arms atop that hospital bed, I knew I couldn't go back to the life I'd led before her arrival. Her eyes wouldn't let me. They were deep, dark, penetrating eyes that didn't know my past life. They didn't make judgments about me the way other people's eyes did. They trusted me in a way that only a baby's eyes can be trusting.

Vanessa's eyes trusted me in much the same way mine had once trusted my father to protect and shelter me from harm. The last thing I wanted to do was let her down the way he had let me down.

Ruth and I didn't have a lot to say to each other in her hospital room that day. She was still recovering from the trauma of childbirth and I was traumatized by the responsibilities of fatherhood. I tried to get by with idle conversation—the kind of empty talk that I usually resorted to when it became too difficult for me to face something head on. But it didn't work. Ruth would have no part of my escapism.

"Look at her," she said. "What are we going to do with this girl?"

"What do you mean?" I asked weakly.

"I mean how are we going to take care of her? I don't want to raise my baby on welfare," Ruth said, her head already shaking from side to side as if to reject the answer I was about to give.

"Who said anything about welfare?" I said defensively.

"I've got a job. And I'm gonna take care of my daughter."

"What are you going to do, caddie the rest of your life?"

"What's wrong with being a caddie? It's a job. It pays good money."

"There's no future in it. I want my baby to have a future. That's all I'm saying."

"Don't worry. She'll have a future" was all the answer I could muster.

The next morning I boarded a bus for Baltimore. The ride home usually took four hours, but this time it seemed much longer. All I could think about as the bus raced south along the New Jersey Turnpike was what Ruth had said about wanting a future for our baby, as if I didn't care. The arguments I couldn't muster in her hospital room the day before started popping into my head as the bus sped along the highway. I was concerned about the future, too. That's why I went to Woodholme in the first place. I'd given up my last four summers to work there. Wasn't that proof enough that I wanted to make something of myself?

Without Ruth there to answer me, my thoughts all made a lot of sense. My parents never had more than forty dollars in their joint checking account at any one time during the last year of their lives. Living that close to the edge must have been unbearably frustrating and demoralizing for them. Just how long they had been teetering on the brink before my father snapped is anybody's guess. I just knew I wasn't going to let my life end up that way. I wasn't going to wander from one dead-end job to another as my father had done. Sure, being a caddie wasn't very glamorous work, but it had rescued me from poverty. How much more could I realistically expect it to do for me?

———

News of my daughter's birth beat me back to Woodholme's caddie shack. When I showed up there the morning after I returned home, the younger guys all congratulated me. The older caddies kept their distance. A lot of them had children of their own. They saw a new baby as just another mouth to feed. If it was a big deal to them at all, it was because they feared I'd try to take money out of their pockets by coming to work earlier and staying later now that I, too, had a baby to feed and clothe.

This time even Pop Henry stayed away from me. I think he finally decided to give me some room. Besides, what more could he say? That was fine with me. I was in no mood to hear another one of his lectures, I told myself. But I wanted to talk to someone about what I was thinking and feeling. I just didn't know who to turn to. I'd walked away from—or turned on—just about everyone at Woodholme who had ever tried to help me. Now I was just beginning to understand that by keeping everyone shut out of my life, I had in effect created a state of emotional isolation that was hard to escape.

In the days following Vanessa's birth I tried desperately to get back into a groove at Woodholme. The time I took off to spend in New York with Ruth during her pregnancy had taken me away from the golf course at its busiest time of the year, and I knew what that was going to cost me.

It would take a while for me to regain my old status. Weeks, maybe even months, before the golf course would once again become a dependable source of income for me. But time was not on my side. Ruth planned to return to Baltimore in the fall and move back in with her mother. She wanted to finish the twelfth grade, which ended abruptly for her in December when she moved to New York. Getting a high-school degree was a big part of the future she wanted for herself and our baby.

I wanted to help her out as much as possible. But with a lot less money coming in than I was used to, it was going to take some time before I could start being the father I wanted to be to my daughter. Besides, I had to think about school, too. If I got my grades up and had a good season with the Douglass varsity basketball team, my chances of getting a college scholarship were good, I thought. That would be a hell of a thing for someone from my neighborhood. A couple of guys from Cherry Hill had gotten a free ride to play football in college, but I didn't know of any who had received one to play basketball. If I could pull that off, I'd really be somebody special.

My daughter was almost a month old the second time I saw her. I caught a bus to New York late one Sunday in August after working all day at Woodholme. Mondays were always slow at the golf course, so most caddies took the day off and Mannion didn't hold it against them. My plan was to catch a bus back to Baltimore late Monday night and be in the caddie shack bright and early Tuesday morning.

A month is a long time in the life of a newborn baby. I was surprised at how different Vanessa looked. The wrinkles in her skin had filled out. The mass of brown hair on her head had grown longer and she was starting to look like me. She had my broad nose. My long eyelashes and fingers. And those little ears that are a trademark of my family.

"There's no way you can deny that child," Vicky said with a laugh. "She's the spittin' image of you."

"You think so?" I answered Vicky with a big smile.

"Oh, yeah, boy. She looks like you just spit her out," she cooed softly.

She was right. Even if I wanted to say Vanessa wasn't my child—and I didn't—there was little chance I'd be believed.

Anyone who got a glimpse of the two of us together would know that we came from the same bloodline. Even so, the chilling reality of what it meant to be a father didn't begin to set in until the moment I saw my daughter that second time.

Later that day I wandered down Stone Avenue, past the corner deli, in the direction of the housing project on the other side of Sutter Avenue. I wasn't headed anywhere in particular, just out for a walk. I ended up on a neighborhood playground shooting a basketball with some guys from the projects. They were good, but I remember thinking that I was better. Before long some other guys showed up and they chose up sides for a pickup game, the kind of school-yard contest that had earned a reputation for me in Cherry Hill.

Right away I tried to establish my dominance, in much the same way that I did back home, by quickly scoring against my opponent. The first time I got hold of the ball I dribbled it casually to the right of the basket and then quickly spun back to the left. The move freed me from the defense and gave me an opening for a jump shot.

Swish.

The ball hit nothing but the strings of the net as it went through the hoop. It was the only goal I scored the entire game. From then on, the guy I was playing against was all over me. He blocked my next two shots and forced me to rush several others that banged off the backboard or just bounced against the rim of the basket before falling harmlessly into the hands of a rebounder. Without much help from me, my team was trounced.

The only thing that changed the next game was that the opposing team had another player guard me. I got off about a dozen shots against him—and made only two. As good as I thought I was, these guys were actually a lot better. When the call came for a third game, I begged off. By then my ego was too badly bruised for me to continue playing.

Up until then I had the rest of my life all figured out. My job at Woodholme would take care of my immediate financial needs—and those of my new baby. And the basketball scholarship my high-school coach had hinted at would take care of our future. That's what I'd thought, anyway. I was at the top of my game when I walked onto that Brooklyn basketball court. But by the time I staggered off it, I understood that my game couldn't lift me high enough.

My future wasn't on a basketball court. The beating I'd just taken wiped out that pipe dream. And deep down inside I was starting to realize the only future I'd find in Woodholme's caddie shack would be no better than my past at the Jewish country club.

I needed to do something to turn my life around—something to bring some discipline and order into it. I knew that wouldn't be easy, but I was determined to try.

CHAPTER 20

The sign atop the small building on the concrete island in the middle of the busy Brooklyn street read: ARMED FORCES RECRUITMENT STATION. Inside, there were four desks, one for each branch of the military. Only two of them—the ones belonging to the Army and Navy—were occupied the Monday morning I walked in. One of the two white men seated at the desks looked at me in the same way that a buzzard eyes a rotting carcass. The other guy didn't seem to care that a potential recruit had just come into the office.

"What can I do for you?" the Army sergeant said as soon as I cleared the door.

"I want to join the Marines," I answered, pointing to the empty desk across from his.

"You sure you wanna do that, son?" the sergeant asked with a straight face. "People like you got a lot more chances to get ahead in the Army," he said. "Why don't you have a seat over here and let me tell you what the Army has to offer?"

I didn't need a high-school degree to decipher what he was trying to say. There were more blacks in the Army than any other branch of the armed services. Every time the subject of the draft came up in the caddie shack, we'd get into an argument about why that was. None of us really knew the answer, but that didn't matter. When it came to choosing a branch of the service our minds were made up. The Marines were our first choice. The Army came in second in those straw polls, followed by the Air Force and then the Navy.

"No thanks. I just want to see the guy from the Marines," I said.

"Well, then have a seat," the sergeant said. "He's due back any time now."

I sat at the Marine Corps recruiter's desk for nearly two hours while guys wandered in and out of the recruiting station to talk to someone about enlisting in the military. The Army recruiter was all over everyone who walked through the door. The Navy recruiter was more selective. He'd talk to anyone who wanted to talk to him, but the only time he really perked up was when someone white was sitting on the other side of his desk. Around noon the office emptied out and the Navy recruiter went to lunch.

I was just about to follow him out the door when a black man wearing a military uniform walked in. The brother was slick. He was one of those spit-'n'-polish servicemen. The creases in his pants were razor-sharp. The sleeves of his crisply starched shirt bent gently under the weight of the five stripes that hung on each of them. And his shoes shone almost as brightly as the buckle on the belt that wrapped neatly around his trim waist. But this guy wasn't a Marine, he was in the Air Force.

"You here to see me, son?" the man asked as he walked over to where I was sitting.

"No . . . I'm here to join the Marines," I answered him.

"What's your name?" he shot back.

"DeWayne . . . DeWayne Wickham," I said, a bit awed by this black man, who, I thought, with so many stripes was surely in charge of something.

"Wickham?" he repeated. "Where's your home?"

"Baltimore."

"I served during the war with a guy from Baltimore named Wickham . . . Johnny was his name. You related to him?"

"He's my father," I said defensively.

"Well, I'll be damned. We were in Africa and Italy together, then I lost track of him. I ran into him once when I was in Baltimore after the war. How is he?"

"He, ah . . ." I started to tell the lie about my father having died in a car crash, but caught myself. "He's dead," I simply said instead.

"I'm sorry to hear that," he responded.

He had spent some time in Baltimore, the sergeant told me, "chasing skirts up and down Pennsylvania Avenue." We talked a lot that afternoon, mostly about things he had done and places he'd seen during a military career he began in the Army before joining the Air Force shortly after its creation in 1947. This was the first black man I'd ever met who had any authority over white people.

When the Navy recruiter returned from lunch, the sergeant said he had to go out to get some papers signed and invited me to ride with him. During the car ride we talked a lot about my reasons for wanting to go into the service. I told him I wanted to do something with my life that would give my daughter a chance at a decent future. And he told me the Air Force treated blacks better than did any other branch of the armed services.

Instead of returning to Baltimore that night, I took Ruth to dinner at Tad's steak house on 34th Street, in Manhattan. That's when I told her I'd decided to enlist in the Air Force.

"When?" she asked in a surprised voice.

"As soon as I can," I answered.

For the first time since Ruth became pregnant, I felt I could hold my head up in a conversation with her. Before, she was making all of the decisions—and rightfully so. She was the one dealing with our baby on a day-to-day basis, feeding and clothing the child and taking care of her emotional needs. I'd given her a few bucks as often as I could, but not nearly enough to meet all her needs. She also got financial help from her mother and sisters.

"Once I get out of basic training we can get married and then the Air Force will send you a check every month."

"For what?"

"You know, for support. To take care of you and the baby. Until then I'll send money home to you."

"And what about school? I thought you were going to finish."

"I am. I can get a GED in the Air Force. This way I can learn a skill that'll get me a decent job when I get out," I reasoned.

What I didn't tell Ruth was that I couldn't get into the Air Force without a waiver, since I hadn't completed high school. To get the waiver, I had to pass a battery of aptitude tests, which would require me to stay in New York for several weeks.

Notice that I passed the tests came in late September, followed a few days later by a letter granting a waiver of the high-school degree requirement for Air Force enlistees. I was ordered to report to the induction center on Whitehall Street, near the southern tip of Manhattan, in two weeks. Everything was happening so quickly and it seemed my future—at least for the next four years—was pretty much set.

While I was waiting for my test results to come back, Charlie paid me five dollars a day to ride shotgun with him on his delivery truck to help with the unloading. In the evenings I usually found a spot atop one of the milk crates outside the apartment and just looked on as people in Browns-ville settled in for the evening. When my induction orders arrived, I caught the Trailways bus home to say my good-byes.

I got together with Danny and Chester almost every night during my short visit to Baltimore. We talked a lot about "the War" that was heating up in Vietnam and the chance that we might all end up there together one day soon. Chester said he was thinking about enlisting in the Army now that he was out of school. Being a Marine was no longer such a glamorous idea. In a war Marines were often the first to fight and the first to die. As I had done earlier, Danny now insisted that only a draft notice would get him into uniform.

As disappointed as André was that I wouldn't be staying at Douglass long enough to get my high-school degree, he seemed relieved to learn I had enlisted in the service. The tension that had been so much a part of our relationship was gone those last days I spent in the town house with him. We talked freely about my decision and the job he had just landed teaching French and Latin to a bunch of rich white boys at a private school. Even Rodney, always the stoic one, opened up to me more than before. It was hardly a flood of conversation, but enough to let me know he'd miss me. That meant a lot to me.

The day before I had to go back to New York for the induction ceremony, I decided to go to Woodholme one last time. On the way, I thought about stopping in to see Mr. Cooper as the No. 7 bus pulled to the curb in front of his store to let off some other passengers. I got up from my seat just as the driver was about to move the bus back into traffic. He saw me and put on the brakes and opened the back door. I didn't move.

"You getting off?" he called back to me.

"No. Not here," I said, slipping back into the seat.

I didn't know how to tell Mr. Cooper that I was quitting school, or that I was the father of a three-month-old daughter.

I knew I was doing the right thing, but I didn't know how to explain it to him. So I decided it would be better to let my actions do the talking for me. Eventually he would understand that I had made the right decision when news got home that I passed my high-school GED and that I was doing well in the service.

For the first time in my life I felt that I was focused more on the future than the past—a future that I now understood could not include Woodholme. For four years it had been my sanctuary, a retreat from all the problems I lacked the courage to face. I went there to get beyond the poverty that entrapped my family, but I stayed there because it served as my emotional hideout, an escape from the painful realities of my life.

But what the deaths of my parents stole from me the birth of my daughter gave back.

Everyone in the caddie shack seemed genuinely happy to see me. They all knew I wouldn't be back for a long time, if ever. So there was a lot of back-slapping and handshaking between us. Mannion even came down and said if I needed some money he'd give me a couple of bags to carry. But I wasn't there for that. I just needed to see the place—and the guys in the caddie shack—one last time.

One of the caddies saw Richard Kress in front of the pro shop and told him I was around back on the patio. I hadn't seen very much of him in the past two years. We'd grown apart almost as quickly as we came together. One moment we were close, the next there was a great distance between us, a creation of my fears and insecurities. But now that I was about to make my final break with Woodholme I wanted to see him once more.

"I hear you're going into the service," Richard said as he approached me, his tone very serious.

"Yeah, that's right," I answered.

"Which branch?"

"The Air Force."

"Did you finish school?"

"No, but I'm gonna get my GED in the service."

"Well, good luck," he said as he reached out to shake my hand.

And with that, Richard turned and walked away. It was all very mechanical. We both seemed to be holding back. He had gotten burned before when he opened himself to me— and I knew that there was little chance I'd ever see him again. So he headed for the golf course and I ducked back into the caddie shack to say goodbye one last time to the guys inside.

Moments later, I left Woodholme the same way I first arrived there, on foot. It was the middle of the day and most of the club's members were at play—on the golf course, at the tennis courts—or lounging around the swimming pool. I walked past the practice tee, pausing for a moment to watch the golfers hit balls in the direction of the young caddies who had been sent out into the field to shag for them.

Then I moved slowly up the footpath toward the Dutch door from behind which Mannion handed out bags of golf clubs to caddies. Pop Henry was there cleaning a bag of clubs.

"Boy, you take care of yo'self," he said, his raspy voice sounding older and more tired than it had the first day we met.

The tee in front of the pro shop was crowded with golfers and the caddies assigned to carry their bags. I waved goodbye one last time and then headed up the walkway that emptied into the parking lot. Business was slow that time of day for the attendants, who lounged around the wooden booth that served as the headquarters of their operation.

As I made my way along the edge of the driveway that curved past the front of Woodholme's clubhouse, I could see a caddie off in the distance with two golf bags on his shoulders walking up the middle of a fairway.

Then, as the road sloped quickly down the hillside and bent around a clump of trees, Woodholme—which had been at the center of my life the past four years—disappeared slowly from view.